Financial Liberalization and Economic Performance in Emerging Countries

Also by Philip Arestis:

THE POLITICAL ECONOMY OF ECONOMIC POLICIES (co-editor with Malcolm Sawyer)

MONEY AND BANKING: Issues for the Twenty-first Century (editor)

MONEY, PRICING, DISTRIBUTION AND ECONOMIC INTEGRATION

RELEVANCE OF KEYNESIAN ECONOMIC POLICIES TODAY (co-editor with Malcolm Sawyer)

WHAT GLOBAL ECONOMIC CRISIS? (co-editor with Michelle Baddeley and John McCombie)

POST-BUBBLE US ECONOMY: Implications for Financial Markets and the Economy (with Elias Karakitsos)

FINANCIAL DEVELOPMENTS IN NATIONAL AND INTERNATIONAL MARKETS (co-editor with Jesus Ferreiro and Felipe Serrano)

ADVANCES IN MONETARY POLICY AND MACROECONOMICS (co-editor with Gennaro Zezza)

ASPECTS OF MODERN MONETARY AND MACROECONOMIC POLICIES (co-editor with Eckhard Hein and Edwin Le Heron)

ON MONEY, METHOD AND KEYNES: Selected Essays (by Victoria Chick, co-editor with Sheila Dow)

IS THERE A NEW CONSENSUS IN MACROECONOMICS? (editor)

FINANCIAL LIBERALIZATION: Beyond Orthodox Concerns (co-editor with Malcolm Sawyer)

POLITICAL ECONOMY OF BRAZIL (co-editor with Alfredo Saad-Filho)

Financial Liberalization and Economic Performance in Emerging Countries

Edited by

Philip Arestis

and

Luiz Fernando de Paula

First published 2008 by
PALGRAVE MACMILLAN
Houndmills, Basingstoke, Hampshire RG21 6XS and
175 Fifth Avenue, New York, N.Y. 10010
Companies and representatives throughout the world

PALGRAVE MACMILLAN is the global academic imprint of the Palgrave
Macmillan division of St. Martin's Press, LLC and of Palgrave Macmillan Ltd.
Macmillan® is a registered trademark in the United States, United Kingdom
and other countries. Palgrave is a registered trademark in the European
Union and other countries.

ISBN-13: 978-0-230-53802-3   hardback
ISBN-10: 0-230-53802-9   hardback

This book is printed on paper suitable for recycling and made from fully
managed and sustained forest sources. Logging, pulping and manufacturing
processes are expected to conform to the environmental regulations of the
country of origin.

A catalogue record for this book is available from the British Library.

Library of Congress Cataloging-in-Publication Data

Financial liberalization and economic performance in emerging
    countries / edited by Philip Arestis and Luiz Fernando de Paula.
        p. cm.
    Includes bibliographical references and index.
    ISBN 0-230-53802-9 (alk. paper)
    1. Finance—Developing countries.   2. Economic development—
    Developing countries.   I. Arestis, Philip, 1941–   II. Paula, Luiz
    Fernando de, 1959–
    HG195.F5354 2008
    332.09172'4—dc22   2008011396

10   9   8   7   6   5   4   3   2   1
17   16   15   14   13   12   11   10   09   08

Printed and bound in Great Britain by
CPI Antony Rowe, Chippenham and Eastbourne

Contents

List of Tables

List of Figures

List of Contributors

Philip Arestis, University Director of Research, Cambridge Centre for Economics and Public Policy, Department of Land Economy, University of Cambridge, UK; Adjunct Professor of Economics, University of Utah, US; Visiting Professor, University of Leeds, UK; and Visiting Professor, School of Oriental and African Studies (SOAS), University of London, UK. He is Chief Academic Adviser to the UK Government Economic Service (GES) on Professional Development in Economics, and Vice-Chair of the ESRC-funded Macroeconomics, Money and Finance Research Group. He was a member of the Economics and Econometrics RAE panel in 1996 and in 2001 a member of the Council of the Royal Economic Society (RES), and Secretary of the RES Standing Conference of Heads of Department in Economics (CHUDE). He has published as sole author or editor, as well as co-author and co-editor, a number of books, contributed in the form of invited chapters to numerous books, produced research reports for research institutes, and has published widely in academic journals.

Luiz Fernando de Paula, Associate Professor of Economics, University of the State of Rio de Janeiro (UERJ) and CNPq Researcher. He is currently a member of the editorial board of the *Brazilian Journal of Political Economy*. His publications include more than 50 articles on banking, financial fragility, economic policy, Post Keynesian theory, Brazilian economy in books and scientific journals, such as *Journal of Post Keynesian Economics, Banca Nationale del Lavoro Quarterly Review, CEPAL Review,* and *Brazilian Journal of Political Economy*. He has also authored, co-authored or edited eight books, including *The Recent Wave of European Banks in Brazil, Monetary Union in South America: Lessons from EMU* and *Economia Monetaria e Financeira*.

Fernando Cardim de Carvalho, Institute of Economics, Federal University of Rio de Janeiro (UFRJ). He was Secretary-Executive of the National Association of Graduate Schools of Economics (ANPEC) and a member of the Advisory Committee in Economics of the National Research Council of Brazil (CNPq). He is currently a member of the editorial boards for the *Brazilian Journal of Political Economy, Estudos Economicos, Revista de Economia Contemporanea* and *Analise Economica*. He has published widely in different journals in Brazil and abroad, such as the *Brazilian Journal of Political Economy, Revista Brasileira de Economia, Estudos Econômicos, Journal of Post Keynesian Economics, Cambridge Journal* *of Economics* and *Banca Nazionale del Lavoro Quarterly Review.* He is also author of the book *Mr. Keynes and the Post Keynesians: Principles of Macroeconomics for a Monetary Production Economy.*

Ricardo Gottschalk, Research Fellow, Institute of Development Studies (IDS). His research interests include the developmental impact of capital flows to emerging economies. His other interests include the empirics of economic growth, macroeconomics of developing countries, economic reforms and sustainability in Latin America, and issues concerning exchange-rate-based stabilization programmes. He was Co-Director of the MPhil in Development Studies from 2001–04. His recent publications include *Overcoming Inequality in Latin America: Issues and Challenges for the Twenty First Century,* with P. Justino (eds), and 'The Macro Content of the PRSPs: Assessing the Need for a More Flexible Macroeconomic Policy Framework', *Development Policy Review* 23(4), 2005.

Hansjörg Herr, Professor of Supranational Integration, Berlin School of Economics, University of Applied Sciences (FHW Berlin). From 1986–93, he was Fellow of the Science Centre for Social Research, Berlin, and from 1981–86 he was Teaching and Research Assistant at the Institute of Theory of Macroeconomic Policy at the Free University of Berlin. He is currently researching China's banking system, and the restructuring of the state-owned companies as well as the monetary policy in the People's Republic of China. His publications include (co-authored with Jan Priewe) *The Macroeconomics of Development and Poverty Reduction. Strategies Beyond the Washington Consensus.* For publications in German, please see http://userpage.fu-berlin.de/~hansherr/.

Jan Kregel, Former Head, Policy Analysis and Development Branch of the United Nations Financing for Development Office. He is Distinguished Research Professor at the Center for Full Employment and Price Stability, University of Missouri, Kansas City and is a Former Chair of Political Economy at the University of Bologna, Italy. He is also Adjunct Professor of International Economics at Johns Hopkins University School of Advanced International Studies where he also served as the Associate Director of its Bologna Centre from 1987–90. His recent publications include *Market Shock: An Agenda for Economic and Social Reconstruction of Central and Eastern Europe,* with E. Matzner and G. Grabher.

Jan Priewe, Professor of Economics, University of Applied Sciences (FHTW Berlin). His research interests include macroeconomics, development economics, money and banking, development finance, macroeconomics of developing countries and the Chinese economy.

His publications include (co-authored with Hansjörg Herr) *The Macroeconomics of Development and Poverty Reduction. Strategies Beyond the Washington Consensus, Capital Account Regimes and Monetary Policy in Developing Countries: Liberalisation with Regulation*, commissioned by the German Ministry of Economic Cooperation and Development. For more detail see www.f3.fhtw-berlin.de/professoren/priewe

Sunanda Sen, Academy of Third World Studies, New Delhi and Visiting Professor at Jamia Millia Islamia University, New Delhi. Her research focuses on development economics with particular reference to finance, trade, labour issues and economic history. Her publications include *Global Finance at Risk: On Real Stagnation and Instability*, and *Trade and Dependence: Essays on the Indian Economy*.

Cecilia Azevedo Sodré, Special Adviser, Secretary of Poverty Reduction, Secretary of Government, Espírito Santo, Brazil. Her research interests include capital flows to developing countries, financial crises in emerging market economies, credit and banking. More recently, she has been involved in research that includes poverty reduction, inequality and growth in Latin America. Her co-authored publications include (with Ricardo Gottschalk) 'Implementation of Basel Rules in Brazil: What are the Implications for Development Finance?', IDS Working Paper, and 'O novo acordo da Basiléia no Brasil e na Índia: uma análise comparada' [The New Capital Accord in Brazil and India: a comparative analysis].

Fatima Cardias Williams, PhD., is a scientist specializing in forest products. She has held research positions at the Instituto Nacional de Pesquisas da Amazonia – INPA, Manaus, Amazon, Brazil, and Bangor University, prior to her current position as scientist at European Plant Science, Bangor, UK. She has led successful research projects, published articles in scientific journals, and worked on various Pan-European and Latin American projects in the fields of science and finance. Her current research interests include statistical analysis of discrete outcomes with specific reference to banking sector consolidation.

Jonathan Williams, Professor in Banking and Finance, Bangor Business School, Bangor University, UK. His research activities span developed and emerging markets and cover financial sector policies, bank efficiency and performance, corporate governance, M&A, price discovery and volatility transmission. Professor Williams is a co-author of *The Monitoring of Structural Changes and Trends in the Internal Market for Financial Services*. He has contributed to several major studies including *Credit Institutions and Banking* and the Cruickshank Report into competition in UK banking.

1
Introduction

Philip Arestis and Luiz Fernando de Paula

Financial globalization and liberalization is related to the global integration of the domestic financial markets, and has reached emerging countries through two main channels: the opening up of the capital account balance of payments; and foreign bank penetration of the domestic banking sector. According to the proponents of the benefits of financial integration, financial liberalization is an inevitable step on the path to development and should therefore be embraced. The main reason is that free movement of capital facilitates an efficient global allocation of savings and helps channel resources into the most productive uses, thereby increasing economic growth and welfare (Fischer, 1998). More specifically, the potential benefits of financial liberalization for emerging countries are related to (i) the greater access of emerging countries to external financial markets, probably at lower cost of capital due to better risk allocation; (ii) the pressure for an improvement in the financial supervision of domestic financial markets; (iii) the greater access to technological know-how and knowledge from other countries through foreign direct investment (transfer of technology); (iv) the development of the financial sector due to the effects of foreign banks' entry on the credit supply, operational efficiency, best practices, and so on; and (v) the market discipline can stimulate more consistent macroeconomic policy as market forces can penalize bad policies (Prasad et al., 2003). In particular, the presence of foreign banks in emerging countries could bring positive effects by increasing the efficiency of the domestic financial system (Peek and Rosengren, 2000).

However, the literature is not conclusive on the positive effects of financial liberalization on economic growth in emerging countries. On the one hand, theoretical studies show that due to the existence of radical uncertainty, asymmetric information and incompleteness of contingent markets, globalized financial markets are prone to herding panics, contagion and boom–bust cycles (Davidson, 2002; Rodrik, 1998). On the other hand, empirical research has shown that there is no robust relationship between financial liberalization and economic growth,[1] while their links with financial crises are quite evident. So, although international financial integration should, in principle, help countries to reduce macroeconomic instability and enhance economic growth, the available evidence suggests that developing countries have not always fully attained these potential benefits. In some cases, it can even be accompanied by increased vulnerability, which can lead to crises. Capital account liberalization in developing countries can damage the development of the domestic financial system due to macroeconomic volatility caused by external capital flows, that are marked procyclical, exacerbating economic fluctuations, when they do not cause them (Stiglitz, 2000, p. 1079). Concerning foreign bank entry in emerging countries, recent experience in Argentina and Brazil showed that there is no evidence that the penetration of foreign banks contributed effectively to the improvement of the macroeconomic efficiency of the financial system.

This book intends to discuss the relationship between financial liberalization, financial deepening and economic performance from both a theoretical and a policy perspective, comparing several 'big' emerging countries – Argentina, Brazil, China, India, Russia and South Africa, and also presenting some case studies (Brazil, China and India). Its main contribution, therefore, is to analyse issues related to financial liberalization in emerging countries focusing on recent experiences. A particular concern of the book is related to the policy dimension of financial liberalization – for instance, the degree of autonomy of domestic economic policy, and the different national policy responses to deal with issues raised by the international financial integration.

The two first chapters concentrate on the general view of financial liberalization and economic policy. In Chapter 2, Jan Kregel assesses the traditional explanation and justification of opening domestic capital markets to improve domestic growth conditions based on the neoclassical theory of market efficiency. He also presents Keynes's analysis of similar proposals in the 1930s, presenting his argument that such policies eliminate domestic 'policy space'. The chapter then presents an alternative justification of the benefits of open international capital markets put forward to solve the conflict between full employment policy and price stability presented in the 1960s, noting that this approach may be considered as providing the initial justification of the application of these policies in Latin American countries in the 1970s, leading to the lost decade of growth and employment in the 1980s. This assertion is supported by reference to the experience of the major Latin American countries, Brazil, Mexico and Argentina, in adopting policies of structural adjustment based on continued opening of domestic markets in the period of the 1980s, and the subsequent financial crises which reduced or eliminated their ability to operate independent domestic policies. Kregel concludes by presenting Keynes's recommendation on how to retain policy autonomy, and assessing the ability of developing countries, particularly in Latin America, to operate autonomous domestic policies in support of full employment in conditions of open international capital markets and potential policy alternatives. He suggests that in a global economy of financial liberalization, preserving policy space in developing countries will require flexible exchange rate, some form of management to prevent exchange rate overvaluation, controls over capital movements, and restricting issue of foreign denominated debt.

Jan Priewe, in Chapter 3, takes stock of the long debates on financial liberalization versus capital controls. He focuses on the theoretical framework for macroeconomic policy under a system of a liberalized capital account (laissez-faire regime) in developing and emerging economies. The starting point is a new interpretation of the 'impossible trinity' which states a policy trilemma between stable exchange rates, autonomous monetary policy and free capital mobility. Turning to a full floating exchange rate regime under capital account liberalization, as often advocated, leads to a sub-optimal policy mix in developing countries with a limited role for monetary policy. To enlarge the room for manoeuvre for central banks, additional policy instruments are needed, especially prudential regulation/supervision of the financial sector, which needs time, and capital controls of various forms (direct and indirect, permanent or temporary) considered as part of monetary policy in a broader context. Taking them together, one can speak of an active management of the capital account under a specific monetary policy regime. This can contribute to mitigate boom–bust cycles of capital flows, thus helping to prevent financial crises by protecting a weak financial sector, attain more stability in the exchange rate, and gain more space for monetary policy adjusted to the domestic needs of the country. The chapter concludes by suggesting that capital controls are an important and indispensable part of the tool-box of economic policies in developing countries geared to actively manage their capital account.

The next three chapters concentrate on a comparative analysis of financial liberalization. In Chapter 4, Luiz Fernando de Paula analyses the relationship between exchange rate regime, capital account convertibility and economic performance within the big emerging countries that constitute what has been called BRIC – Brazil, Russia, India and China. In particular, the chapter deals with the way macroeconomic policy regimes and the management of economic policies have determined the success or otherwise of an economic environment that has contributed to a higher (or lower) economic performance and macroeconomic stability in the BRIC countries. The chapter provides evidence that economic performance of BRIC countries is the result, at least partially, of the quality of the macroeconomic policy management adopted in each country, in which exchange rate policy, capital account convertibility and the degree of external vulnerability play a key role. China, India and Russia manage their exchange rate regimes with controlled capital account convertibility, and have been successful cases of macroeconomic policy management where the stability of the exchange rate has a crucial role and seeks to create a stable environment for economic growth. Brazil, on the other hand, has adopted a more liberal and orthodox economic policy, that includes a less interventionist approach relating to exchange rate policy and a very open capital account. This has resulted in higher exchange rate volatility, higher interest rates, and a poor economic performance. The chapter concludes that the recent experience of the BRIC countries shows the importance of having a gradual process of capital account liberalization combined with a managed floating exchange regime in order to achieve a better performance of economic policy for economic growth and stability purposes.

Ricardo Gottschalk and Cecilia Azevedo Sodré in Chapter 5 examine the experience with the liberalization of capital outflows in Brazil, India and South Africa in the 1990s and early this century. The authors discuss in particular the similarities and differences among the three countries through examining the specific measures these countries' authorities adopted on the liberalization of capital outflows by individuals, corporations and institutional investors. They also analyse these countries' sources of strengths and vulnerabilities, and ask the question of whether it is appropriate to fully liberalize the capital account even where all possible sources of vulnerabilities have been eliminated. The chapter shows that, of the three countries, Brazil went furthest in liberalizing capital outflows during the 1990s, especially for corporations and individuals. By contrast, South Africa and especially India adopted a more cautious liberalization strategy. This seems to have had positive consequences in terms of reducing these countries' vulnerabilities to the various international financial crises that occurred during the period. Turning to the early part of this century, the chapter shows that these countries have undertaken further liberalization attempts, this time in a more benign international financial environment. India, moreover, has signalled the intention of further liberalizing the capital account, as it emerges as a major force in the global economy. The authors conclude that in the three countries important sources of vulnerabilities still remain, thus suggesting caution to further capital account liberalization.

Fernando Cardim de Carvalho, in Chapter 6, analyses the experiences of Brazil and Argentina with financial liberalization, which both countries embraced from the late 1980s. Financial liberalization produced great expectations that these economies would be able to unleash their entrepreneurial energies and reach a sustained high growth path supported by external savings. The author examines the extent to which these expectations were confirmed or disappointed. Indeed, financial liberalization in the 1980s and 1990s in both countries followed the standards proposed by the theory of financial repression, beginning by freeing interest, deregulating banking and securities markets and allowing the creation of universal banks. Some important differences, on the other hand, existed between the two processes, the most important of which was probably the role reserved to foreign banking institutions. Argentina adopted radical entry liberalization measures, which coupled with the impulse to privatize state-owned banks in the 1990s, led to the disappearance of domestic banks in leading positions in the industry. In Brazil, entry of foreign banks was controlled and as a result the sector is led by strong local, private and public, banks. The liberalization process was conducted with the goal of increasing savings and investment and deepening financial intermediation. The chapter concludes that expectations related to financial liberalization were disappointed. This was due to the investment rate remaining low and growth was not resumed in Brazil, while in Argentina it was resumed only after the 2001 crisis that led to the repudiation of some liberalization measures and to greater government intervention in the economy.

The remaining chapters comprise case studies of countries, which have had different experiences with financial liberalization. In Chapter 7, Hansjörg Herr analyses the Chinese capital controls as part of an overall development regime geared towards economic growth and relative economic independence. Contrary to the so called Washington Consensus, Chinese development is characterized by active government interventions in many areas. Of key importance were and are strict capital import and export controls which protected and allowed the positive economic development in China. Capital controls prevented destabilizing capital imports which led in so many countries to boom–bust cycles, exchange rate volatility and foreign debt crises. China never experienced a currency crisis or a twin-crisis. In China the structure of capital inflows was geared towards foreign direct investment and away from portfolio investment and international credits. Last, but not least, capital controls allowed a domestic oriented monetary policy and the stimulation of a domestically based Schumpeterian–Keynesian credit-investment-income-creation process. Large central bank interventions and sterilization policies as well as the strategy to defend current account surpluses and to follow export-led growth are part of the Chinese economic regime. According to the author developing countries can learn from China that a combination of capital controls, central bank interventions and sterilization and the prevention of destabilizing current account deficits create a stable external environment for positive domestic development. Furthermore, an intermediate exchange rate regime can be combined with the policies mentioned above.

Sunanda Sen in Chapter 8, draws attention to the links between deregulated finance and industrial growth, and its impact on deregulated labour markets, with special focus on the experience of the Indian economy. The arguments dwell on the frequently observed phenomenon of booming finance in the presence of a stagnating real economy, and the related portfolio adjustments, which siphon off funds from real activities to speculation, with reactions on part of industry to practise cost cutting by using labour in its most adaptable and flexible form while minimizing additional job creation. According to the author, countries' experiences show that financial deregulation is neither necessary nor sufficient to generate and sustain growth in real terms. It can be pointed out that while propelling swings in financial markets, deregulation does not necessarily generate real activities. This is because these financial booms are often driven by speculations on financial assets, a large part of which are not backed by real assets. New investments in the secondary market for stocks or in the real estate market do not mean new real activity, as in construction of plants or new constructions of industrial plants. It is also important to analyse the structural impact of financial deregulation on different segments of the economy, which include those on employment as well as investments in industrial activities. In this connection, the chapter focuses its attention on the status of labour in the major Indian industries under deregulated finance. This relates to India's labour market, which is laden with flexibility under economic reforms. It is concluded that the 'immiserization' of labour in India's manufacturing industries can be linked to both the flexibilization of labour and the 'financialization' process, with disparate profit opportunities between the real and the financial investments. The latter leads to the drive on the part of employers to invest heavily in financial assets while making good in the real sector by using labour in the most profitable way.

Finally, Fatima Cardias Williams and Jonathan Williams, in Chapter 8, analyse the extent to which ownership explains bank merger and acquisitions in the recent experience of banking consolidation in Brazil. In Brazil, like other emerging countries, the consolidation process was used to restructure market banking sector following episodes of financial crisis. Indeed, since the mid-1990s, an extensive consolidation process has swept across the Brazilian banking sector, with domestic restructuring and foreign bank penetration reshaping the industrial structure. This chapter attempts to determine whether acquiring and targeting banks are distinguishable from non-merging banks in terms of financial profile, and, if found, whether differences exist across bank ownership – between domestic-owned and foreign-owned buyers and targets. The authors contend that bank financial profile determines participation in mergers and acquisitions (M&A), and that the characteristics of participants are sensitive to bank ownership, domestic or foreign. To test the hypothesis, a multinomial logit model is applied to a sample of commercial banks between 1992 and 2005. The results suggest there are common factors which explain the probability of a bank being a buyer, irrespective of ownership. However, domestic and foreign buyers acquire target banks that have contrasting profiles: domestic buyers tend to buy underperforming banks whereas foreign buyers tend to acquire large, slow growing institutions. This suggests domestic buyers behave in accordance with the efficient operation of the market for corporate control, while foreign banks use M&A as a vehicle to increase bank size and market share. The findings indicate a clear pattern in the M&A strategies of banks operating in Brazil. The authors conclude that one can make inferences concerning the continuing consolidation process in the Brazilian banking sector.

We wish to thank all the staff at Palgrave Macmillan for their encouragement and close collaboration on this and, of course, on many other projects. As always we are hugely grateful to all of them. Most of the chapters included in this volume were presented to a conference at the Centre for Brazilian Studies, University of Oxford, in November 2006. We are grateful to the Centre for Brazilian Studies, especially to its Director, Professor Leslie Bethell, and to the staff of the Centre for their encouragement and for their hospitality over the duration of the conference.

Note

1. Prasad et al. (2003) summarize the empirical findings of the literature: 'a systematic examination of the evidence suggests that it is difficult to establish a robust causal relationship between the degree of financial integration and output growth performance' (p. 3).

References

Davidson, P. (2002), *Financial Market, Money and the Real World*, Cheltenham: Edward Elgar Publishing.

Fischer, S. (1998), 'Capital-account Liberalization and the Role of the IMF', *Essays in International Finance,* n° 207, 1–10.

Peek, J. and Rosengren, E.S. (2000), 'Implications of the Globalization of the Banking Sector: The Latin American Experience', *New England Economic Review*, Federal Reserve Bank of Boston, September, 45–62.

Prasad, E., Rogoff, K., Wei, S., and Kose, M. (2003), 'Effects of Financial Globalization on Developing Countries: Some Empirical Evidence', http://www.imf.org/external/np/apd/seminars/2003/newdelhi/prasad.pdf

Rodrik, D. (1998), 'Who Needs Capital-account Convertibility?', *Essays in International Finance*, n° 207, 55–65.

Stiglitz, J. (2000). 'Capital Market Liberalization, Economic Growth, and Instability', *World Development*, 28(6), 1075–86.

2
Financial Liberalization and Domestic Policy Space: Theory and Practice with Reference to Latin America

Jan Kregel

2.1 Introduction

Although they were not included in the original policy proposals of the Washington Consensus, opening domestic capital markets to foreign capital inflows and deregulation of domestic capital markets have been a crucial element of structural adjustment policies practised by Latin American developing countries and as part of the conditionality attached to IMF and World Bank lending programmes starting in the 1970s. Support for these measures comes from a straightforward application of the neoclassical approach to efficient distribution of economic resources on a global level. This position still dominates the thinking of multilateral institutions, despite the fact that it is based on a faulty theoretical justification, as demonstrated by the 1960s Cambridge Controversies in the theory of capital.

Even before the theoretical debates in capital theory, Keynes had criticized similar policies in the 1930s. He reached the conclusion that such policies would eliminate what is now called a country's domestic 'policy space', that is, its ability to pursue domestic economic policies directed at maximizing output and employment.

This chapter will present and assess the traditional explanation and justification of opening domestic capital markets to improve domestic growth conditions, and outline the criticism based on the Cambridge Capital debates. It will also present Keynes's analysis of similar proposals in the 1930s, presenting his argument that such policies eliminate domestic 'policy space'. It will then present an alternative justification of the benefits of open international capital markets put forward to solve the conflict between full employment policy and price stability presented in the 1960s, noting that this approach may be considered as providing the initial justification of the application of these policies in Latin American countries in the 1970s, leading to the lost decade of growth and employment in the 1980s. This assertion is supported by reference to the experience of the major Latin American countries – Brazil, Mexico and Argentina – in adopting policies of structural adjustment based on continued opening of domestic markets in the period of the 1980s, and the subsequent financial crises which reduced or eliminated their ability to operate independent domestic policies. It concludes by presenting Keynes's recommendation on how to retain policy autonomy, and assesses the ability of developing countries, particularly in Latin America, to operate autonomous domestic policies in support of full employment in conditions of open international capital markets and potential policy alternatives.

2.2   Theoretical support for global financial liberalization

The theoretical support for global financial liberalization is to be found in the basic neoclassical theory of market efficiency. One of the first to support the continued existence of free international capital flows in the postwar period, in contrast to those who believed that international capital flows should be mediated by governments through the new Bretton Woods multilateral financial institutions, was Jacob Viner. In Viner's words 'The basic argument for international investment of capital is that under normal conditions it results in the movement of capital from countries in which its marginal value productivity is low to countries in which its marginal value productivity is high and that it thus tends toward an equalization of marginal value productivity of capital throughout the world and consequently toward a maximum contribution of the world's capital resources to world production and income' (Viner, 1947, p. 98).

The veracity of this position that follows from the assumption of the efficient distribution of resources by international capital markets, has never really been questioned. But there is an implicit assumption that lies behind this reasoning, as it applies to the flows of capital between developed and developing countries. That implicit assumption is that the return on investment is higher in developing countries than it is in developed countries. The reason for this is usually supported by reference to the longer experience of capital accumulation, and thus the greater accumulation of capital and higher capital intensity of production believed to prevail in developed countries. Higher per capita incomes in developed countries are thought to provide higher savings ratios than in lower per capita income developing countries. Finally, developed countries are thought to be experiencing declining labour forces and aging populations, relative to young, larger populations in developing countries. Thus, transferring financial resources from high saving, capital-rich aging developed countries provides them with a means of increasing returns, assuring their income in retirement, while increasing income growth and employment by providing the financing for investment in higher return endeavours in developing countries.

However, this approach, based on the maximization of the return to capital resulting from free international capital flows relies on the number of subsidiary assumptions such as:

1. A negative relation between capital intensity and rate of return.
2. It is possible to identify differences in capital intensity between developed and developing countries.
3. Foreign capital inflows from developed countries are in fact used to increase productive domestic investment.
4. If foreign capital inflows do not satisfy point 3, and are primarily invested in financial assets, then there is a high elasticity of substitution between financial and real assets.
5. Fixed exchange rates or insurable exchange rate risk.

However, as a result of the Cambridge controversies in capital theory show, few of these implicit assumptions are generally valid. We now know:

1. The theorems on capital reversal and double switching show that it is possible for increasing capital intensity to be associated with higher, rather than lower rates of return to capital, and that the same rate of return may be associated with the same degree of capital intensity. As a result it is impossible to establish a general relation between capital intensity and rate of return. This means that the returns to capital in developing countries may be lower even if capital intensity there is lower. Simply, there is no univocal relation between capital intensity and value productivity of capital.
2. Because capital is a produced good, its value depends on the prices of the capital and labour inputs necessary to produce it. Because it is a durable good, its value depends on the rate of return used to calculate present values. It is thus impossible to measure capital intensity unambiguously.[1]

In addition to the capital theory debates history has suggested several reasons to be sceptical about the traditional view.

3. Foreign capital inflows tend to have little impact on rates of domestic investment. Most studies suggest that the impact is marginal. On the other hand, there is evidence that increased foreign capital inflows are associated with increasing domestic consumption.
4. Finally, the impact of capital flows tends to be concentrated in investment in financial assets, and the impact on domestic financial conditions does not produce a change in the relative prices of financial and real assets that leads to a substitution of the former for the latter. The majority of foreign inflows are attracted by high domestic policy rates on financial assets, and because these are policy rates their impact on domestic monetary conditions is offset by the monetary authorities.

2.2.1   A modern version of the Viner postulate

There is however a more modern justification for financial liberalization that deals not with capital flows themselves but with the liberalization of the movement of financial institutions. In the words of Lawrence Summers, former deputy Secretary of United States Treasury:

> The case for capital account liberalization is a case for capital seeking the highest productivity investments. We have seen in recent months in Asia – as at many points in the past in other countries – the danger of opening up the capital account when incentives are distorted and domestic regulation and supervision is inadequate. Inflows in search of fairly valued economic opportunities are one thing. Inflows in search of government guarantees or undertaken in the belief that they are immune from the standard risks are quite another. The right response to these experiences is much less to slow the pace of capital account liberalization than to accelerate the pace of creating an environment in which capital will flow to its highest return use. And one of the best ways to accelerate the process of developing such a system is to open up to foreign financial service providers, and all the competition, capital and expertise which they bring with them. The recently concluded global financial services agreement demonstrates that countries recognize these beneficial effects of external liberalization. (Summers, 1998)

Here the argument is that the success of financial liberalization requires domestic institutions and monitoring that can best be provided by the free entry of foreign financial service providers. While this argument does not provide a response to the criticisms just noted of the implicit assumption that lies behind the theoretical support of financial liberalization, its empirical support is equally suspect. We know from the report of the Argentine parliament that foreign banks operating in Argentina were the first to exit in 2001, and that not only did they transfer their capital out of the country, they also provided the means for their clients to exit after the imposition of the 'corralito'.[2] They clearly did not contribute to creating a stable domestic environment (Tonveronachi, 2006).

In addition, there is substantial evidence that foreign banks operating in Brazil are less efficient that domestic banks[3] and that when foreign banks are allowed to take over or merge with domestic banks in Latin America, they tend to do so with the best performing banks, rather than improving the operation of badly performing domestic banks (Williams and Williams, 2007).

2.3 Keynes's position on financial liberalization

In an extension of a view that had already taken shape in the 1920s Keynes's *Treatise on Money* Volume II subtitled the 'Applied Theory of Money' undertakes a detailed analysis of the impact of an international system with global financial flows under an international standard such as the Gold Standard. Keynes's criticism here is more mundane – dealing with asymmetric adjustment in different aspects of the economic system.

In discussion of a return to the degree of financial liberalization implicit in the operation of the pre-war gold standard he raises:

> a doubt whether it is wise to have a currency system with a much wider ambit than our Banking System, our Tariff System and our Wage System. Can we afford to allow a disproportionate degree of mobility to a single element in an economic system which we leave extremely rigid in several other respects? If there was the same mobility internationally in all other respects as there is nationally, it might be a different matter. But to introduce a mobile element, highly sensitive to outside influences, as a connected part of the machine which the other parts of which are much more rigid, may invite breakages. It is, therefore, a serious question whether it is right to adopt an international standard, which will allow an extreme mobility and sensitiveness of foreign lending, while the remaining elements of the economic complex remain exceedingly rigid. If it were as easy to put wages up and down as it is to put bank rate up and down, well and good. But this

is not the actual situation. A change in international financial conditions or in the wind and weather of speculative sentiment may alter the volume of foreign lending, if nothing is done to counteract it, by tens of millions in a few weeks. (Keynes, 1930, Chapter 36)

The major difficulty with financial globalization was that it implied uniform rates of interest in all countries and thus the loss of national policy autonomy. The quotation given above comes from Chapter 36 of the *Treatise on Money* and bears the title 'National Policy Autonomy'. There he gives a very clear assessment of the impact of international capital flows on domestic economic conditions. He notes the conflict between policy to support international investment flows and policy to offset the impact on the economy of the cyclical behaviour of domestic investment decisions. In the discussions of development theory we would today talk of 'national policy space' for developing countries. Keynes is arguing that financial liberalization precludes a country from using monetary policy to offset fluctuations in domestic investment, rather requiring the use of interest rates to influence international capital inflows. The loss of policy autonomy was thus caused by a policy conflict – low interest rates, required to offset a decline in domestic investment would cause a decline in foreign investment.

2.4   Policy paradoxes in the US in the 1960s

These types of conflict restricting policy autonomy are not new. In the United States, after the dollar shortage had been replaced by a dollar glut, there was also policy conflict between internal and external equilibrium. This conflict concerned both monetary and fiscal policy. If the external account is in equilibrium at less than full employment, expanding demand by active fiscal policy produces an external deficit, but if the external account is in deficit at full employment, restrictive fiscal policy reduces domestic demand and raises unemployment.

This conflict was resolved by the Fleming–Mundell[4] creation of policy space through external capital inflows. This approach proposed that monetary policy be used to attract capital inflows to finance the current account deficit that would occur at full employment produced by the use of expansionary fiscal policy. External capital flows in open capital markets thus provided policy space if the 'assignment problem' was suitably resolved to use the fiscal instrument to target domestic equilibrium and the interest rate to target external equilibrium.

2.5 Solving policy paradoxes after the Latin American debt crisis of the 1980s

The same sort of justification was used in 1980s to provide policy space for Latin American countries facing unsustainable debt burdens built up during the large increase in international financial liberalization in the 1970s. After the failure of the attempts by these countries to generate sufficiently large current account surpluses to meet their debt service obligations because of the reduction in growth rates that this required, the Baker Plan was replaced by the Brady Plan, which proposed the use of domestic policies and financial derivative structures to allow countries to eliminate inflation and support growth by allowing them to return to international capital markets to once again borrow the funds needed to service debt.

These policies included a fixed exchange rate regime to provide an exchange rate anchor to inflation expectations; the deregulation and development of domestic capital and equity markets, supported by the creation of private assets through the privatization of state-owned enterprises and other quasi-government activities; the full liberalization of external trade and external capital inflows to allow foreign investment in the newly liberated capital markets; the removal of controls and restrictions over domestic financial institutions and the liberalization of domestic interest rates to be set by international markets; and the use of tight monetary policy and restrictive fiscal policy to reduce domestic demand and fight inflation.

In some countries such as Mexico, Argentina and Brazil the return of capital inflows created 'policy space' and success in providing for a rapid elimination of inflation. The policies were also accompanied by a rise in domestic purchasing power and in domestic consumption which led to a recovery in domestic growth rates.

However, the success has hidden within it some unanticipated and unintended consequences. The increasing capital inflows led to an increase in external debt, much of it denominated in foreign currency, the recovery in domestic consumption with open domestic markets leading to an increasing commercial account deficit. Since capital inflows often exceeded the financing requirements for the rising external deficit, the result was an overvaluation of exchange rate, sometimes in nominal, but in all cases in real, terms. Tight domestic monetary policy created large international interest rate differentials that supported the capital inflows and also led to large incentives to borrow in foreign currency at lower interest rates that led to currency mismatch in financial and non-financial sector balance sheets. The rising level of debt, with high interest rates, led to a rising debt service that increased domestic fiscal deficits and produced financial sector weakness. Eventually, capital inflows reversed and produced financial sector and exchange rate crisis, which eliminated any increase in policy space and once again reduced policy space to zero.

Thus developing countries faced a new policy conflict. Inflation would not have been reduced without the existence of the exchange rate anchor and the return of capital inflows in quantities sufficient to prevent external deficit from creating an exchange rate crisis. But capital inflows financed increased domestic consumption not investment, while the high interest rates required to sustain them and currency overvaluation that they produced reduced the competitiveness of domestic producers. Solving the policy conflict to combine growth and price stability became hostage to the willingness of international investors to continue to maintain their investments. Or, As Keynes had already noted, monetary policy had become the hostage of international capital markets.

This loss of policy control, which resulted from the very success of the economic policies that accompanied the Brady Plan,[5] thus led to domestic monetary policy being determined by foreign investors as domestic interest rates had to be sufficiently high to ensure the capital inflows needed to meet debt service and the commercial deficit. Nominal fiscal balances went out of control as they came to be increasing determined by the level of interest rates required by foreign investors. The overvaluation of real exchange rates, the liberalization of domestic markets and high interest rates made it increasingly difficult for domestic producers to restructure to meet international competition. Finally, the external balance came to be driven increasingly by debt service, and thus less responsive to traditional policy measures such as reduced domestic demand. All of these factors can be seen in the experiences of the major Latin American economies who applied these structural adjustment policies as part of their Brady Plan exit from the debt crisis of the 1980s (UNCTAD, 1998).

2.6   Resolving the policy conflict: the Mexican experience

In Mexico licensing and other controls and restrictions on imports were substituted by tariffs starting around the time of the mid-1985 devaluation, followed by a series of sharp reductions in tariffs starting in 1987 leading to a rapid increase in imports.[6] At the same time regulations on foreign direct investment were liberalized and by 1989 authorization became nearly automatic.[7] The new Salinas government proceeded with the privatization of state-owned enterprises (small and medium-sized enterprises had already been wound up or sold starting in 1983), deregulation of the banking system and the liberalization of domestic financial markets. Tight monetary policy produced large interest rate differentials that allowed the deregulated banks to fund sharply increased domestic lending with foreign borrowing, while international investors produced boom conditions in domestic equity and bond markets and a sharp real appreciation of exchange rate. The foreign inflows led to a return of rising external indebtedness that the introduction of the Brady Plan had reduced at the same time as it bolstered central bank foreign exchange reserves.[8] At the same time, the wild expansion of bank lending – largely designed to beef up balance sheets to attract foreign partners – led to a sharp increase in non-performing assets in conditions of substantial currency mismatch for domestic financial and non-financial borrowers and rising overvaluation of the currency.[9] The introduction of NAFTA at the same time as a new government was taking office in conditions of domestic political unrest led to a sharp exit of institutional investors in peso denominated domestic assets. The reports of $29 billion of dollar-indexed short-term Tesobonos dwarfed the existing foreign exchange reserves that had fallen from a peak of around $25 billion in 1993 to around a fifth of that amount. The risk was not just the collapse of the exchange rate, it was of convertibility itself. The resulting Tequila Crisis led to a collapse of the domestic banking system, which has now come to be majority controlled by external financial institutions.

2.7 The Argentine experience

Argentina went through a very similar experience with the exception of a fixed peg to the US dollar through a currency board arrangement as its exchange rate anchor. While this prevented nominal appreciation, it aggravated real appreciation of the exchange rate. Trade liberalization started in the late 1980s with unilateral reductions of tariffs, that is, without any reciprocal concessions from its trading partners, but under unconditional most-favoured nation status. The currency board was instituted in 1991 on the grounds that this would bring about reductions in interest rates since the peso was as reliable as the dollar. However, although inflation did decline to near zero in around two years, large interest rate differentials prevailed, leading to large capital inflows and substantial real appreciation of exchange rate. At the same time all state-owned enterprises were privatized and all state controls were eliminated. The decline in debt that had occurred by the end of the 1990s was reversed and despite the elimination of the losses from state-owned industry from the government's balance sheet (indeed it had benefited substantially from the receipts from privatization), fiscal deficits soon returned. Hit by contagion from the crisis in Mexico and under pressure from the IMF to reduce fiscal deficits, the new De La Rua government continued policies of fiscal austerity[10] that plunged the economy into an ever deepening recession.[11] As receipts fell more rapidly than the government could introduce expenditure cuts, international investors eventually lost confidence in the government and the policy tricks introduced by Cavallo, called back to his former post of Minister of Economics, were unable to stem a capital reversal which produced bankruptcy of the banking and pension system, a collapse of the currency board and the largest sovereign default in history.[12]

2.8   The Brazilian experience

Brazil began its experience of trade liberalization under the Collor government in the late 1980s. After a long series of adjustment plans, in 1994 the Real Plan provided for a new 'real' value of the domestic currency and a fixed exchange rate.[13] The sharp decline in the rate of inflation produced an increase in domestic purchasing power and an increase in domestic consumption at the same time as it produced first a nominal and then a real appreciation in the exchange rate. Domestic monetary and fiscal policy remained highly restrictive in support of the Real Plan, leading to large interest rate differentials that led to high capital inflows, rising external debt and rising fiscal deficits. Capital inflows continued in the face of a rising internal and external deficit, as an election approached at the end of 1998. An IMF support loan provided the external reserves necessary to reassure foreign investors that the exchange regime would be maintained, but after the elections, a foreign exchange crisis brought depreciation in January 1999 that allowed a loosening of the restrictive policies and some recovery in growth. In contrast to the other two countries, the banking system emerged unscathed; in fact it earned substantial profits speculating on the depreciation.

This marks a significant difference between Brazil and Mexico and Argentina on the one hand, and the Asian countries after the 1997 crisis on the other. This is for two reasons. First, Brazil employed a restructuring of the financial system as part of the Real Plan. Through the Proer and Proes programmes[14] the government committed around 11 per cent of GDP to close insolvent private and state-owned banks and restructure the balance sheets of those remaining.[15] In addition, after the restructuring the central bank and the central government offered exchange rate and interest rate linked debt which became the major investment in the banks' portfolios, thus insulating them from both the risk of monetary policy to defend the exchange rate and the impact of the devaluation when it finally occurred. Indeed, since there was widespread expectation that the exchange rate was being defended for electoral purposes – in the campaign for the November 1998 election the sitting President ran on a platform that presented the defence of the exchange rate as protection against the return of hyper-inflation – banks engaged in extensive hedging and speculative positions in derivatives markets that allowed them to earn record profits after the devaluation in January.

2.9 The illusion of creating domestic policy space through foreign borrowing

Thus, throughout Latin America, increased external capital flows were used to emerge from the crisis of the 1980s and provide the policy space to combine growth with price stability. However, none of them were sustainable and this led to capital account crises.

How did this happen? The simple answer is that the Fleming–Mundell solution has an inherent flaw, just as the position put forward by Viner had an implicit assumption. The Fleming–Mundell analysis is a flow analysis dealing only with the short term. It ignores the impact of capital inflows on debt stock and the increase in the debt stock on debt service.[16] Further, there is no impact analysis of the high interest rates required to insure the capital inflows on the amount of debt service on the increasing debt stocks. And thus, no analysis of impact of rising debt service on current account balance, and no analysis of rising debt stocks on risk premia on external borrowing and thus on the interest rates that have to be paid on foreign lending. Simply, it assumes that capital flows can be maintained indefinitely, irrespective of the size of the accumulated debt and the interest rates to be paid on this debt. The result is that an externally financed policy space was a short-term illusion that simply delayed the problems caused by the inherent policy conflict.

Keynes had already warned about the false illusion of National Policy Autonomy financed by external borrowing. As he had noted, a single international monetary standard requires the Central Bank to relinquish control over domestic interest rates and implies a uniform rate of interest across countries. In the case of developed countries, this was probably the case. In the case of developing countries, there is no tendency towards uniformity, large interest differentials remain, but so does the loss of national policy autonomy. Indeed, this position is much the worse since it creates the factors noted above caused by persistent international interest rate differentials.

Any attempt to use interest rates to offset domestic fluctuations in investment would create interest rate differentials and international capital flows that would eventually undermine the country's commitment to the international standard. To resolve this policy conflict Keynes suggests the control of net capital flows – the foreign capital balance.[17]

2.10   Keynes's proposals

2.10.1   Long-term capital flow controls

As remedy to the loss of National Policy Autonomy, in Chapter 36 of the *Treatise* Keynes recommends formal controls over long-term capital flows. He notes that most countries have always had registration requirements for capital issues in their own markets and that these could be expanded internationally. He also suggests a tax on purchase of foreign securities not listed in the UK market of 10 per cent.

2.10.2   Supported by short-term controls

But, long-term controls have to be supported by short-term controls. To influence short-term flows he recommends a dual rate structure that differentiates between financial flows and trade finance, given preference to the later. He also recommends a more flexible exchange rate structure through variation in the rates at which the central bank sets bid and offer rates within the gold points.

Keynes also recommends the active use of intervention in the forward market, a suggestion that was first made in the *Tract on Monetary Reform*, to influence short-term interest rates on short-term capital transactions. Keynes's conclusion is that central banks should use bank rate, the forward rate and flexibility in its bid and offer rates to influence short-term flows.

2.10.3   The ideal international financial system

However, Keynes's implicit acceptance of a gold standard system is predicated on the fact that the United Kingdom had by that time already decided to return to the gold standard. Nonetheless, he notes that in his view an ideal system would be one with flexible exchange rates. From the time of the *Tract on Monetary Reform* Keynes argued that a flexible exchange rate system was preferable to a fixed rate system as long as there was a forward foreign exchange market in which traders could cover their exchange risks. This is basically the same position that was incorporated in the proposal for the Clearing Union and the position that he took to the Bretton Woods Negotiations in 1944.[18]

2.10.4 Implications of this analysis for current financial globalization

The most important point of Keynes's analysis of these issues for current conditions is his implicit acceptance of the position that dominated pre-war thinking on these issues: external capital flows determine domestic conditions and trade flows, rather than the other way around.

In Keynes's words from the *Treatise on Money*:

> The belief in an extreme mobility of international lending and a policy of unmitigated laissez-faire towards foreign loans has been based on too simple a view of the causal relations between foreign lending and foreign investment. Because net foreign lending and net foreign investment must always exactly balance, it has been assumed that no serious problem presents itself. Since lending and investment must be equal, an increase of lending must cause an increase of investment, and a decrease of lending must cause a decrease of investment; indeed, the argument sometimes goes further, and – instead of being limited to net foreign lending – even maintains that the making of an individual foreign loan has in itself the effect of increasing our exports.
>
> All this, however, neglects the painful, and perhaps violent, reactions of the mechanism which has to be brought into play in order to force net foreign lending and net foreign investment into equality. ... I do not know why this should not be considered obvious. If English investors, not liking the outlook at home, fearing labor disputes or nervous about a change of government, begin to buy more American securities than before, why should it be supposed that this will be naturally balanced by increased British exports? For, of course, it will not. It will, in the first instance, set up a serious instability of the domestic credit system – the ultimate working out of which it is difficult or impossible to predict. Or, if American investors take a fancy to British ordinary shares, is this going, in any direct way, to decrease British exports? (Keynes, 1930, pp. 335–6)

2.10.5   Will flexible exchange rates produce policy space?

Many developing countries introduced flexibility in exchange rates after the financial crises that followed their successful stabilization policies. Many have now introduced inflation targeting and primary surplus targets as a substitute for the fixed exchange rate policy anchor. Also, a number have managed to create commercial and capital account surpluses. Yet, their debt stocks remain high and nominal deficits are not being reduced, because of the persistence of high interest rate differentials, while growth rates remain low. This would all suggest that Keynes's original recommendation still holds and that some form of management of the foreign balance is still required.

2.11   Conclusion

We can thus conclude that in a global economy of financial liberalization, preserving policy space in developing countries will require:

• Flexible exchange rates. In all of the cases of financial crisis following financial liberalization in Latin America, the destabilizing capital flows result from either an implicit or explicit exchange rate guarantee. Indeed, in most cases, the opening of domestic markets to international capital flows produced inflows that more than offset the increasing external financing needs, and thus created either real or nominal appreciation of the currency. Foreign investors, or domestic financial institutions thus had a double advantage – a large positive interest rate differential that could be exploited by borrowing abroad at low rates and investing domestically at high rates, plus the exchange rate appreciation that multiplied these already high returns.

• Thus avoiding these destabilizing arbitrage flows will require some form of management to prevent overvaluation and a one way bet that supports the returns on foreign borrowing that naturally exists from the interest rate differential.

• Controls over capital flows to allow management of interest rates and exchange rates. As long as developing countries use domestic restriction on monetary or fiscal policy they will suffer an interest policy determined interest rate differential. To prevent capital flows being driven by this differential, which has no impact on domestic interest rates or investment, will require some sort of control over international capital flows.

• Restricting issue of foreign denominated debt by both the public and the private sectors to ensure the effective management of foreign capital inflows. Since a major source of the speculative flows comes from the ability to raise funds in foreign currency – whether speculative or used to finance domestic productive activity creating a currency mismatch for non-financial corporations – eliminating the source will require controls over the ability of domestic financial and non-financial corporations to borrow in foreign currency. This means strengthening the domestic financial sector. Unfortunately, this will not be easy, since the policies followed by governments to ensure the sale of government debt mean that banks can maximize profits by lending to government rather than to the private sector. Statistics suggest that post-financial crisis Latin American financial institutions no longer lend to the non-financial sector. To the extent that foreign banks have been granted increased access as a means of restructuring after crises, their lending has tended to be for consumer and mortgage lending, again leaving the business sector without sources of finance.

Finally, the pressure on most countries to deregulate the financial system has led to the elimination of national development banks which in the past had provided lending to industry.[19]

Notes

1. For a summary of the results of these debates see Harcourt (1971). It is interesting that despite the fact that these conclusions have now been accepted by all sides in the debates, they have been ignored in the development literature, and in most of the modern macroeconomic literature.
2. See the official report of the Comisión Especial de la Cámara de Diputados, República Argentina (2005).
3. See Guimarães (2002), de Paula (2002) and de Paula and Alves Jr (2007).
4. The original papers were developed by both economists when they were working for the International Monetary Fund and were published virtually simultaneously. See Fleming (1962) and Mundell (1962).
5. In fact they closely resemble what came to be codified as 'Washington Consensus' policies of structural adjustment, but with the exception of the exchange rate anchor and financial liberalization – two aspects that were crucial to their success. See, e.g. Kregel (1999).
6. See Kate (1990).
7. See Guillén (1995).
8. See Mantey (1998).
9. See Correa (1996).
10. For a revealing discussion of the views of the Fund in this period see the book of interviews with Claudio Loser who was responsible for Fund policy in Latin America at the time in Tenembaum (2004).

11. See for example, Cafiero and Llorens (2002), and Sevares (2002).
12. A review of Argentine policy leading up to the crisis is available in Kregel (2003).
13. For a detailed comparison of the plans proposed prior to 1994 see Modenesi (2005, pp. 290–5).
14. See Maia (1999) for more information on the details of these programmes.
15. See Sáinz and Calcagno (1999) who note that this restructuring was a major source of the increased government indebtedness after the Real Plan, but also prevented the collapse of the system after the devaluation of 1999.
16. A more extensive analytical criticism of this approach may be found in Kregel (2007).
17. In chapter 2 of *A Tract on Monetary Reform* Keynes (1923) had already recommended a capital levy on bondholders as the most appropriate method for dealing with the 'progressive and catastrophic inflations' in Central and Eastern Europe, and in 1924 he had recommended capital controls as a way of reducing deflationary pressure due to the return to gold. See Skidelsky (2000, p. 191).
18. See for example the discussion in Skidelsky (2000, p. 191).
19. Brazil remains the exception in this regard, although a number of Latin American countries are considering resurrecting national development banks.

References

Cafiero, M. and Llorens, J. (2002), *La Argentina Robada – El corralito, los bancos y el vaciamento del system financiero argentine*, Buenos Aires: Ediciones Macchi.

Comisión Especial de la Cámara de Diputados, República Argentina (2005), *Fuga de Divisas en la Argentina: Informe Final*. Buenos Aires, Comisión Latinoamérica de Ciencias Sociales (Clacso) and Siglo XXI.

Correa, E. (1996), 'Cartera vencida y salida de la Crisis Bancaria', in Girón, A. and E. Correa (eds) *Crisis Bancaria y Carteras Vencidas*. Ed. UAM-IIEc-UNAM-La Jornada. México.

Fleming, M. (1962), 'Domestic Financial Policy under Fixed and under Floating Exchange Rates', *IMF Staff Papers*, Vol. 9, pp. 369–79.

Guillén, H. (1995), 'El Consenso de Washington en México', in Jose Luis Calza, *Problemas Macroeconomicos de México* – Vol. 1, Mexico City: UAM.

Guimarães, P. (2002), 'How does foreign entry affect domestic banking market? The Brazilian case', *Latin American Business Review*, vol 3 (4), pp. 121–40.

Harcourt, G.C. (1971), *Some Cambridge Controversies in the Theory of Capital*, Cambridge: Cambridge University Press.

Kate, A.K. (1990), 'La aperture commercial de Mexico – experiencias y lecciones', in Eduardo Gitli (ed.) Estudios sobre el sector external Mexicano, Mexico City: Serie Economia UAM Azcapotzalco.

Keynes, J.M. (1923), *A Tract on Monetary Reform* (*Collected Writings*, Vol. IV).

Keynes, J.M. (1930), *A Treatise on Money*, Volume II, London: Macmillan.

Kregel, J.M. (1999), 'Alternative to the Brazilian Crisis', *Revista de Economia Política Brazilian Journal of Political Economy*, vol. 19, no. 3 (75) July, pp. 23–38.

Kregel, J. (2003), 'An alternative view of the Argentine Crisis: Structural flaws in structural adjustment policy', *Investigación Económica*, January, No. 243, pp. 15–49.

Kregel, J. (2007), 'Keynes, Globalisation and "National Policy Space"' forthcoming in a book edited by João Sicsú, Carlos Vidotto and João Saboia Commemorating the 70th Anniversary of the General Theory, to be published by Editora Campus-Elsevier.

Maia, G. (1999), 'Restructuring the banking system – the case of Brazil', Bank for International Settlement, http://www.bis.org/publ/plcy06b.pdf.

Mantey, G. (1998), 'Efectos de la liberalización financiera en la deuda pública de México', in Alicia Giron and Eugenia Correa (eds) *Crisis Financiera: Mercado sin Fronteras*, Mexico City: UNAM-IIE, DGAPA, Ediciones Caballito.

Modenesi, A.M. (2005), *Regimes Monetários – Teoria e a Experiência do Real*, Tambore, SP, Editoria Manole.

Mundell, R. (1962), 'The Appropriate Use of Monetary and Fiscal Policy under Fixed Exchange Rates', *IMF Staff Papers*, Vol. 9, pp. 70–9.

de Paula, L.F. (2002), 'Expansion strategies of European banks to Brazil and their impacts on the Brazilian banking sector', *Latin American Business Review*, vol. 3 (4), pp. 59–91.

de Paula, L.F. and Alves Jr, A.J. (2007), 'The Determinants and Effects of Foreign Bank Entry in Argentina and Brazil: A Comparative Analysis', *Investigación Económica*, vol. LXVI, n. 259, pp. 65–104, January.

Sáinz, P. and Calcagno, A. (1999), 'La economía brasileña ante el Plan Real y su crisis', *Temas de Coyuntura*, No. 4, CEPAL, Santiago de Chile, July.

Sevares, J. (2002), *Por qué Cayó La Argentina*, Buenos Aires: Grupo Normal.

Skidelsky, R. (2000), *John Maynard Keynes – Fighting for Freedom, 1937–1946*, London: Penguin.

Summers, L. (1998), US Government Press Release, 2286, March 9, 1998: 'Deputy Secretary Summers Remarks before the International Monetary Fund', http://www.ustreas.gov/press/releases/rr2286.htm.

Tenembaum, E. (2004), *Enemigos*, Buenos Aires: Grupo Norma.

Tonveronachi, M. (2006), 'The Role of Foreign Banks in Emerging Countries – The Case of Argentina, 1993–2000', *Investigación Económica*, vol. LXV (255), January, pp. 97–107.

UNCTAD (1998), *Trade and Development Report*, Chapter III, section B, 'Anatomy of the crises in the post-Bretton Woods period for a discussion of the similarity in these crises from the Southern Cone crisis of the early 1990s to the Asian Crises of 1997–8'.

Viner, J. (1947). 'International Finance in the postwar World', *Journal of Political Economy*, 55, April, pp. 97–107.

Williams, J. and Williams, F. (2007), 'Does ownership explain bank M&A? The case of domestic banks and foreign banks in Brazil', Chapter 9, this volume.

3
Capital Account Management or Laissez-faire of Capital Flows in Developing Countries

Jan Priewe

3.1 Introduction: Where do we stand after the long debates on capital controls?

The academic and political debates on the issue of capital controls versus capital account liberalization in developing countries seem to be never-ending. When the Bretton Woods institutions were founded a vast majority was in favour of control, at least for the option of control, although the global commercial financial markets did not play a significant role for developing countries at that time. Keynes was not the only critic of unfettered capital flows in the postwar world economy (Boughton 2002). He promoted the priority of trade, while the supposed volatile commercial capital flows were seen as a disturbing, not a supporting, factor for the real economy.

In the wave of the global liberalization of exchange rates, capital flows and many other regulations throughout the 1970s, a gradual lifting of domestic and cross-border financial controls took place. Some developing countries were considered emerging economies and as potential recipients of financial investments from the perspective of the financial industry in the developed world. With the spread of the neoclassical counter-revolution in economic thinking, capital account liberalization[1] (CAL) as a complement to trade liberalization has become a promising tenet for many international economists. As global capital flows increased in the course of financial globalization after the early 1980s, the thrust of the pro-liberalization arguments increased until 1998, when, at the peak of the Asian crisis, leading stakeholders in the IMF attempted to promote an amendment to the statutes making free capital flows a binding goal for all fund members and the fund's policy. The failure of this endeavour marks the watershed in the debates. The pro voices became less vocal, the sceptics ever more, and dozens of mainly empirical studies were conducted. The results were staggering for the proponents because a robust positive relationship between the liberalization of capital flows and economic growth could not be proven in numerous cross-country econometric studies, comprising both developed and developing countries.

However, cross-country studies suffer from serious shortcomings. Firstly, suppose one finds clear-cut relationships between two or more variables and causality can be detected. There may also be one or more countries which have fared very well in the opposite direction, presumably due to country-specific institutions or policies. Of course they will not change their policies to follow a general concept based on the relationship of the majority. Hence positive deviations from standard patterns deserve discriminating attention as they could be models for other countries. Secondly, suppose again that a clear relationship was found, but that average economic performance was meagre and there was no positive deviating case. One must not exclude the possibility that in the future countries will explore other patterns with contrasting policies which will yield better results. Thirdly, one might question whether there is a general, historically invariant pattern of development, some kind of 'law of motion'; it must not be ruled out that complex historically unique and idiosyncratic patterns exist which may not be transferable to other countries. Hence one should have in mind the limitations of the methodology of cross-country analyses. Therefore country studies can be much more enlightening than the often fruitless cross-country studies that are much too crude to capture the complexity of factors involved (Epstein et al., 2005; Edwards 2007).

It can be said that most empirical investigations (Prasad et al., 2004, Stiglitz 2004, Kose et al., 2006) seem to agree on the following: (i) There is no general robust relationship between capital account liberalization and growth. (ii) Strong growth records have been found in countries with and without capital controls, weak performances respectively. (iii) There is also no clear general relationship between capital account opening and financial crises. (iv) The composition of capital flows matters, with long-term equity being more conducive for growth and external debt more risky. (v) Fixed or fairly stable exchange rates are now harder to maintain under capital flow liberalization than under controls. (vi) Liberalization impacts monetary and fiscal policy. (viii) The outcome of cross-border liberalization of capital flows differs according to financial sector stability, macro stability and the quality of institutions (whatever this is and whatever the appropriate measure); the less developed the latter three items are, the more critical the outcome of liberalization, and this calls for a threshold or sequencing concept. Seldom addressed explicitly, any general policy conclusion drawn from this mixed and shaky empirical knowledge is inconclusive and fragile at best.

Those inspired by orthodox neoclassical theory have been confronted with a predicament since the promises of the theory are clear-cut, and after so much empirical research must come to the surface sooner or later, assuming the theory is right. In fact, the basic premises of the underlying theories are disputable. The most current deviation is to accept the empirical results, contend obliviously the orthodox theories but point out so-called 'collateral benefits' (Kose et al., 2006): in a catalytic manner capital account liberalization is supposed to indirectly improve the quality of the domestic financial sector, the quality of institutions and macroeconomic discipline in general. This way liberalization is the whip for discipline that in the end exacts higher growth. If this were true, sooner or later growth effects would have to show up in the empirical studies regardless of whether they were directly or indirectly effectuated. Or might this be the hope for the *very* long run? The apologetic bias is easily discernible. Some twist the argument, maintaining that sacrifices for financial integration are inevitable in order to progress from under-development to the stage of an emerging economy and finally to a developed country, just as crises are the pavement on the road to historic progress. But perhaps there are more favourable alternatives for development; some countries, such as China and India have proven that these exist.

There is good reason to believe that the empirical findings mentioned reflect severe shortcomings of the basic propositions of orthodox theories and in turn give support to those who have questioned them.

Within an alternative conceptual framework – as unfolded in what follows – it can be shown that capital controls can potentially have beneficial effects on the growth performance of developing countries. What is presented in the following is a re-interpretation of the 'impossible trinity' as a heuristic for the discussion of the benefits of capital controls. The proper use of capital controls changes the policy mix, and so does capital account liberalization, albeit in another, less favourable direction. By contrast to the notion of 'collateral benefits' through financial integration, 'collateral damage' by reduced policy options and a distorted policy mix is deemed more realistic. This is the main proposition put forward here.

In this chapter I first review the definition of capital controls; the simple issue, mostly ignored, turns out to be reasonably complex and involves far-reaching consequences. Next, I re-interpret the 'impossible trinity'. When liberalization is opted for in this framework, a policy tool is missing which leads to a sub-optimal policy-mix. In this case, financial sector reforms could be the missing tool. Whether or not this is a proper substitute for capital controls in developing countries is addressed in section 3.4. Section 3.5 disputes the theoretically asserted benefits of capital account liberalization, and section 3.6 summarizes the conclusions.[2]

3.2 What really are capital controls? A narrow and broad understanding

It is surprising that most studies on capital controls neglect to define the key term in a coherent way. Most authors follow the definitions of the IMF's 'Annual Reports on Exchange Arrangements and Exchange Restrictions' (IMF AREAER) and the OECD's 'Code of liberalization of Capital Movements' (OECD 2004) which provide only an enumeration of dozens of specific and direct regulations, comprising quantitative controls, prohibitions, but also some so-called market-based measures, such as unremunerated reserve requirements for short-term inflows or a Tobin-tax. In this focus, *indirect* ways to exert influence on cross-border capital flows or foreign exchange transactions are excluded. Such indirect effects can stem from five types of policy which are normally not considered as capital controls:

(i) prudential regulation of the financial sector, bank and non-bank supervision, etc., e.g. prescriptions for hedging requirements against currency mismatch risks, limitations to open positions, regulations for banks and non-banks to contain foreign-exchange risks, capital adequacy ratios, measures which regulate (allow or constrain) the use of foreign currency in the country;

(ii) the monetary policy of the central bank can use the fixing of interest rates to attract or deter capital inflows for various purposes;

(iii) by the choice of the exchange rate regime and the respective exchange rate policy, the central bank exerts massive influence on the flow of capital; most importantly, under fixed exchange rates or managed floating measures to avoid appreciation (depreciation) induce increasing (decreasing) reserves and hence impact official capital flows;

(iv) fiscal policy can use domestic or foreign debt with the choice of various maturities which has a vast impact on capital flows and the balance of payment, also indirect effects on the exchange rate, the country rating of creditworthiness and hence on private capital flows;

(v) tax laws and related administrative rules for their implementation can impact cross-border capital flows, either in inflow-promoting directions (e.g. tax havens, off-shore banking, preferential taxation for inward foreign direct investment) or in outflow-alleviation or hindrance through lax or strict implementation of laws, tolerated or closed loopholes, existence or non-existence of double-taxation agreements, etc.

There is no doubt that the indirect five channels can have a strong impact and magnitude on cross-border flows, often bigger than the direct channels. There is an analogy to non-tariff barriers to the trade of commodities as compared to direct barriers, i.e. tariffs. In developing countries, the capacity to actively use these channels is less developed or coupled with drawbacks for the domestic economy (e.g. tight monetary or fiscal policy, or the strict implementation of hedging obligations for enterprises and banks). Because of these shortcomings they often use administrative or occasionally some market-based controls of capital flows.

The AREAER- and OECD-definitions are narrow insofar as they exclude the five channels mentioned. The focus stems from a predominant view on administrative, non-market based command-and-control measures, although market-based measures are included in the AREAER-list and in the OECD-classification, especially if they relate to exchange rates (such as dual or multiple exchange rates). But market-based controls play only a minor role in most developing countries, including emerging economies. The absence of administrative and certain market-based controls defines capital-account liberalization in this view. CAL would then be compatible with the capital-flow effects of sector policies (such as prudential regulation, taxation) and macro policies (monetary, exchange rate, fiscal policy) although the latter can have a strong impact on cross-border capital flows. They can be considered potential substitutes for the traditional direct forms of capital controls. A more radical understanding of CAL would, in addition, call for independently floating exchange rates so as to minimize governmental influence of private capital flows.

A wide definition of capital controls includes all governmental measures (including those of the central bank) which directly or indirectly, intentionally or unintentionally influence cross-border capital-flows.[3]

Most countries, developed and developing alike, use some form of capital controls in this sense. This definition makes the term CAL more or less meaningless.

Another approach is to use a very narrow definition of capital controls by confining them to administrative measures. Market-based measures are then regarded as parts of monetary, exchange rate or tax policy, strictly separated from quantitative controls. CAL in this sense simply means the abolition of administrative controls, but is compatible with all other forms of capital account management. CAL implies that other policies can substitute for the administrative measures.

One might prefer to contend that capital controls are all measures that treat private international capital flows in a different and therefore discriminatory way as compared to flows within the domestic economy. Hence CAL would abolish all border controls for private capital movements. This approach applies, however, only to a monetary union with a single monetary policy, a single capital market, including the same (or very similar) type(s) of prudential regulations, taxation of capital income (or international tax agreements). The existence of nation states with their own currency and hence with separate foreign exchange markets, sovereign monetary policy, national regulatory policies, national taxation rules, etc. poses important differences for cross-border flows as compared to regional flows within an economy. One might argue less stringently and allow for cross-border capital flows between countries with very similar regulations, policies, etc. This may pertain to the similarity of capital flows between OECD countries, but the analogy certainly does not hold for capital flows between developing and developed countries. This makes clear that the notion of absolutely free and solely market-determined cross-border capital flows as envisaged by the proponents of CAL is erroneous.

All three definitions presented here (administrative controls, administrative controls plus market-based controls, or the latter controls plus all indirect controls) are not fully satisfactory. A solution could be to shift to the term *active capital account management* through the various channels and instruments mentioned, in contrast to a *laissez-faire regime* which bans all direct and intentional measures of regulating cross-border capital flows. The old issue of whether or not capital controls are conducive for development boils down to the following questions: should there be an active capital account management rather than a laissez-faire regime? What policies and instruments are appropriate if the former approach is chosen? Are administrative controls dispensable for developing countries? Which forms of capital controls or regulations are the best and which involve the fewest opportunity costs for which country group? Is there an optimal policy mix? In the following I adhere to the standard definition of capital controls.

3.3   Re-interpreting the 'impossible trinity' as a heuristic for understanding capital controls

The theorem of the 'impossible trinity' (or the 'open economy trilemma') can be used to demonstrate the potential benefits of capital controls (or of an active management of the capital account). The well-known theorem states that all countries tend to be in favour of three goals – sovereign monetary policy adjusted to the domestic needs, stable exchange rates regardless of the type of the exchange rate regime, and free mobility of private capital (cp. Obstfeld and Taylor 1998). No country can realize all three goals at the same time, only two are possible – this is the message of the theorem. There are two underlying trade-offs: first, monetary policy can either be aligned to fulfil internal macro stabilization (predominantly price stability and avoiding output gaps) or it can serve external stability, i.e. guaranteeing stability of the nominal exchange rate at an appropriate level, under conditions of CAL. Second, with full capital mobility, exchange rates tend to be unstable unless stabilized by monetary policy. Conversely, exchange rate stability can be achieved either by monetary policy or by capital controls.

Hence, each country has three options for the policy-mix: (i) monetary policy autonomy plus free capital mobility but floating exchange rates (e.g. the US option); (ii) stable or even fixed exchange rates plus capital mobility, but no autonomous monetary policy (e.g. Argentina under the currency board until 2001); (iii) monetary policy autonomy plus stable exchange rates but constrained capital mobility (e.g. China option). Put differently, capital controls are the missing policy tool that can possibly help avoid the monetary policy trade-off between fulfilling internal or external stabilization.

Let us look at three implications of the theorem. First, the dilemma between internal and external stabilization can be shown by the Taylor-rule for monetary policy. The Taylor-rule suggests that monetary policy should set real short-term interest rates according to the equilibrium real short-term interest rate unless there is an inflation gap and/or an output gap. If inflation is higher than target inflation and output higher than potential output, the central bank interest rate has to be tightened, and vice versa. The weights assigned to the inflation gap and the output gap are constant (Taylor assumed 50 per cent each for the US). This rule presumes the prevalence of domestic targets, i.e. internal stabilization of prices and output. If an external goal is added like a target nominal exchange rate which permanently or occasionally gains priority (to avoid risks of financial crisis), monetary policy becomes inconsistent as it is impossible to assign constant weights to the three goals (or external stabilization becomes the only goal).[4]

Another implication of the theorem is that exchange rate stabilization by means of monetary policy under full CAL is considered possible. This corner solution bias concerning exchange rates regards currency boards or similar regimes (e.g. official dollarization) as feasible without considering the specific preconditions which only few countries have in fact met thus far. Following the theorem, the other corner solution, full floating, enables full monetary policy autonomy, a long-standing notion of monetary theory, for instance implicit in the Mundell–Fleming model. However, for countries with high stocks of external debt in foreign currency, normally not sufficiently hedged against exchange rate risks, strong exchange rate fluctuations are not affordable, so that monetary policy is not free to benignly neglect exchange rates. This is the menace of original sin.

A third noteworthy implication of the theorem is the proposition that the lifting of capital controls has no impact on the stance of monetary policy. Evidence from developing countries shows that very often real interest rates rise. Monetary policy becomes tighter, which often reflects the problem of defending the exchange rate when full floating is not acceptable. Conversely, the option of capital controls plus the autonomy of monetary policy generates the possibility of de-linking interest rates from global financial markets; the uncovered interest rate parity theory is, of course, not applicable under segmented capital or money markets. Interest rates can, in principle, be adjusted to the needs of the country. What is sometimes blamed as manipulation or distortion of interest rates reflects monetary policy autonomy backed and effectuated by capital controls.

One might doubt whether the theorem is suitable as a theoretical base for the debate about the merits or costs of capital controls. It could be contended that the theorem is bound to be a short-run analysis as exchange rates tend to be stable according to the purchasing power parity theory in the long run, whereas in the short term overshooting prevails. It goes without saying that this exchange rate theory is highly contentious as it implies that capital flows follow rational expectations governed by real-economy fundamentals. But even if the concept were tenable, short run fluctuations could trigger crises with lasting collateral damages.

The importance of monetary policy autonomy and exchange rate policy could also be questioned. If they were neutral with respect to output growth, it would not be a loss if they were turned down. However, there is abundant evidence that both policies *do* matter, at least for the short and medium term, and financial crises normally have effects of a rather long duration. From a Keynesian point of view, a short-run disequilibrium can linger long without corrective forces at work. There is the risk that long-run steady state equilibrium is never reached. Without delving more deeply into this, it can be argued that the output effects of monetary and exchange rate policies are long and enduring enough to be relevant for policy making.

The predominant interpretation of the theorem is that countries are pushed in the corner solutions of exchange rate regimes, either absolutely fixed or fully floating exchange rates if capital controls are completely lifted (Fischer 2001). And the erosion of the latter is often considered an inevitable necessity enforced by markets and technology (or by 'globalization'). For Fischer, the main argument for the corner solution is – apart from the evidence over the last few decades – the risk of speculative attacks under intermediate exchange rate regimes, full capital mobility presumed. But for developing countries the reality and the options are different. The two largest Third World countries still use pervasive capital controls, although with decreasing intensity, and many others do so to some extent, and stubbornly refrain from full floating but practise managed floating.

Although the impossible-trinity theorem is a well-suited starting point for the analysis of capital controls, it requires some revisions when applied to developing countries. My re-interpretation addresses two major shortcomings.

First, the theorem addresses corner solutions with respect to the three goals. Either they are achieved fully or not at all, especially regarding the exchange rate goal. But the core idea of the theorem, in my understanding, is to show trade-offs which of course also exist if intermediate solutions, partial fulfilment of one, two or all goals are included. For instance, a country may have something from all three goals as a compromise. If for example a country implements some capital controls while other parts of the capital account are left open, it can achieve a higher degree of exchange rate stability, such as intermediate regimes, and enjoy a monetary policy which under normal circumstances can care effectively for internal stabilization. To assume either full capital controls or unconstrained capital mobility disregards the various options between the corners (cp. Williamson 2000 as a proponent of intermediate regimes).

Second, developing countries are unlikely to accomplish two of the three goals unless they opt for capital controls. Applying the theorem to developing countries poses a difference as compared to developed countries, and this on four counts: (i) Most developing countries are net debtor countries – in foreign currency – as a result of long-standing current account deficits in the past, and most developed countries are net creditors or countries with only temporarily small negative current accounts; the US is an exceptional case as it is indebted in its own currency; countries within a currency union are another exception. Net debtor economies are much more sensitive towards exchange rate fluctuations, particularly devaluations. In other words, they are stuck in 'original sin' (Eichengreen et al., 2002) as they are generally unable to issue debt in their own currency, and the ways for redemption are limited. (ii) The quality of the money is much lower as compared to the OECD currencies which are on top of the currency hierarchy; this poses a risk premium in credit contracts. (iii) The quality of the financial sector is considerably worse than in developed countries, measured by creditworthiness indicators or by the quality of the prudential regulation and supervision of financial institutions. (iv) Most developing countries, even the larger ones except China and India, are small, open economies strongly dependent on trade and finance (in the case of CAL) on global commodity and financial markets, dominated by OECD countries. Taking these four features seriously implies that these countries do not have the choice for autonomy of monetary plus capital mobility while neglecting the exchange rate. They can only endure a limited amount of exchange rate fluctuation, and if they have more, it harms financial stability and output growth severely. Full monetary autonomy under CAL is the privilege of the countries with the leading currencies; for developing countries the US option is elusive. If, on the other hand, only a few countries with specific characteristics fulfil the preconditions for absolutely fixed exchange rates (currency board, official dollarization), the Argentina option is also unavailable for most developing countries (and Argentina failed). The result is that those countries that opt for full capital account liberalization realize this goal only, gaining neither stable exchange rates nor monetary autonomy.

Combining the two reservations of the theorem leads to the conclusion that developing countries that opt for full-fledged CAL achieve only a low degree of monetary autonomy – monetary policy is doomed to followership vis à vis leading central banks – and are faced with a lower degree of exchange rate stability. Both options, the US and the Argentinean, are simply not available for them, apart from exceptions. If capital mobility remains restricted through selective capital controls (long-standing or temporary), a higher degree of exchange rate stability – including the option for intermediate regimes – and monetary autonomy can be gained, albeit not fully. Of course, this result is only valid if there are no severe negative impacts or costs of capital controls and if the latter can be applied in a prudent way, avoiding abuses.

Under full CAL there is little policy space for monetary policy if there is a flexible exchange rate regime, since fluctuations of the exchange rate *must* to be limited, hence external stability has priority. This has two critical consequences. For the purpose of internal stabilization fiscal policy has to take over the role of monetary policy. But this can hardly be considered a second best option for reasons not discussed here. Now it is up to wage and price flexibility, which have to take care of internal and external stabilization (to adjust the real exchange rate if necessary, should monetary policy be occupied to stabilize the nominal rate) as well. In this assignment, markets are supposed to substitute paralysed or sub-optimal policies. Following Keynes, there are good reasons to believe that wage and price flexibility are weak and improper stopgaps for policy. Hence, if monetary policy cannot fulfil its function of internal stabilization, more inflation or deflation are the likely consequences. Thus, macro management deteriorates under a laissez-faire arrangement.

The second critical consequence of a full CAL pertains to a situation with a comparatively weak financial sector, including systems of prudential regulation which are not as good as in developed countries. It is not the weakness as such, but the *differential* that is important here. Abandoning capital controls leads to a risk premium on domestic interest rates. Now markets reveal all the weaknesses and evaluate them; before the lifting they were covered or concealed by the protective function of the controls.[5]

The risk premium reflects the relative weakness of the financial sector of developing countries as compared to developed countries, and assigns financial products which are otherwise identical with those in developed countries a country-specific stigma. The risk premium is not stable, falls normally in good times – often dependent on the world business conjuncture – and rises in bad. The consequences of CAL are higher interest rates, often hailed as the whip of financial globalization which compels countries to adhere to stronger monetary discipline. In reality, however, the opposite is true: monetary policy is forced to greater tightness, fiscal policy too, and the policy mix deteriorates; furthermore, if less exchange rate stability is the outcome despite the preoccupation of monetary policy with external stabilization, the financial sector is exposed to more stress and its weaknesses increase further.

On the other hand, capital controls can drive a wedge between foreign and domestic interest rates and exchange rates can be kept more stable. Monetary policy is capable of determining autonomously the magnitude of the wedge. The wedge can be positive or negative, domestic interest rates can be above or below world market rates, assuming competitive domestic financial markets, i.e. abolition of 'financial repression' on domestic markets. It is likely that there are limits to the wedge, as very high interest rates induce illegal capital inflows and very low rates elicit capital outflows. Under strong differentials the tightness of the controls is contested. Full and efficient capital controls would erase the country risk premium, although it may exist notionally but is not reflected in interest rates.

If capital controls are selective but efficient enough to stabilize intermediate exchange rate regimes (e.g. adjustable pegs, crawling pegs, etc.) corner solutions in exchange rate policy which are problematic for most developing countries can be avoided.

In short, capital controls in developing countries, analysed in the framework of the 'impossible trinity', in the case of prudent application can contribute to (i) greater autonomy of monetary policy, (ii) facilitate more stability of exchange rates including intermediate options, (iii) reduce or abandon the country risk premium on interest rates and protect an immature, underdeveloped financial sector. As a result, boom–bust cycles of capital inflows and outflows with the risk of comprehensive financial crises can be mitigated. The capital account would be well-managed. Again, these benefits can only be reaped if no severe opportunity costs of capital controls exist.

Before I address the issue of the benefits and costs, it should be discussed whether the role of capital controls (again: in the standard understanding of the term) can be replaced by other policies that can be associated with the broader definition of capital controls. If this cannot be done easily, but instead involves high costs and risks, developing countries cannot be considered ready for CAL.

3.4 Can financial sector reforms or other policies replace capital controls?

As mentioned in section 3.2, five other policies can exert indirect influence on a country's cross-border capital flows. The most important candidate is the prudential regulation of the financial sector, or put differently, financial sector reforms. Before I come to this, I will appraise the aptitude of the other four policies.

Monetary policy could potentially stem overly strong capital inflows with a loose stance. Since strong inflows occur in times when output thrives and overheating is imminent, this would thwart internal stabilization; tight fiscal policy is sub-optimal in such a situation. Under strong pressure for capital outflows, especially the sudden reversal of capital inflows, even a very tight monetary policy is unable to stem outflows and avoid or limit depreciation of the currency. The momentum of outflows is simply too strong as demonstrated on numerous occasions.

Turning to *exchange rate policy*, can high reserves be used to defend the exchange rate in the case of excessive outflows? With traditional measures for the appropriateness of foreign exchange reserves of central banks, using reserves to defend the exchange rate can yield at best a short-term deceleration of outflows. Although super-large reserves may deter speculators, they involve other problems. Accumulating very high reserves, as some countries have practised in the last few years, is costly, requires vast sterilization measures to mop up excessive domestic liquidity, the outcome in a crisis remains uncertain, and it can lead to global imbalances if many or several large countries follow this policy (Stiglitz 2006, pp. 245 ff.).

Many contend that floating exchange rates, meaning revaluation, are the appropriate remedy against booming capital inflows, and fixed but maladjusted exchange rates – as in Thailand in 1997 – are the true culprits for financial crises. However, the maladjustment of exchange rates can even be reinforced, as in the case of full floating, because revaluation would not be sustainable and is likely to be followed by an even stronger devaluation. If financial investors foresee the problem, they have incentives for short-run inflows and subsequent outflows. It would be a simplistic explanation of Thailand's 1997 financial crisis to believe that floating exchange rates could have prevented the disaster.

Fiscal policy, in particular if it focuses on the currency denomination of budget deficits, can contribute to financial stability by avoiding or limiting currency mismatch, that is giving preference to domestic currency borrowing. This normally has a strong impact on the current account balance which would be improved if domestic finance was used. Although this may involve severe follow-up problems, to a limited extent it could replace – or complement – capital controls. But even if this can be done, the *stock* of public debt is normally mainly external debt so that the country is highly sensitive to any depreciation of the currency.

Tax policy and its proper implementation can help to curb capital outflows and possibly dampen the level of financial inflows, but is not
designed to cope with strong fluctuations of inflows or outflows. For
low-income countries usually not subject to commercial capital inflows,
effective taxation may alleviate the drain of savings and contribute to
deepened domestic financial markets. To some extent they have similar
functions as capital export controls, especially in low income countries,
but are hard to implement.

Most proponents of CAL count on *financial sector reforms* which are
considered prerequisites for lifting capital controls. They comprise prudential regulation of financial markets and institutions, especially bank
and non-bank supervision. Such reforms encompass those of accounting and auditing standards of enterprises, bankruptcy rules, information
disclosure requirements, implementing appropriate capital adequacy
standards for banks, non-banks and enterprises as well, provisions for
non-performing loans, and so on. Many of the reformers point to the
necessity to privatize state-owned banks as they are seen as undermining
sound banking and competition in the financial sector. Generally speaking, financial sector reforms serve to transit from soft to hard budget
constraints for enterprises and financial institutions.

The field in which financial sector reforms overlap with capital controls pertain mainly to measures that avoid non-hedged currency and
maturity mismatch in the balance sheets of financial institutions and,
more generally, measures against incurring too many risks that make
banks and non-banks vulnerable. Although, in principle, all this is necessary, the outreach of prudential regulations is limited, even if they can
be implemented within a short period; they cannot fully replace capital
controls for the following reasons:

• First of all, they are microeconomic measures aiming to prevent the
  failure of a single financial institution, but not systemic financial
  crises. Of course, micro reforms that encompass *all* institutions can
  gain macro importance, but this needs time. Apart from this, even
  if financial institutions are stabilized according to all standards, their
  clients may not be, so that the vulnerability of enterprises can spill
  over to banks or banks can resort to a credit crunch vis à vis bad
  debtors. The nature of systemic risks differs from micro risks. Even if
  the financial sector is fairly stable (as in Argentina in the 1990s) massive shocks such as sudden capital inflow reversals and subsequent
  unanticipated currency devaluations can shatter the financial sector.
  The peculiar magnitude of the shocks stems, at least to some degree,

from the shallow domestic financial markets which are swamped by comparatively huge waves of inflows and subsequent outflows.

- The logic of banking reforms for risk assessment is different from what is needed to avoid financial crises. For instance, as long-term assets are regarded in banking supervision as riskier than short-term assets, short-term lending is favoured which can reinforce macro instability. Or: the focus on capital-adequacy standards can induce procyclical lending and borrowing (Ishii and Habermeier, 2002, p. 45).

- Prudential regulations of the financial sector are not geared for discretionary measures to stabilize the whole economy in periods of stress, such as excessive capital inflows or outflows. They are made to set long-standing rules to foster the resilience of the financial sector, but they do not target the prevention or alleviation of the shocks themselves. The origin of the latter may perhaps lie in certain events or changes in behaviour or attitudes outside the country, e.g. swings in external investors' sentiments, which affect the host countries so massively that even fairly robust financial institutions are not robust enough. In such cases discretionary policy is needed for a rush defence of the financial sector as a whole.

- Because of the net debtor status in the foreign currency of most developing countries, their exposure to sudden blown-up currency mismatch risks triggered by strong devaluations is not comparable to developed countries with (predominantly) a net creditor position. Hence prudential regulations would have to erase original sin by hedging all stocks of debt. Pervasive balance sheet management is called for, in financial institutions, enterprises and governmental authorities as well. Particularly currency mismatch in the state budget (or the government's balance sheet) is not subject to prudential regulations.

- In the logic of prudential regulations, to cope better with currency mismatch risks, financial institutions may favour the use of hard currency on the asset *and* liability side of their balance sheets unless this is hindered by the authorities. Such a practice would promote unofficial dollarization, which is counter-productive for the stability of the financial system for several reasons. Normally this weakens the external value of the local currency, is likely to reinforce inflation, impairs or even paralyses the use of monetary policy and makes the financial system, in general, more fragile (Priewe and Herr 2005, pp. 159 ff.).

A brief look at the quality of the financial sector in developing countries shows the immense gap vis à vis developed nations. This also holds true for most emerging economies. There is a strong correlation between the creditworthiness of countries, evaluated by rating institutions, and the income per capita.[6] The extent of compliance with international standards (i.e. developed countries' standards) in banking supervision, accounting, bankruptcy law, and so on, is low, even when Basle I standards are taken as a measure (Powell, 2004). There is nothing to add to Eichengreen's comment: 'But the sad truth in all too many countries is that banks have a limited capacity to manage risk and that regulators have limited capacity to supervise their actions. In a sense, this limited capacity is the very definition of a financially underdeveloped, or less-developed, or developing economy' (Eichengreen, 1999, p. 11). In other words, to call for a big leap in the quality of the financial sector is to call for making developing countries suddenly developed. If a shock strategy is to be avoided, patient gradualism is needed.

Goldstein and Turner (2004, pp. 3 ff.) offer proposals for far-reaching policy reforms to cope with currency mismatch, including the extension of a currency-mismatch assessment to the clients of banks, and an IMF reporting system. Meanwhile, the IMF has also acknowledged the currency mismatch in the so-called 'Balance Sheet Approach' (IMF 2003). It is to be integrated in the Financial Sector Assessment Program (FSAP) and the framework for the Debt Sustainability Analysis of the Fund. Financial Soundness Indicators have been developed (Carson and Ingves 2003). At first glance this appears to be a big step forward. However, the crucial guideline prevails: 'the private sector is responsible for protecting its balance sheets against shocks' (IMF 2003, no. 12). According to this document, policies should promote buffering and hedging on private balance sheets by (i) abandoning implicit promises of government bailouts, (ii) changing the tax system that favours debt over equity, elimination of tax distortions, (iii) reduced government involvement in private sector investments, (iv) more flexible exchange rates, and (v) a general strengthening of prudential regulation and supervision. It has to be added that international bail-outs would also have to be prohibited to prevent vast moral hazards leading to too much risk-taking on the part of international investors (Diaz-Alejandro, 1985). Such policy proposals either deliberately accept the risk of severe adjustment problems which dampen economic growth or are not fully aware of the drastic consequences of the restructuring of the financial sector and the sectors of its clients. Or it needs to be spelt out that such reforms require long-lasting gradualism.

To sum up, if tight and thorough financial sector reforms are implemented within a short time, it will probably lead to a fierce tightening of the financial sector: hard budget constraints have to be rigorously instituted, financial institutions which cannot pass muster have to be closed or downsized, sales to foreign banks seem necessary, credit rationing is likely to increase. Financial stabilization and adjustment would be imposed at the expense of financial deepening. 'Narrow banking' could be a likely outcome (World Bank, 2001, pp. 90 ff.). To put it differently: the financial sector has to adjust to the rules prevalent in highly developed countries although the country hosting the financial institutions lags far behind and the potential shocks are stronger. On the whole, the concept of quickly instituting deep financial sector reforms is burdened with the tasks it can hardly solve without high economic and social costs. So this substitute for capital controls is the Achilles' heel of the capital account liberalization policy package.[7] Only if there are very strong benefits to be expected from CAL, could the high adjustment costs be justified.

3.5   The costs of capital controls and the elusive promises of financial liberalization

Of course, the proponents of CAL see the main opportunity costs of capital controls in the foregone benefits of the financial integration of developing countries. The benefits promised can be characterized as gains from an optimal international allocation of capital; they embrace chiefly five parts (Dooley, 1996; Fischer et al., 1998; World Bank, 1997): (i) increased net capital inflows considered as promoters of economic growth; (ii) reduced cost of capital due to its diminished scarcity; (iii) intertemporal smoothing of consumption; (iv) better risk diversification in the wealth portfolios of financial investors; (v) improved governance due to enhanced discipline in economic policies. The argumentation is rooted in orthodox neoclassical theory, tied to a host of restrictive assumptions. In general, the theoretical foundation is surprisingly weak and the empirical evidence is dubious.

The notion that 'capital' flows from the capital-rich to the capital-poor countries if capital mobility exists, is tied to a comparatively higher marginal productivity of capital. However, there is no sound theoretical connection between capital intensity and returns on physical capital. A globally uniform production function, the absence of externalities and permanently sufficient aggregate demand are assumed, global full employment also. By 'capital' is meant 'capital goods', which are added to the capital stock in the poorer country, or finance that translates fully into capital goods, nothing into consumption or simply the money stock. There is no crowding out of domestic capital formation by foreign inflows. Even if all this happened, the result would be a long-standing current account deficit financed by capital inflows without any ensuing problems. If this occurs too, only a temporary once-off level effect in the output of the receiving country takes place, as marginal productivity of capital is assumed to fall (Gouranchas and Jeanne, 2004). Permanently higher growth would only follow if the inflows incorporate and trigger a continuous flow of technical progress. The concept likens the often-criticized saving-gap theory of under-development, which contends that poor countries save insufficiently for higher growth and require external saving. A key weakness of this concept is that capital inflows are not differentiated into FDI, short-term equity, debt, and so on. Rather than anything else it could apply to FDI inflows, which tend to be growth-enhancing, but even this at least to some extent is questionable (Moran et al., 2005).

From the viewpoint of the endogenous growth theory, capital flows also depend on human capital, infrastructure endowments, the capacity to generate technical progress, and so on, which may lead to increasing returns to scale; hence there can also be a capital flow from capital-poor to capital-rich countries. If, however, labour is comparatively immobile and therefore locked-in due to regulations as capital tends to flow out, under-development is reinforced by capital mobility. The latter is obviously not one-way traffic.

The notion of an interest rate-reducing capacity of capital inflows to developing economies disregards the monetary determinants of interest rates, particularly country risk premia, besides monetary policy. In reality, as mentioned previously, CAL often comes along with rising real interest rates, in contrast with what orthodox theory upholds. Apart from this, if interest rates would fall due to capital inflows they would at the same time lower or prevent the incentives from flowing in. When strong capital inflows occur, asset prices often soar, signalling falling interest rates, albeit often only temporarily, followed by the bursting of the bubble. The volatility of financial flows is not captured properly as the focus of the orthodox theory is on the 'real economy'.

Capital inflows are attributed to the ability to smooth consumption over time. Even at a low-income stage, economies can maintain a higher consumption level than without capital inflows as foreign saving substitutes domestic, and at a higher stage of development more domestic saving is necessary to pay for external debt. Also, short-run income fluctuations need not impact expenditure if buffered by fluctuations of external capital inflows. Admittedly, in this case inflows may also be used for consumption, at least temporarily. Even if consumption were smoothed it is not apt to enhance the growth trend. Empirical evidence shows that inflows often feed consumption (particularly government consumption) and that consumption can become more volatile rather than smoothed (Williamson 2005, p. 29).

Cross-border capital mobility is supposed to support the diversification of the portfolios of the wealth owners, in rich and poor countries alike. From the viewpoint of developed countries, the inclination and ability to take and manage risks increases with a higher level of wealth, and developing countries pose different risks than developed. And, of course, developing countries need capital ready to take risks. Conversely, wealth owners in poor countries may also want to add foreign assets to their portfolio, but the weight of inflows is regarded bigger. First of all, the risk diversification argument pertains to the microeconomic rationale of individual wealth owners. What is perhaps wealth-enhancing for them, is not necessarily good for the developing economy. Furthermore, diversification of risks of individual wealth owners can generate new macroeconomic risks, such as speculative bubbles, exchange-rate risks, country-specific risk premia, currency mismatch, and so on. Finally, the argument assumes that risk assessment and hedging capacities exist on both sides, that of the financial investors and the host country. It is likely that the distribution of these capacities is unequal. In short, maturity, soundness and resilience of the financial sector in the developing country are presumed for the validity of the argument.

It is one of the most popular arguments put forward for abolishing capital controls that the exposure of a developing economy to the world financial markets exerts a salutary impact by rewarding good economic governance and punishing bad (e.g. Weizsäcker, 1999, pp. 112 f.; Siebert, 1997; Prasad et al., 2004, pp. 14 ff.). The governance addressed here mainly concerns macroeconomic policy and the achievement of macro targets, mainly price stability and fiscal 'soundness', perhaps also other sectors of policy such as corruption, transparency, and banking sector stability, and so on. These arguments are flawed in many respects:

- Whether or not 'appropriate' policies are rewarded depends on the effectiveness of the channels (i) to (iv). So it is presupposed that capital account liberalization is a wholesale good thing: hence the argument cannot be used to prove what is preconceived.
- The punishment through capital markets can be so disastrous with irreversible collateral damages, that it turns out to be *destructive*. If this indeed is the case, the argument can be twisted in favour of capital controls to avoid such devastating effects.

- It is presumed that there is no doubt what the appropriate policies or good governance in this respect really are. It is likely that the policy space shrinks under CAL and thus impairs prudent macro-policies and distorts the policy mix.
- Sanctions for misbehaviour are only sensible, of course, if the incriminated misconduct is the unambiguous cause of the problems, for instance, a financial crisis. But often the cause-and-effect nexus is more complex and subject to contrasting interpretations, and besides this, the causes for problems can lie far beyond the scope of governance in developing countries. It can be the whims and sentiments of global financial markets, or the change in macroeconomic conditions (or policies) in the financial centres of the world economy that induce external shocks.
- The argument seems to presume that the global financial markets behave rationally and that their judgements are infallible. But often enough market reactions are myopic, driven by extreme short-termism, truncated by information asymmetries, speculation, herd behaviour and contagion defects, using biased information filters and screening methods – on the whole not always a good or even impartial referee or judge. There seems to be blind trust in the infallibility of global financial markets.

  Of all the arguments in favour of capital account liberalization this is the weakest and unequivocally of a highly ideological nature (cp. similar conclusions of Williamson, 2005, pp. 31 ff., and Stiglitz, 2004, p. 62).

Apart from the alleged benefits of CAL, capital controls are rebutted for being ineffective and costly. The argument has three facets: first, it is contended that capital controls cannot be sufficiently enforced and are therefore ineffective in the sense that they do not accomplish their goals. This implies that the goals are legitimate. Second, there are costs of bureaucracy in organizing and conducting controls. Third, the controls have distorting effects that cause the sub-optimal allocation of resources with growth dampening effects. The last argument hinges of course on the hypothesis that capital account liberalization has positive effects on capital allocation and growth. Thus it is recourse to the above mentioned channels and adds nothing new. The first argument has to be taken seriously, but it requires detailed analyses of the proper instruments and the way they work, knowledge about what they can achieve and what not. It is an essentially empirical and practical question. Also, the often held assertion that controls can be bypassed the longer they exist requires empirical vindication. Loopholes must certainly be closed and an active enforcement policy has to permanently control circumvention activities, as is the case with all government regulations, especially in the banking sector. It should also be mentioned that capital controls do not have to be implemented with a perfect keeping to the rules, although this is desirable from a legal perspective. The critical point is to achieve the economic targets as is also the case, analogously, with taxation, which is always at risk of being undermined by tax evasion. Sceptics underline that in the modern age of open borders, easy transportation technology and electronic communication, capital controls cannot be maintained much longer. But it can also be argued conversely: with electronic means and strong capital concentration, transparency and control of commercial activities have become much easier and less costly. It is likely that market-based controls like the Chilean unremunerated, required reserves, cash-reserve requirements for liabilities incurred vis à vis non-residents or withholding taxes on inflows and outflows are more efficient than broad-based administrative controls. But this issue is not the subject of this chapter. That capital controls can be efficient at least to some extent can be learnt from China, India, Malaysia, Singapore and Chile, to name the most important examples.

Certainly, capital controls involve costs of implementation. Administrative controls most probably induce microeconomic misallocation by discriminating against certain agents affected more than others (Forbes 2005). Compared with the costs of financial crises – assuming that capital controls contribute to preventing crises – the costs are almost negligible if the lost GDP over the years 1997 to 2000 in per cent of a year's GDP is taken as an indicator (e.g. for Thailand 108.9, Indonesia 87.8, South Korea 49.0 (Williamson 2005, p. 16)). Of course, capital control measures can be abused or used imprudently to conserve inconsistent policies and to prevent painful adjustments, such as unavoidable exchange rate readjustments, the restructuring of enterprises, fighting corruption and rent seeking, and so on. But all this applies to many policy tools which can be used either with foresight or not.

3.6   Conclusions

The notion of full financial integration where capital can flow across the borders of nations as freely as it can flow within a national economy is elusive. Capital account liberalization in this sense exists nowhere as exchange rate markets, national monetary policy and national regulations generate conspicuous differences, even if all administrative controls are lifted. Cross-border capital flows are indirectly influenced, sometimes to a strong extent, by monetary and exchange rate policy, especially in the case of interventions and subsequent changes in reserves, but also by fiscal and tax policies. The view that only direct measures of the state influence capital flows, i.e. administrative restrictions and/or market-based controls, and thus hinder full financial integration implies too narrow an understanding of capital flow restrictions. Therefore the full array of direct and indirect measures that influence capital flows has to be considered. The comprehensive use of these measures can be called capital account management. The contentious issue is whether active management should be conducted and which policy tools are to be included, especially concerning direct measures.

The so-called concept of the 'impossible trinity' can be used as a heuristic to ascertain that direct capital controls can be used by developing countries to stabilize exchange rates, e.g. to facilitate intermediate regimes which under CAL are not attainable, and to gain a higher degree of monetary policy autonomy. This does not necessarily imply full control of capital flows but can also relate to selective and temporary measures; even if full monetary policy and fixed exchange rates may not be feasible under partial controls, a considerable degree of stability or autonomy may be achievable. This has several far-reaching implications. A better policy-mix between monetary and fiscal policy is possible if the monetary policy is geared to domestic needs of price and output stabilization. And with stable but adjustable exchange rates more policy space can also be gained. Moreover, with capital controls interest rates can be decoupled, at least to some extent, from the global level governed by the leading currency countries. Hence lower (or if necessary higher) real interest can be achieved than under CAL which leads to an increased risk premium as the weaknesses of the domestic financial system are brought to the fore. With controls, the under-developed financial sector can be protected so as to use time to reform it deliberately and gradually in tandem with the real economy. Overall, the proper use of capital controls can facilitate a more comprehensive policy package with more options than under CAL.

Developing countries normally do not have the choice of two goals out of the three of the 'impossible trinity' if they opt for full financial integration. In the latter case they gain only CAL but neither a combination with stable exchange rates nor one with autonomous monetary policy. Under CAL, monetary policy is overburdened to defend the exchange rate, and a net debtor country with a high stock of hard currency debt cannot enjoy monetary policy autonomy with strong exchange rate fluctuations. This would risk financial stability and depress output growth severely. Opting for full CAL narrows the policy space, distorts the policy-mix and overstrains financial sector reforms. Full financial integration pushes developing countries to resort to unfavourable corner solutions of exchange rate regimes. There is no active capital account management, the 'activities' are governed by the financial markets, characterized by strong volatility with boom-and-bust cyclicity. As often contended, a sound and stable financial sector and disciplined macro policy are regarded as preconditions for full CAL; put differently: in case this threshold has not yet been reached, capital controls are necessary. But the punch line is that full financial liberalization – if it comes as a pre-maturity – impairs the macroeconomic management of the central bank and the financial authorities and overburdens the financial sector.

Given the overall weak features of the financial sector in most developing countries, deeply rooted in structural characteristics of underdevelopment, reforms of the financial sector in the short or medium term involve most probably high opportunity costs as thorough structural complementary adjustments in the non-financial sectors are inevitable. Hence these reforms can hardly be considered a substitute for capital controls, at least not in the short or medium term.

Most of the promises of CAL are derived from a theoretical model of a global 'real' – i.e. non-monetary – economy which abstracts from money, exchange rates and finance, and in so doing, from reality. In a global monetary economy the alleged gains from CAL pertain at best and under certain conditions to FDI inflows among all capital inflows, and the asserted benefits from improved risk diversification require, *inter alia*, a stable and mature financial sector.

The essential function of capital controls is a *'third line of defence'* (Eichengreen 1999, p. 12) of the financial sector against external disturbances: the first line of defence is the risk-protection by the banks themselves; the second is the prudential regulation and supervision of financial institutions and markets; and the third are direct capital controls. The first line should include enterprises and private and public households as well.

Although not a subject of this essay, market-based controls for inflows and outflows, which should be regarded as a special monetary policy instrument, seem superior to administrative controls. The latter are more difficult to handle, loopholes and distorting microeconomic effects are more likely, and discretionary short-term alterations are difficult. To cope better with the boom–bust cycles of cross-border flows requires temporary discretionary adjustments with high flexibility. Generally speaking, emerging economies should be more concerned with inflow regulations, poorer developing countries with outflow regulations. Comprehensive administrative controls might be useful as a contingency plan for cases of emergency.

Capital controls are an important and indispensable part of the tool box of economic policies in developing countries geared to actively manage their capital account.

Notes

1. The term is used here interchangeably with global financial integration.
2. This chapter draws on a comprehensive study (co-authored with Hansjörg Herr) commissioned by the German Ministry of Economic Cooperation and Development (Herr and Priewe 2006).
3. A narrower definition of capital controls would include only the *intentional* measures, but the distinction between intended and non-intended forms is difficult or impossible. Another attempt to taper the definition could be to exclude all official cross-border transactions of capitals (reserve policy, budgetary policy, etc.), but – directly or indirectly – these measures impact private capital transactions.
4. The normal Taylor-rule would be extended to $r_T = r^* + \alpha(\pi - \pi^*) + \beta[(Y - Y^*)/Y^*] + \gamma(e - e^*)$. r_T is the central bank's target interest rate, π is the actual inflation, π^* is target inflation, Y and Y^* are output and potential output, e and e^* the actual and the target exchange rate, α, β and γ are weights which add to one. In the case of solely external stabilization, α and β are zero.
5. The uncovered interest rate parity changes to $i_D = i_F + \hat{e}_e + R$, with i_D as the domestic interest rate, i_F the interest rate in the leading foreign countries, $\hat{e}$ the expected appreciation or depreciation of the exchange rate (depreciation is positive); R, the risk premium, is added compared to the conventional interest rate parity.
6. For example, the index of creditworthiness of the Institutional Investors' Index 2002 comprises 142 countries with a maximum rating of 100. The weakest OECD country (excluding Turkey and Mexico) is Greece with slightly more than 70, the best upper middle income country is the Czech Republic with roughly 65; China is the strongest lower middle income country with 60; India is the strongest low income country with 48; Vietnam reaches, as the second best in this group, 38. The rest of the low income countries range between 7 and 37 (cp. Institutional Investor 2003).
7. Goldstein and Turner (2004) argue against the original sin hypothesis of Eichengreen et al. (2002 and 2003) and use instead the concept of currency mismatch as an antidote. The proponents of the original-sin-hypothesis are more pessimistic and point to policies beyond the scope of developing countries (supply-side measures in developed countries).

References

Boughton, J. (2002), 'Why White, Not Keynes? Inventing the Post-war International Monetary System', in Arnon, A. and W. Young (eds), *The Open Economy Macromodel: Past, Present and Future*, Boston: Kluwer Academic Publisher, pp. 73–96.

Carson, C.S. and Ingves, S. (2003), *Financial Soundness Indicators*. International Monetary Fund. 14 May, Washington, DC: IMF.

Diaz-Alejandro, C. (1985), 'Good-bye Financial Repression, Hello Financial Crash', in *Journal of Development Economics*, No. 19, pp. 1–24.

Dooley, M.P. (1996), 'A Survey of Literature on Controls over International Capital Transactions', *IMF Staff Papers*, Vol. 43, pp. 639–87.

Edwards, S. (ed.) (2007), *Capital Controls and Capital Flows in Emerging Economies: Policies, Practices, and Consequences*. Chicago: University of Chicago Press.

Eichengreen, B. (1999), *Towards A New International Financial Architecture. A Practical Post-Asia Agenda*. Washington, DC: Institute for International Economics.

Eichengreen, B. et al. (2002), 'Original Sin: The Pain, the Mystery, and the Road to Redemption', Paper presented at a conference on Currency and Maturity Mismatching: Redeeming Debt from Original Sin. Inter-American Development Bank, 21–22 November, Washington, DC.

Eichengreen, B. et al. (2003), 'Currency Mismatches, Debt Intolerance, and Original Sin: Why They Are Not the Same and Why It Matters', *NBER Working Paper* No. 10036. Cambridge, MA.

Epstein, G. et al. (2005), 'Capital management techniques in developing countries', in Epstein, G. (ed.), *Capital Flight and Capital Controls in Developing Countries*. Cheltenham/Northampton: Edward Elgar.

Fischer, S. et al. (1998), 'Should the IMF Pursue Capital Account Convertibility?' *Essays in International Finance* No. 207, Princeton University, Princeton.

Fischer, S. (2001), 'Exchange Rate Regimes: Is the Bipolar View Correct?' *Journal of Economic Perspectives*, Vol. 15(2), pp. 3–24.

Forbes, K. (2005), 'The Microeconomic Evidence on Capital Controls: No Free Lunch', *NBER Working Paper* No. 11372, Cambridge, MA.

Goldstein, M. and Turner, P. (2004), *Controlling Currency Mismatches in Emerging Markets*. Washington, DC: Institute for International Economics.

Gouranchas, P.-O. and Jeanne, O. (2004), 'The Elusive Gains From International Financial Integration', *IMF Working Paper* WP/04/74.

Herr, H. and Priewe J. (2006), 'Capital Account Regimes and Monetary Policy in Developing Countries – Liberalization with Regulation', Berlin, unpublished.

IMF (2003), 'The Balance Sheet Approach and its Application at the Fund', Paper prepared by the Policy Development and Review Department, 30 June.

IMF: AREAER – *Annual Report on Exchange Rate Arrangements and Exchange Restrictions*, several issues, IMF, Washington DC.

Institutional Investor (2003), Country Credit Ratings. http://www.institutional-investor.com.

Ishii, S. and Habermeier, K. (2002), 'Capital Account Liberalization and Financial Sector Stability', *IMF Occasional Paper* 211. Washington DC.

Kose, M.A. et al. (2006), 'Financial Globalization: A Reappraisal'. *NBER Working Paper* No. 12484, Cambridge, MA.

Moran, T.M. et al. (eds) (2005), *Does Foreign Direct Investment Promote Development?* Washington DC: Institute for International Economics.

Obstfeld, M. and A. Taylor (1998), 'The Great Depression as a Watershed: International Capital Mobility over the Long Run', in, M.Bordo et al. (eds), *The Defining Moment: The Great Depression and the American Economy in the Twentieth Century*, Chicago: University of Chicago Press, pp. 353–402.

OECD (2004), OECD Code of Liberalization of Capital Movements (September 2004). Paris. (www.oecd.org, 4 August 2005)

Powell, A. (2004), Basel II and Developing Countries: Sailing Through the Sea of Standards. Universidad Torcuato Di Tella and World Bank. Washington, DC.

Prasad, E., Rogoff, K., Wei, Sh.-J. and Kose, M.A. (2004), 'Financial Globalization, Growth and Volatility in Developing Countries', *NBER Working Paper Series* 10942.

Priewe, J. and Herr, H. (2005), *The Macroeconomics of Development and Poverty Reduction. Strategies Beyond the Washington Consensus*, Baden-Baden: Nomos.

Siebert, H. (1997), 'Disziplinierung der nationalen Wirtschaftspolitik durch die internationale Kapitalmobilität', in Duwendag, D. (ed.), *Finanzmärkte im Spannungsfeld von Globalisierung, Regulierung und Geldpolitik*. Berlin, pp. 41–68.

Stiglitz, J. (2004), 'Capital-Market Liberalization, Globalization, and the IMF', *Oxford Review of Economic Policy*, Vol. 20(1), pp. 57–71.

Stiglitz, J.E. (2006), *Making Globalization Work. The Next Steps to Global Justice*. London: W.W. Norton.

Weizsäcker, C.C. (1999), *Logik der Globalisierung*. Göttingen: Vandenhoeck & Ruprecht.

Williamson, J. (2000), *Exchange Rate Regimes for Emerging Markets: Reviving the Intermediate Option*, Washington DC: Institute for International Economics.

Williamson, J. (2005), *Curbing the Boom–Bust Cycle: Stabilizing Capital Flows to Emerging Markets*, Washington DC: Institute of International Economics.

World Bank (1997), *Private Capital Flows to Developing Countries: The Road to Financial Integration*. Oxford: Oxford University Press.

4
Financial Liberalization, Exchange Rate Regime and Economic Performance in BRICs Countries[1]

Luiz Fernando de Paula

4.1 Introduction

In October 2003, a Goldman Sachs report (Purushothaman and Wilson, 2003), using the demographic projections and a model of capital accumulation and productivity growth, mapped out GDP growth, income per capita and currency movements of the BRICs countries (Brazil, Russia, India and China) until 2050. Based on some assumptions, the report forecast that in less than 40 years the BRICs countries together could be larger than the G6 in US dollar terms and by 2025 they could account for over half the size of the G6 (currently they are worth less than 15 per cent). However, as the report recognizes, there is no guarantee that the economic growth of these countries will reach what is forecast by the study, as such behaviour depends on a set of factors, which includes macro stability (understood as price stability), development of good institutions (legal system, functioning markets, educational systems, financial institutions, etc.), openness to trade and FDI, and improvement in education level of the population – all known development policies supported by multilateral institutions, such as the World Bank.

Although such a forecast is exposed to criticism, there is no doubt that due to their geographic and population size and GDP dimension (current and potential), in spite of the problems of social inequality and even poverty that the BRICs countries face nowadays, one cannot disregard the importance and potentiality of these economies. Looking at the GDP growth performance of the BRICs countries, one can see that since 1990 GDP growth has differed among the countries: average GDP growth in China in 1990–2006 was 9.8 per cent, in India 6.1 per cent, Brazil 2.2 per cent and Russia −0.1 per cent. If we compare the BRICs countries only in the recent period (1999–2006), that is, after the 1998 Russian crisis,

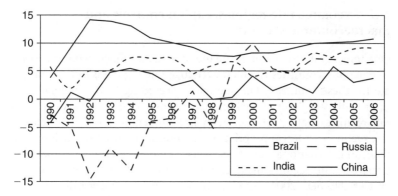

Figure 4.1 GDP growth (%) of BRICs countries
Source: IMF, IPEADATA (Brazil) and DB Research (Russia).

the economic performance changes: 9.3 per cent in China, 6.8 per cent in India, 6.7 per cent in Russia and 2.8 per cent in Brazil (see Figure 4.1).

Why have economic performance and macroeconomic stability[2] differed among the BRICs countries? More specifically, in which ways have macroeconomic policy regime and the management of the economic policy defined an economic environment that has contributed to a higher (or lower) economic performance and macroeconomic stability of the BRICs countries?

The chapter aims at analysing the relationship between exchange rate regime, capital account convertibility and economic performance within the big emerging countries that constitute what has been called BRIC – Brazil, Russia, India and China, during the period of capital account liberalization that has happened in broader terms since beginning of the 1990s. The main hypothesis developed in the chapter is that economic performance of BRICs countries is the result, at least partially, of the quality of the macroeconomic policy management adopted in each country, in which exchange rate policy, capital account convertibility and the degree of external vulnerability play a key role.

The chapter is divided into three sections. Section 4.2 discusses the relationship between capital account convertibility, exchange rate regime and macroeconomic stability in emerging countries, while section 4.3 focuses the analysis on the recent experience of each BRIC country. Section 4.4 briefly compares such experiences and seeks to extract some conclusions.

4.2   Exchange rate regimes, capital controls and macroeconomic stability

One important discussion in the literature about macroeconomic issues in emerging countries is which exchange rate regime is more appropriate for these countries. On one hand, according to the 'bipolar' view intermediary regimes – which involve all sorts of intermediary exchange rate regimes, that is, between freely floating regime and fixed exchange rate regime – are less appropriate for economies with substantial involvement in international capital markets. The main argument is that such exchange rate regimes make countries more vulnerable to speculative attacks (Fischer, 2001). On the other hand, the view called 'fear of floating' points out that many emerging countries that adopt flexible exchange rate regime in practice seek to limit exchange rate movements. Such resistance to floating arises from their low policy and institutional credibility and high degree of pass-through of exchange rate changes into domestic prices, among other factors (Calvo and Reinhart, 2002). Other reasons why monetary authorities avoid exchange rate movements are related to the effects of excessive exchange rate volatility (mainly devaluation) on the outstanding foreign currency debts of banks and the corporate sectors with unhedged foreign currency liabilities. In addition, exchange rate fluctuations may generate uncertainties that could impede trade. For instance, prolonged real appreciation associated with large capital inflows can adversely affect export competitiveness and investment in the external sector.

Fixed exchange regime has the advantage of eliminating the exchange rate risk that affects the decisions of exporters and importers and domestic borrowers in international financial markets, and also converging domestic inflation with external inflation. However, such regime has also high risks for bigger emerging countries, as it results in the loss of economic policy flexibility in facing external shocks, mainly when economic authorities do not have enough exchange reserves to intervene in the exchange market and/or there is a confidence crisis associated with the lack of government capability in maintaining the pegged exchange rate; under these conditions, the adjustment costs can be very high. Fixed exchange rate may encourage borrowers to be too confident in taking out foreign-exchange-denominated loans, making very painful any change in the exchange rate regime.[3]

One could argue that the adoption of a freely flexible exchange regime by emerging countries could isolate these countries from speculative attacks on domestic currency as government has no commitment to any level of exchange rate. Besides, floating exchange regime could increase the autonomy of monetary policy, overcoming the 'impossible trinity' that says a country cannot have at the same time capital account convertibility, fixed exchange rate regime and monetary policy autonomy in order to achieve domestic objectives. However, floating exchange regime frequently works in the real world differently from what is supposed in the textbooks. According to Grenville (2000), fundamentals cannot explain the behaviour of exchange rate over a short/medium term horizon, that is, exchange rates have at times exhibited long-lived swings with no apparent changes in fundamentals significant enough to justify them. The problems related to the exchange rate volatility are greater for emerging countries, as they have: (i) no long historical experience of market-determined exchange rate; (ii) few Friedmanite stabilizing speculators acting in the exchange market (that is, there has been a lack of players willing take contrarian foreign exchange positions in emerging countries); and (iii) much larger and volatile capital flows, in relation to the size of their capital markets and economies more generally (Grenville, 2000). According to Ho and McCauley's data (2003), despite the rapid growth in activity during the 1990s, foreign exchange markets in most emerging countries continue to be relatively small with less liquidity than their counterparts in the industrial world. This suggests that emerging foreign exchange markets are more prone to one-sided bets and instability, because they are thin and subject to a high degree of uncertainty and information asymmetries (Moreno, 2005, p. 10).

Flexibility in the operation of floating exchange regimes can be helpful in absorbing the capital inflow, in buffering external shocks, and responding to the changing productive capacity of emerging economies; it can also inhibit some short-term flows, by serving as a constant reminder that exchange rate volatility can outweigh the interest rate advantage of foreign currency borrowings (Grenville, 2000, p. 59). Some sort of managed floating exchange rates regime can be useful if the objective of the central bank is to reduce the exchange rate volatility and also influence somehow the real exchange rate for international trade purposes. Central bank intervenes in foreign exchange markets to achieve a variety of macroeconomic objectives, such as controlling inflation, maintaining external competitiveness and/or maintaining financial stability. Differently from a pegged exchange rate, authorities' interventions to limit exchange rate movements may not target a certain level of the exchange rate, allowing nominal exchange rate to float in order to discourage speculative capital flows, but may influence its path.

The preservation of a competitive and stable real exchange rate can be used as an intermediate target of macroeconomic policies oriented to employment and growth objectives.[4]

In order to enhance the possibility of a successful management of exchange rate regime in emerging markets some measures can be necessary to reduce the volatility of capital flows and the likehood of speculative attack on domestic currency. One possibility is the use of official intervention in the foreign exchange market, which may exert direct influence on nominal exchange rate as it alters the relative supply of domestic and foreign currency assets. On one hand, the countries' ability to resist currency depreciation is limited by its stock of foreign exchange reserves and its access to potential credit lines. Reserve accumulation can be seen as an insurance against future negative shocks and speculative attack on domestic currency, as emerging economies have limited access to international capital markets. On the other hand, the ability to avoid currency appreciation may require the use of sterilized intervention. The accumulation of reserves requires some sort of financing due to the excess of foreign currency reserves over domestic currency in circulation. The central bank can finance this gap by issuing domestic monetary liabilities. If central banks have a target for the short-term rate, then they can attempt to offset increases in bank reserves selling domestic assets or issuing their own securities (Mohanty and Turner, 2006).

There are some concerns about the prolonged use of foreign exchange intervention to resist currency appreciation. One concern is related to the fact that a large portfolio currency asset exposes the central bank to potential valuation losses for currency appreciation. A second concern is related to the carrying costs of reserves, which are determined by the difference between the return on domestic assets and foreign assets.[5] Finally, continuous reserve accumulation might at some point raise problems for the central bank in controlling monetary growth. The assessment of the recent experience of exchange reserve accumulation in emerging countries shows evidence that such countries have so far been successful in sterilizing reserve operations (Mohanty and Scatigna, 2005; Mohanty and Turner, 2006). On one hand, carrying costs have been low or even negative in an important number of countries (including China, India and South Korea), although they have been high in some countries (Brazil and Indonesia). On the other hand, many central banks may have used reserve accumulation to expand the monetary base to deliberately ease monetary policy in an environment of low inflation and large excess capacity. Owing to the effectiveness of official foreign exchange intervention and low inflation environment, real exchange rates have not risen significantly (or even fallen) in many countries with large and persistent current account surpluses.

Another opportunity to enhance the management of exchange rate regime (that is, not excluding official intervention) in emerging countries is the use of 'capital management techniques', which include 'capital controls', that is, norms that manage volume, composition, and/or allocation of international private capital flows, and/or 'prudential domestic financial regulations' that refer to policies, such as capital-adequacy standards, reporting requirements, or restrictions on the ability and terms under which domestic financial institutions can provide to certain types of projects[6] (Epstein et al., 2003, pp. 6–7). Capital controls can be used for different, sometimes related, objectives, such as (i) to reduce the vulnerability of a country to financial crises, including capital flight during any currency crisis; (ii) to drive a wedge between onshore and offshore interest rates in order to provide monetary authorities with some policy autonomy at least in the short run; (iii) to maintain some short-term stability of nominal exchange rate and to reduce exchange rate pressures derived from excessive capital inflows. For this purpose capital controls can be used to change the composition and maturity structure of flows (towards longer maturity flows) and to enhance monetary authorities' ability to act in the exchange foreign market.

Although the effectiveness of capital controls is very controversial,[7] evidence suggests that the macroeconomic benefits of capital management techniques can outweigh the microeconomic costs as some recent experiences show. Magud and Reinhart (2006) review more than 30 papers that evaluate capital controls either on inflows or outflows around the world (the evaluation excludes countries with comprehensive capital controls, such as China and India), making use of a capital controls effectiveness index in order to standardize the results of the empirical studies. They conclude that 'capital controls on inflows seem to make monetary policy more independent; alter the composition of capital flow; reduce real exchange rate pressures (although the evidence is more controversial)', but 'seem not to reduce the volume of net flows (and hence, the current account balance)' (Magud and Reinhart, 2006, p. 26), while limiting private external borrowing in the 'good times' can play an important prudential role more often than not in countries that are 'debt intolerant' (Magud and Reinhart, 2006, pp. 26–7). Similarly, Ho and McCauley (2003, p. 34) conclude that 'recent experience has shown that capital controls, if properly designed and applied, can be helpful in protecting the economy against the destabilizing aspects of capital flows, supporting the implementation of other policies and even resolving certain types of policy dilemma'.

4.3   Exchange rate regimes, capital account convertibility and economic performance: the recent experience of BRICs countries

4.3.1   Brazil

Since beginning of the 1980s, the Brazilian economy has had a low and volatile growth: between 1981 and 2006, the average GDP growth

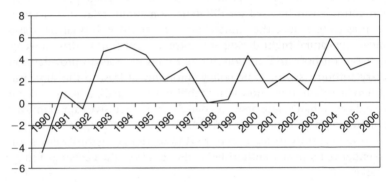

Figure 4.2   Brazil – real GDP growth (%)
Source: IPEADATA.

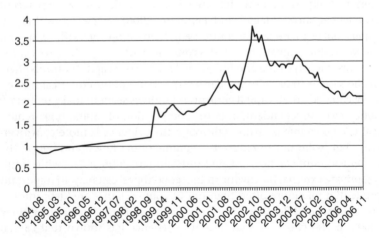

Figure 4.3   Brazil – nominal exchange rate
Source: Central Bank of Brazil.

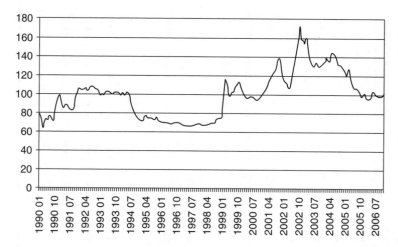

Figure 4.4   Brazil – real effective exchange rate (June 1994 = 100)
Source: Central Bank of Brazil.

was 2.2 per cent, contrasting with economic growth of 7.1 per cent in 1947–80, which was during the period of import substitution industrialization (ISI). Low economic growth (2.1 per cent in 1990–2006; see Figure 4.2) has been the result of high inflation (until June 1994), the external vulnerability caused by the financing needs of balance of payments (at least until 2002) and also by the effects of the very high real interest rates (around 11 per cent in 1999–2006 on average). As a result investment rate has been low and stable for years (Table 4.1). On the other hand, after three decades of high inflation, the combination of de-indexation of the economy, huge reduction of import taxes, high interest rates and exchange rate appreciation, under the auspices of the Real Plan, launched in July 1994, resulted in the sharp decrease of inflation: in 1995, consumer price index fell to 22.4 per cent, and in 1998 reached 1.7 per cent (Table 4.1). Indeed, since beginning of the 1990s, Brazil has followed a pattern of economic development, which in broader terms was inspired by Washington Consensus, that includes a set of liberalizing and market friendly policies such as privatization, trade liberalization, stimulus to foreign direct investment (FDI), financial liberalization, social security reform, and price stabilization.

Since the beginning of the 1990s until nowadays, Brazil implemented different strategies of economic policy: in the 1990–94 period economic policy was based on a crawling peg exchange rate regime with nominal diary devaluations, that resulted in a depreciated real exchange rate,[8]

Table 4.1 Brazil – basic economic indicators

	1990	1991	1992	1993	1994	1995	1996	1997	1998	1999	2000	2001	2002	2003	2004	2005
GDP real growth (% p.a.)	−4.4	1.0	−0.5	4.7	5.3	4.4	2.2	3.4	0.0	0.3	4.3	1.3	2.7	1.2	5.7	2.9
Gross fixed capital formation (% GDP)	17.3	18.3	18.4	19.3	20.7	20.5	19.3	19.9	19.7	18.9	19.3	19.5	18.3	17.8	19.6	19.9
Consumer price index (% p.a.)	1621.0	472.7	1119.1	2477.1	916.5	22.4	9.6	5.2	1.7	8.9	6.0	7.7	12.5	9.3	7.6	5.7
Fiscal balance (% of GDP)	–	26.5	44.3	59.6	24.7	6.6	5.3	5.5	7.0	5.3	3.4	3.3	4.2	4.7	2.4	3.0
Public debt (% of GDP)	42.01	34.14	37.06	32.56	30.01	27.98	30.72	31.83	38.94	44.53	45.54	48.44	50.46	52.36	46.99	46.45
Exchange rate average (real/USD)	0.0000	0.0001	0.0016	0.0322	0.6393	0.9177	1.0051	1.0780	1.1605	1.8147	1.8301	2.3577	2.9208	3.0771	2.9251	2.4344
International reserves (excl. gold, USD million)	7441	8033	22521	30604	37070	49708	58323	50827	42580	34796	32488	35739	37684	49111	52740	53574
Current account (% of GDP)	−0.8	−0.4	1.6	−0.2	−0.3	−2.4	−2.8	−3.5	−4.0	−4.3	−3.8	−4.2	−1.5	0.75	1.6	1.2
International reserves (% of imports)	36.0	38.2	109.6	121.2	112.1	99.5	109.3	85.1	73.7	70.6	58.2	64.3	79.8	101.7	84.0	72.8
External debt (% of GDP)	26.3	30.5	35.1	33.9	27.3	20.1	21.4	23.0	28.6	41.1	36.6	37.9	41.8	38.8	30.3	19.2
External debt/exports ratio	3.9	3.9	3.8	3.8	3.4	3.4	3.8	3.8	4.7	5.0	4.3	3.6	3.5	2.9	2.1	1.4
Income debt (% of exports)	40.6	33.4	25.5	30.2	25.9	31.3	36.7	40.9	48.0	47.4	39.0	39.5	35.6	30.0	24.6	24.6
Trade balance (USD million)	10747	10578	15239	14329	10861	−3157	−5453	−6652	−6603	−1261	−698	2650	13121	24794	33666	44757
Current account (USD million)	−3823	−1450	6089	20	−1153	−18136	−23248	−30491	−33829	−25400	−24225	−23215	−7636.6	4177.29	11737.6	14198.9

Source: IMF – International Financial Statistics; IPEADATA (GDP growth, CPI, fiscal balance and public debt).

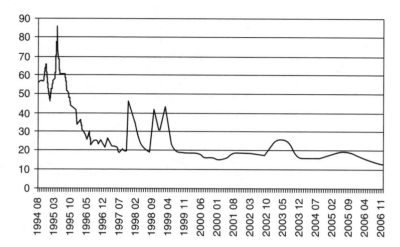

Figure 4.5   Brazil – Selic interest rate (% p.a.)
Source: Central Bank of Brazil.

and a policy of high real interest rates; such a policy generated both high
trade balance surplus and the attraction of capital flows, at the costs of a
very high inflation (Table 4.1). The period from July 1994 until January
1999, the period of the Real Plan, is characterized by the use of a nominal
anchor (a crawling exchange rate band) for stabilization purposes and
the implementation of a very tight monetary policy, which resulted in a
huge exchange rate overvaluation, and the consequent increase of both
trade deficits and capital inflows. This period is also marked by the con-
tagious external crises, such as the Mexican crisis, the Asian crisis and the
Russian crisis. In the context of the semi-pegged exchange rate, Central
Bank of Brazil (BCB) reacted to the capital flight by sharply increasing
interest rates in order to seek reverting capital outflows (Figure 4.5).

After the Brazilian currency crisis in January 1999, Brazil adopted a
new economic policy based on the following guides: floating exchange
rate regime, inflation targeting regime and the generation of primary fiscal surpluses,[9] which has resulted in interest rates lower than the former
period (1995–98) but still high, and volatile exchange rates. In general
inflation rate has been higher than the former period while since 2002
there is a remarkable improvement in the external sector balance due
to the increase of the trade balance surplus favoured initially by the
exchange rate devaluation and later by the increase in both demand and
prices of the commodities in the international trade. The *modus operandi*
of inflation targeting regime plus the a floating exchange rate regime,

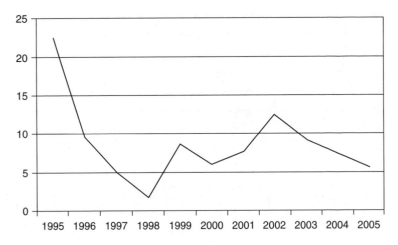

Figure 4.6   Brazil – consumer price index (% p.a.)
Source: IMF.

under the conditions of operation of (almost) full opening of the capital account, has resulted in a sharp instability of the nominal exchange rate (Figure 4.3). Capital flight induced an exchange rate devaluation that affected domestic prices, which frequently jeopardized the BCB's inflation target: the targets were missed in 2001–03.[10] Under these conditions, BCB has been compelled to increase the interest rate in order to seek to reduce the 'pass through effect' – as was the case in 2001, in view of the turbulence of international markets, and again in 2002–03, due to the confidence crisis related to the election of the leftist President Lula da Silva. The BCB's reaction to exchange rate movements has frequently caused a decline in output and employment, increasing at the same time the volume of public debt (see Table 4.1). More recently, favoured by the benign international environment, BCB has gradually reduced short-term interest rate.

Capital flows legislation in Brazil was introduced in the 1960s, governing which foreign capital flows should be registered in order to obtain permission for associated outflows (profits, interests, royalties, and repatriation). Since the end of the 1980s an increasing trend can be noted towards capital account liberalization in Brazil. Early 1990s foreign direct investment (FDI) was further liberalized as prohibition on FDI into certain sectors was lifted and bureaucratic obstacles were reduced. In 1991 the Brazilian government permitted the acquisition by foreign institutional investors of equities of domestic firms. In 1992

BCB allowed a broad liberalization of capital outflows as it permitted a special non-resident account called CC5 to be operated more freely by foreign financial institutions as a result of acquisition or sale of foreign currencies. This exception created a privileged way to short-term capital flight that was used very often during periods of speculative attacks on domestic currency and represented the introduction of de facto convertibility as, in practice, residents could deposit in a non-resident bank's account held in a domestic bank, which could convert domestic into foreign currency: residents could transfer resources abroad making these deposits and asking the non-resident financial institution to buy foreign currency to deposit in an account abroad.[11] In April 1994 the Brady Plan converted the external loans into debt securities, helping to overcome the external debt crisis that had contributed somehow to the 'stagflation' environment of Brazil since 1981. In 1994 BCB implemented a financial transaction tax[12] and increased the minimum maturity requirements for capital inflows in order to reduce upward pressure on the exchange rate, to minimize the cost of sterilization and to give some degree of freedom in monetary policy.[13] At the same time, measures aimed to stimulate outflows – including the permission for prepayment of foreign borrowing and import finance – were also adopted.

After the 1999 Brazilian currency crisis and the adoption of a floating exchange regime, economic authorities implemented many norms that resulted in further financial liberalization (mainly related to capital outflows) and greater flexibility in foreign exchange market, including the unification of the exchange rate markets (floating and free ones), the reduction and later elimination of both the minimum average maturity for external loans and the financial transaction tax on capital inflows, the elimination of the restrictions on investments in the securities markets by foreign investors, and the simplification of the procedures related to the capital remittance to other countries.[14] In November 1999 Brazil accepted the obligations under Article VIII of the IMF, which precludes the country members from imposing restrictions on the meaning of payments and transfers for current international transactions. More recently, in August 2006, the Brazilian government introduced more flexibility on export operations' exchange rate coverage as now Brazilian exporters are allowed to maintain abroad a maximum of 30 per cent of their export incomes.

There are some controversies related to the macroeconomic effects of financial liberalization in Brazil. Goldfajn and Minella (2005, p. 37), for instance, support that, in order to reap the benefits of capital account liberalization, such liberalization should be accompanied by a broad range of reforms to improve and foster stronger institutions – such as approval of de jure central bank independence. However, the empirical findings suggest that financial liberalization in Brazil resulted in greater exchange rate volatility and higher domestic interest rate – probably as consequence of the reduction of barriers to capital outflows. Ono et al. (2005), using a VAR model with the objective to evaluate the relation between capital controls, exchange rate and interest rate in Brazil during 1990–2001, found the following results: (i) the relation between short-term interest rate (Selic) and capital controls is negative, so that an increase (decrease) in the former should result in the reduction (increase) in the interest rate; (ii) nominal exchange rate does not respond to the variations in the capital controls, which suggests that there is no evidence that capital controls generate an increase in exchange rate volatility, a hypothesis suggested by some Brazilian economists (Arida, 2004).

As we have seen, during the period of semi-pegged exchange rate regime BCB defined the nominal exchange rate inside a narrow band; after the 1999 devaluation of the *real* (Brazilian currency), however, BCB has had no commitment to determine exchange rate (both nominal and real), although it has operated occasionally in the exchange foreign markets in periods of greater capital flows volatility and more recently according to its policy of accumulating exchange reserves.[15] Therefore, Brazilian exchange rate regime is not a freely floating exchange regime, as BCB eventually intervenes in foreign exchange market, but it is closer to a floating exchange regime than other emerging countries. Since end of 2002 real exchange rate has had an overvalued trend due to both increase of trade surplus and capital flows. The latter has been attracted by high yield differentials between domestic and foreign bonds. As can be seen in Figure 4.7, the resumption of capital flows was dominated by portfolio investment (equity and debt securities) until 1994, while the decline in the capital flows was commanded by portfolio investments and other investments.[16] Portfolio investments have played a crucial role in the large capital flow swings associated with the financial crisis. Since 1998 FDI has prevailed as the main source of capital flows. According to ECLAC (2000, pp. 35–6), since 1996 Brazil was the second-largest destination for FDI among developing countries, although as can be seen in Figure 4.7, the volume of FDI has declined more recently.

External vulnerability is a marked feature in Brazil since the mid-1990s due mainly to the dependence on foreign capital in order to reach some equilibrium in the balance of payments and also as a result of the gradual but increasing opening up of capital account. Indeed, the ratio external indebtedness to exports, a traditional indicator of external solvency, was

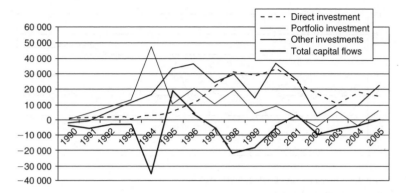

Figure 4.7 Brazil – capital flows (liabilities, US$ million)
Source: IMF.

up to 3.0 per cent until 2002. Due to the current account deficits, that reached more than 4 per cent in 1998, the Brazilian economy was very dependent on foreign capital by the end of the 1990s, which left the economy vulnerable to external contagions (Paula and Alves Jr, 2000). Even after the adoption of a floating exchange regime in 1999, the Brazilian economy suffered strong speculative pressures in 2001 and 2002, when there was eventually a situation of 'sudden stop' of capital as a result of the loss of confidence of investors in the likely election of Lula's candidate. The growth of exports since 2002 and the quick reduction of external indebtedness have resulted in an improvement in the indicators of external vulnerability: the ratio of foreign debt over exports declined from 2.5 per cent in 2002 to 1.4 per cent in 2005. At the same time, foreign reserves have increased due to the foreign reserve accumulation policy implemented by BCB. However, sterilization operations have been costly for the Brazilian government, due to the high interest rate differential between domestic and international bonds – public debt has been more or less at the same level despite the fiscal primary surplus.

4.3.2 Russia

Russia, from 1990 to 2006, had on average a negative economic growth of minus 0.1 per cent. However, if we divide the Russian economy growth into two periods, that is, before and after the 1998 Russian crisis, we have quite different periods: while from 1990 until 1998 GDP real growth accumulated a fall of around 45 per cent, the average GDP growth from 1999 until 2006 (6.7%) performed well. Figure 4.8 presents the behaviour of GDP growth in Russia in the 1990–2006 period. After the 1998 Russian

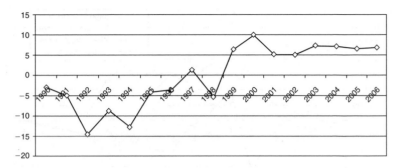

Figure 4.8   Russia – real GDP growth (%)
Source: Deutsche Bank Research.

financial crisis the rebound of the economy has been faster and stronger than could ever have been predicted. Indeed, recent Russian economic performance corresponds closely to the notion of a 'growth acceleration', as defined by Hausmann et al. (2004), that is, at least eight years of sustainable economic growth.

According to Berengaut and Elborgh-Woytek (2005) this radically different performance can be explained by the fact that during 1990–98 the main reason why the Russian economy presented so poor a performance is related to the transition from a planning and centralized economy to a market economy. The Russian economy after 1990 experimented with a rapid process of economic change, that did not succeed, which included privatization of state-owned firms with no clear rules and no property rights, abrupt price liberalization, and a quick process of trade liberalization and financial liberalization. The collapse of the old system and the slow adjustment to a new one imposed heavy social costs in terms of unemployment, living standards and distribution of income.[17] The priority of economic policy at that time was to bring down a continuing high rate of inflation, which in 1994 was still over 300 per cent. For this purpose government decided to use exchange rate as a 'nominal anchor' for monetary policy: exchange rate was kept pledged within a pre-announced corridor, with a depreciation well bellow the inflation rate, which resulted in real exchange rate appreciation (Figures 4.9 and 4.10). The Russian government started a gradual liberalization of restrictions on non-resident portfolio investment in 1994 that was completed in early 1998.[18] The weak performance of trade combined with a tight monetary policy, within a context of disordered transition to capitalism, contributed to the poor economic performance in the 1990–98 period.

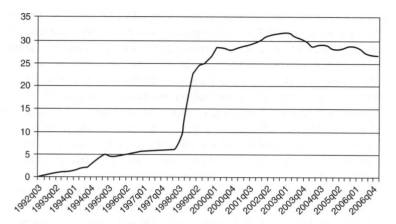

Figure 4.9　Russia – official exchange rate (roubles per USD – period average)
Source: IMF.

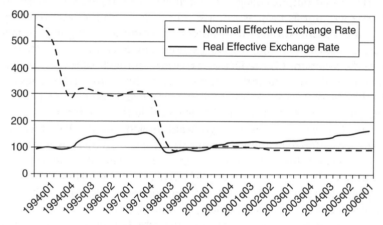

Figure 4.10　Russia – NBER and REER (period average; index number 2000 = 100)
Source: IMF.

According to Owen and Robinson (2003, pp. 25–6), the seeds of the 1998 Russian financial crisis were related to some economic imbalances: a large budget deficit (7.4 per cent of GDP in 1996) arising from the government inability to collect taxes and contain expenditure; a large short-term domestic debt; and the lack of structural reform in banking, natural monopoly, and agricultural sectors. Furthermore, by contributing to weakening commodity prices (especially oil), the Asian crisis sparked a sharp deterioration in Russia's terms of trade – which resulted in a sudden decline in the trade balance from US$ 21.6 billion in 1996 to US$ 14.9 billion in 1997; the contagions of the Asian crisis substantially increased the cost of access and reduced the volume of foreign capital (Owen and Robinson, 2003, p. 5). In such an environment, Russian authorities secured a financing package with the IMF, the World Bank and Japan, and announced emergency measures in August 1998 that included a default on rouble-denominated government debt maturing before end-1999, an adjustment to the exchange rate band from 5.3-7.1 roubles to 6.0–9.5 roubles, and the reintensification of capital controls, in an attempt to quell the pressure on reserves. However, negative market reaction, reflecting the residual fragile fiscal situation, forced the rouble to fall quickly to the edge of the new exchange band; the band was abandoned on 2 September, leaving the exchange rate to float. Losses in international reserves were US$ 5.1 billion in 1998 and consumer prices rose very sharply, with inflation reaching 86 per cent p.a. in 1999 (Table 4.2).

The initial output collapse that followed the August 1998 crisis in Russia was not as deep as in most other crisis countries and recovery was quicker and stronger than other crisis countries owing to a set factors that include: (i) import substitution stimulated by large exchange rate depreciation; (ii) the fact that channels through shocks are generally transmitted to the real economy in crisis situations was less relevant in the case of Russia than in other emerging market economies, because private sector wealth was largely held outside the banking sector, and relatively few enterprises had significant foreign currency liabilities not matched by foreign currency income streams; and (iii) the positive terms of trade change from rising oil prices gave a further boost to the economy from mid-1999 and allowed a quick recovery of international reserves (Owen and Robinson, 2003, pp. 7–9). Furthermore, the Bank of Russia – Russia's central bank – acted quickly to address the problems in the banking sector, rapidly improving the liquidity situation of the banks, which avoided a general run on deposits and at the same time enhanced the payments system.

As we have already stressed, growth performance after the Russian crisis has been strong contrasting with the pre-crisis period. By 2000 high oil prices – the average oil price increased from US$ 12.8 in 1998 to US$ 28.4 in 2000 – contributed to a quick rise in investment rate of the economy (Table 4.2). Furthermore, the rise of aggregate demand also contributed to boosting economic growth, favoured by the increase in both pensions and wages, the increase of net exports, and the decline of interest rates due to the adoption of a more expansionary monetary policy (Figure 4.12), that has stimulated the increase of banking credit,

Table 4.2 Russia – basic economic indicators

	1993	1994	1995	1996	1997	1998	1999	2000	2001	2002	2003	2004	2005
GDP real growth (% p.a.)	−8.7	−12.7	−4.1	−3.6	1.4	−5.3	6.4	10.0	5.1	4.7	7.3	7.2	6.4
Gross fixed capital formation (% GDP)	20.4	21.8	21.1	20.0	18.3	16.1	14.4	16.9	18.9	17.9	18.4	18.3	18.2
Consumer price index (% p.a.)	874.6	304.6	197.5	47.7	14.8	27.7	85.7	20.8	21.5	15.8	13.7	10.9	12.7
Fiscal balance (% of GDP)	–	–	−4.9	−7.4	−6.4	−4.8	−1.2	2.4	3.1	1.7	2.4	4.9	7.5
Public debt (% of GDP)	65.1	45.7	40.7	32.8	55	79.4	88.8	56.8	42.9	36.6	31.9	24.5	16.6
Oil price, brent blend (USD/bbl)	17.1	15.96	17	20.6	19.2	12.8	17.8	28.4	24.4	24.9	28.8	38.2	54.4
Exchange rate average (ruble/USD)	1.0	2.2	4.6	5.2	5.8	9.7	24.6	28.1	29.2	31.3	30.7	28.8	28.3
International reserves (excl. gold, USD million)	5835	3980	14383	11276	12895	7801	8457	24264	32542	44054	73175	120809	175891
Current account (% of GDP)	24.7	4.6	2.3	3.0	0.0	0.2	13.8	18.1	11.4	8.5	7.9	9.6	11.1
International reserves (% of imports)	–	11.7	–	20.5	22.6	19.2	28.6	56.9	61.9	71.3	92.0	116.3	132.4
External debt (% of GDP)	–	–	39.3	34.6	31.4	115.4	–	–	–	33.8	24.0	–	10.2
External debt/exports ratio	–	–	1.5	1.4	1.4	2.0	–	–	–	1.1	0.8	–	0.3
Income debt (% of exports)	–	7.9	9.2	10.8	14.7	21.5	15.3	10.9	10.8	11.4	17.8	13.7	15.2
Trade balance (USD million)	–	16928	19816	21591	14913	16429	36014	60172	48121	46335	59860	85825	118266
Current account (USD million)	–	7844	6965	10847	−80	219	24616	46839	33935	29116	35410	58592	83184

Source: IMF – International Financial Statistics; Deutsche Bank Research (GDP, oil price and public debt).

from 12 per cent of GDP in 1999 to 22 per cent in 2003 (IMF, 2004, p. 10). Energy sector has had a direct impact on output growth as it contributes about 20 per cent of GDP, and indirectly as it pushes other industrial sectors (such as construction and machinery). However, the economic recovery was broad-based as the marked real exchange rate depreciation in late 1998 provided a strong boost to the competitiveness of the tradable sector, which was translated into a surge in the output in many sectors of the economy (Owen and Robinson, 2003, p. 51).

Pushed by the increase in the oil prices (US$ 54.4 in 2005), trade balance increased from US$ 16.4 billion in 1998 to US$ 36.0 billion in 1999, rising steadily to reach US$ 118.3 billion in 2005, despite the recent deterioration of non-fuel trade balance; as a result, the ratio current account over GDP increased from 0.2 per cent in 1998 to 11.1 per cent in 2005. Foreign reserves until 1999 were relatively low to satisfy the needs of imports of goods by the Russian economy, as they covered on average only 20 per cent of the Russian imports. However, since 2002, the ratio of international reserves to imports has been around 88 per cent on average. The continuous and sharp increase of foreign reserves, from US$ 8.5 billion in 1999 to US$ 175.0 billion in 2005, is due to an aggressive foreign reserves accumulation policy within a context of high current account surplus and capital flows reversal after 2002. Indeed, all the external vulnerability indicators have shown a very clear improvement since 1999, as can be seen in Table 4.2. In particular, the external debt-to-exports ratio declined from 2.0 in 1998 to only 0.3 in 2005. After many years of massive capital outflows, capital flows changed course in 2002, with significant reduction in capital outflows and a surge in capital inflows, including higher borrowing (see Figure 4.11). The combination of a prolonged period of high world energy prices with some capital account surplus has generated a real exchange rate trend, that has gradually returned to its pre-crisis level, despite the efforts of the Bank of Russia to attenuate this trend (see Figure 4.10). As nominal exchange rate has been stable, due to the active performance of the Bank of Russia in the foreign exchange market, the bulk of real appreciation took the form of a persistently high inflation differential. The continued real appreciation, although partly neutralized by productivity gains, has raised the risk of 'Dutch disease' that can reduce the efforts of diversification of Russia's production and export structure – a current concern of the Russian government.

After the 1998 crisis Russia adopted an administered floating exchange regime, in the context of capital account partial convertibility. The Bank of Russia has pursued multiple objectives, avoiding an unnecessarily tight monetary policy for fear of slowing output growth. The main goal

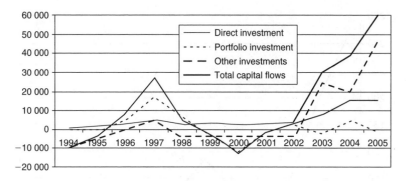

Figure 4.11 Russia – capital flows (liabilities, US$ million)
Source: IMF.

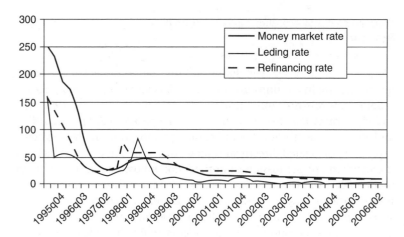

Figure 4.12 Russia – interest rates (%)
Source: IMF.

of the Bank of Russia has been to accumulate reserves, and to prevent overly rapid real exchange rate appreciation, by maintaining a stable nominal effective exchange rate, in an effort to preserve the competitiveness of the manufacturing sector, and also to smooth the path of exchange-rate adjustment, while guiding down inflation has been an important, but secondary, objective.[19] Inflation, though still high, has continued to edge downwards each year despite relatively lax monetary conditions (Figure 4.13). The decline in inflation reflects the effect of

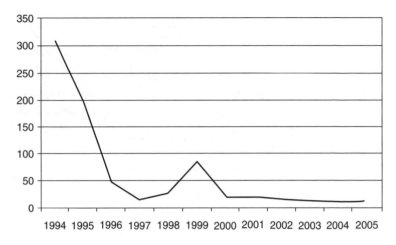

Figure 4.13   Russia – consumer price index (% p.a.)
Source: IMF.

REER appreciation, reduced duties on importation of beef above quota, lower increase in administered prices, and a cap on petroleum prices.

Some controls on capital flows were introduced after the 1998 crisis to help protect the Russian currency from speculative capital outflows and also to protect the still weak banking sector from the more volatile capital flows. Related directly to capital outflows, such controls included the requirement permission from the Bank of Russia to portfolio investment abroad and the need that Russian credit institutions have to create reserves for operations with offshore residents. Designed to dissuade speculative inflows into the rouble, in 2004 the Bank of Russia created a system of five accounts for non-residents, which included 'S accounts' to purchase rouble-denominated government debt – such accounts were subject to reserve requirements of 15 per cent for a year in 2005.[20] However, since June 2005 residents may open foreign exchange accounts with authorized banks without restriction. In July 2006 the Russian government announced the gradual introduction of rouble convertibility by eliminating all restrictions on non-resident transactions in domestic securities (in practice, eliminating the Bank of Russia's system of accounts), a political decision as the Kremlin wants to establish the rouble as a strong international currency.[21]

Large-scale foreign exchange purchases by the Bank of Russia – via unsterilized interventions – that have resulted in a rapid growth of monetary aggregates, have been combined with large fiscal surplus. According to Owen and Robinson (2002, p. 12), fiscal restraint in the face of burgeoning oil revenues allowed the government to quickly rebuild international reserves while slowing the real appreciation of the rouble. Since 1999 fiscal position strengthened due to a remarkable fiscal adjustment of 9.5 per cent of GDP from 1997 to 2001, which resulted from both higher oil revenues and a reduction of real government expenditures. While in 2002 and 2003 fiscal surplus declined compared with the previous period, it increased sharply in 2004 and 2005 (4.9 per cent and 7.5 per cent of GDP, respectively), due to the extra fiscal revenue arising from higher oil prices since 2002.

The Oil Stabilization Fund,[22] established in 2004, in which the bulk of the windfall fiscal revenue is accumulated, plays a crucial role in maintaining the fiscal surplus. In 2005, around two-thirds of the increase in revenues from oil, gas and oil product exports was actually sterilized through the Stabilization Fund. Some flexibility in the fiscal policy was introduced in 2006 with the creation of an Investment Fund in the federal budget. The aim of the fund is to finance infrastructure investment and innovation related projects in joint public–private partnerships (PPPs). The sums involved have been relatively small – around 0.26 per cent of projected GDP for 2006 and 0.34 per cent in 2007.

4.3.3 India

After years of low economic growth and after facing a financial crisis in 1991, India has had a dramatic change in economic growth: the real GDP growth was on average 6.5 per cent in 1990–2006 (Figure 4.14), while it was 3.1 per cent in 1971–80 and 4.7 per cent in 1981–90 (Ariff and Khalid, 2005, p. 97). Although India still has an enormous lack of infrastructure,

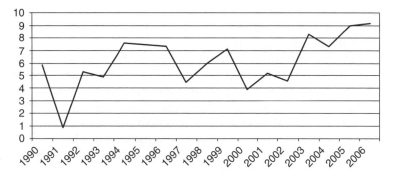

Figure 4.14 India – GDP real growth (% p.a.)
Source: IMF.

investment rate has increased from around 22 per cent in the first half of the 1990s to around 24 per cent during the 2000s (Table 4.3). This good economic performance has been the result, among other factors, of the enormous potential of its domestic consumer market, the existence of a segment of well-qualified workers, the strong productivity growth (more than 3.5 per cent over the course of the 1990s), the management of a well-coordinated economic policy, and the implementation of economic reforms. Capital account liberalization has been part of a broad-based programme of economic reform, that included the abolishment of industrial license, the sharp reduction in import taxes, liberalization of the transactions related to the current account and a more limited liberalization of the capital flows related to the capital account.

Economic liberalization accelerated after the external debt crisis of 1991, when the *rupee*, the domestic currency, was depreciated in two steps by almost 20 per cent against the US dollar (see Figure 4.15). Liberalization began with a dramatic process of trade liberalization; as a result, the imports tariffs reduced from 87.0 per cent on average in 1991 to 25.0 per cent on average in 1997 (IMF, 2001, p. 32). In the context of economic reform, capital account has been gradually liberalized and the exchange rate regime changed from a pegged exchange rate to a managed floating exchange regime. This change began with the transition of a managed floating related to a basket of currencies to a dual exchange rate regime in March 1992. Finally, India adopted a floating and unified exchange rate regime in March 1993. The change in the exchange rate regime was followed step-by-step by flexibility on current account transactions, which resulted in the acceptance of full convertibility of current account in August 1994, that is, the formal acceptance of the obligations of the IMF's Article VII. Although India formally adopted a floating exchange regime, in practice it is a quasi-managed float where the Reserve Bank of India (RBI) plays a crucial role in the foreign exchange market. Indeed, RBI has been an important player in the foreign exchange market, acting to avoid that some big transactions in this market can increase the exchange rate volatility, and at the same time seeking to affect the real effective exchange rate trajectory in the long run. For this purpose, RBI makes use of a very large range of tools operating in the spot and derivative markets, and even making use of administered measures. Such management has been possible because of the existence of extensive capital controls that result in limited integration into international financial markets.

Compared with other countries that adopted floating exchange regime, the volatility of nominal exchange rate has been lower in India

Table 4.3 India – basic economic indicators

	1990	1991	1992	1993	1994	1995	1996	1997	1998	1999	2000	2001	2002	2003	2004	2005
GDP real growth (% p.a.)	5.8	0.9	5.3	4.9	7.6	7.5	7.4	4.5	6.0	7.1	3.9	5.2	4.6	8.3	7.3	9.0
Gross fixed capital formation (% GDP)	22.9	22.0	22.4	21.4	21.9	24.4	22.8	21.7	21.5	23.3	22.7	23.1	24.1	24.7	25.9	–
Consumer price index (% p.a.)	9.0	13.9	11.8	6.4	10.2	10.2	9.0	7.2	13.2	4.7	4.0	3.7	4.4	3.8	3.8	4.2
Fiscal balance (% of GDP)	–7.6	–5.5	–5.3	–7.0	–5.6	–5.0	–4.9	–4.9	–5.3	–5.4	–5.2	–4.7	–5.9	–4.5	–4.0	–4.1
Public debt (% of GDP)	–	–	84.5	83.9	77.9	71.4	67.8	68.3	69.5	69.9	71.1	82.7	85.5	82.1	86.0	83.1
Exchange rate average (rupee/USD)	17.5	22.7	25.9	30.5	31.4	32.4	35.4	36.3	41.3	43.1	44.9	47.2	48.6	46.6	45.3	44.1
International reserves (excl. gold, USD million)	5504	6841	8961	13916	23366	22046	24212	27933	30216	35744	40793	48819	71049	103582	131830	136932
Current account (% of GDP)	–2.2	–1.7	–1.6	–0.7	–0.5	–1.6	–1.6	–0.8	–1.7	–0.7	–1.0	0.3	1.4	1.1	–	–
International reserves (% imports)	23.5	32.4	39.1	57.7	78.7	58.1	55.3	61.1	67.4	78.5	75.7	95.3	129.9	151.9	–	–
External debt (% of GDP)	26.7	32.5	37.6	34.9	32.2	26.9	24.5	23.2	23.8	22.2	21.8	20.5	20.7	18.8	17.9	–
External debt/exports ratio	3.2	2.7	2.3	2.6	2.8	3.4	3.7	4.0	4.0	4.3	4.4	4.7	4.6	5.1	5.2	–
Income debt (% of exports)	20.6	23.9	21.8	19.1	17.5	17.0	14.1	14.3	16.3	15.8	17.5	17.7	14.1	14.0	–	–
Long-term debt (% external debt)	86.6	87.7	87.6	90.8	91.6	92.1	91.4	93.9	95.3	96.0	96.5	97.0	96.1	95.4	93.5	–
Trade balance (USD million)	–5150.9	–2992	–2911.2	–2092.5	–4150.1	–6718.8	–10052	–10028	–10752	–8678.9	–10640	–6417.9	–3559.3	–8870.2	–	–
Current account (USD million)	–7037	–4292	–4485	–1876	–1676	–5563	–5956	–2965	–6903	–3228	–4601	1410	7060	6853	–	–

Source: IMF – International Financial Statistics; ADB (fiscal balance in 2002–2005; external debt).

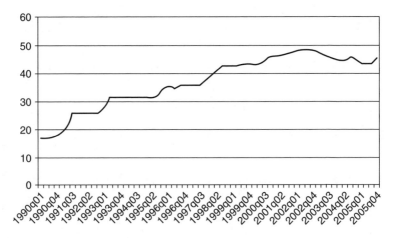

Figure 4.15   India – nominal exchange rate (rupee/dollar)
Source: Reserve Bank of India.

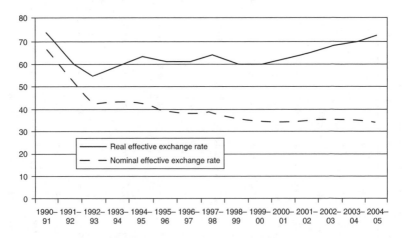

Figure 4.16   India – REER and NEER (export-based weights, annual average)
Source: Reserve Bank of India.

(IMF, 2001, p. 152). Exchange rate has been used in India, combined with other extra-exchange rate tools, to absorb external shocks. As a general trend, nominal exchange rate has been gradually devaluated since 1996 (Figure 4.15 and 4.16). Real effective exchange rate has been most time stable, while recently there is a gradual appreciation trend. Indeed, during the 1990s RBI followed a PPP rule whereby the nominal exchange rate was indexed to the price level to target the real exchange rate (Kohli, 2005, p. 153). Since the end of the 1990s, exchange rate policy has begun to change course a little, shifting from stabilizing the real exchange rate towards a more flexible rate regime with no fixed target, but still concerned in curbing excessive volatility and calibrating temporary mismatches in the demand and supply of foreign exchange.

As already stressed, after the 1991 external debt crisis, India began a gradual but rapid process of liberalization of current account, that included the end of the foreign exchange budget and the elimination of controls on current transactions. Although some norms related to long-term capital flows have been loosened, including the limits of ownership share related to foreign direct investment, short-term capital controls are still significant. The approach to capital account liberalization in India has been cautious: what was liberalized has been specified while everything else remained restricted or prohibited. The contours of liberalization were in large part shaped by the lessons of the 1991 external debt crisis – mainly problems related to roll over short-term debt and capital flight due to deposit withdrawals by non-resident Indians.

The Indian approach of gradual and limited liberalization of capital account has emphasized opening up the economy to foreign direct investment and portfolio equity investment, instead of external debt, with the objective of reducing the country's vulnerability to external crises by reducing reliance on volatile short-term debt flows that characterized the 1980s (Habermeier, 2000, p. 80). First, concerning capital inflows, financial liberalization began in July 1991 with a more flexible policy related to foreign direct investment (FDI) when FDI with up to 51 per cent equity was to receive automatic approval in 35 selected high priority industries subject only to a registration procedure with the RBI, while access through the automatic route has been progressively enlarged over time. Secondly, liberalization was extended to portfolio investment in September 1992, when foreign institutional investors were allowed to invest in the domestic capital market, first in the secondary market for equity subject to a ceiling of 5 per cent and later in the primary market (maximum limit of 15 per cent of the new issue). Thirdly, liberalization in the sphere of external commercial borrowings (ECBs) has been limited, selective and variable. Commercial borrowings require case-by-case approval from the government where the decision depends upon the amount borrowed, the maturity period and the proposed utilization. Deregulation of ECBs has been subject to annual ceilings decided on the basis of the country's external debt and balance of payments position. Finally, concerning non-resident deposits, in order to avoid capital flight, the Indian government reduced the interest rate differentials (typical of the 1980s), so that interest rates offered to these deposits were gradually aligned with international rates, and RBI has no longer underwritten the exchange rate risk (Nayyar, 2002).

Capital controls in India have been well-designed and are clearly effective in limiting measured capital flows. There has been a predominance of quantitative capital controls rather than those market based, administratively enforced, and clearly demarcating the distinction between resident (with more strict controls) and non-resident transactions. On the other hand, there are more extensive controls on capital outflows and considerable liberalization on capital inflows. In particular, capital outflows related to residents are more limited: while they are very restricted to individuals, for domestic firms capital outflows are possible within some limits stipulated by the government. More recently, restrictions on individuals and domestic corporates have been loosened to allow investments abroad.[23] Capital controls in India have also been dynamic, that is, government tends to tighten capital controls on outflows during speculative periods and to loosen them after that (Epstein et al., 2003, p. 30).

Due mainly to the increase of foreign exchange reserves and the limits to accumulation of foreign debt (mostly short-term ones), most external vulnerability indicators show a remarkable and continuous improvement since 1991: the ratio current account over GDP has been below to −2.0 per cent, and since 2001 the ratio has been positive, due mainly to the increase of services and income and current transfers.[24] Although the traditional external solvency indicator (external debt over exports) gradually increased during the 1990s, the external indebtedness declined markedly, from a peak of 38 per cent of GDP in 1992 to less than 25 per cent in 1996, while the income debt ratio over exports declined sharply in the early to mid-1990s. Furthermore, since 1993 the share of the long-term debt on the total external debt has been more than 90 per cent – clear evidence that the reorientation of capital account policy towards non-debt creating inflows and FDI since 1991 succeeded. Finally, the international reserves-to-imports ratio increased to more than 100 per cent by 2002, compared with less than 40 per cent in the beginning of the 1990s. Indeed international reserves rose from US$ 30.2 billion in 1998 to US$ 136.9 billion in 2005 – an increase of 453 per cent in just seven years – owing to RBI's more aggressive exchange reserve accumulation policy (Table 4.3). Summing up, the improvement of external vulnerability indexes in India resulted mainly from the low current account deficit, a declining external debt and the increasing level of foreign reserves.

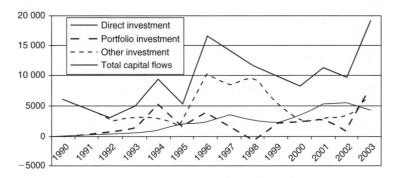

Figure 4.17 India – capital flows (liabilities, USD million)
Source: IMF.

The nature and pace of capital account liberalization exercised an influence on the dimensions and the composition of private foreign capital inflows to, and outflows from, India – a shift from debt creating to non-debt creating capital flows (Figure 4.17). Capital flows has increased a great deal during the 1990s, followed by a sharp change in their composition: until 1993 there was a predominance of other investments (which include, among other items, non-resident Indian deposits – NRI – and foreign loans) while other types of capital flows were almost non-existent; since 1994 capital flows have increased and diversified owing to the increase of portfolio investments, other investments and foreign direct investment. However, financial integration of the Indian economy into international capital markets has still been slow and limited: FDI has been increasing during 1990s, but it is low compared with other 'big' emerging countries; according to IMF (2005, p. 20), the ratio FDI over GDP in 2002 was 3.7 per cent in China, 3.1 per cent in Brazil, 2.1 per cent in Mexico and only 0.6 per cent in India.

Owing to the adoption of a managed floating exchange regime, which has resulted in a stable nominal exchange rate, domestic interest rate has had a more unstable behaviour, probably because interest rate has been used as a tool to stabilize nominal exchange rate and also because of non-sterilized operations related to foreign exchange accumulation policy. Figure 4.18 shows that there was a remarkable declining trend of interest rate in India after the adoption of the managed floating exchange rate regime in 1993 and the steady reduction of the cash reserves requirement since 1991. Such interest rate reduction has stimulated credit expansion under a market based credit system. It seems that in India capital controls have been used not only to reduce external vulnerability and to avoid

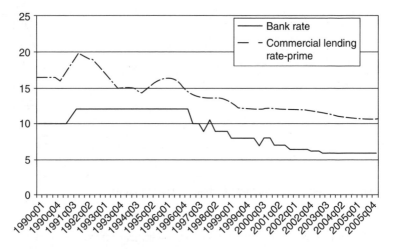

Figure 4.18   India – interest rate (% p.a.)
Source: IMF.

currency crises, but also to drive a wedge between domestic and external interest rates in order to provide RBI discretion to achieve some monetary policy autonomy.

Finally, concerning inflation, there is a general declining trend in the consumer prices index, for which the combination between trade liberalisation with (the more recent) exchange rate appreciation has contributed somehow. Fiscal deficit has been high (Table 4.3), that is, higher than 4.0 per cent of GDP (but declining more recently), and public debt has also been very high (more than 80 per cent of GDP); however, it is mostly domestic, denominated in rupee and with the predominance of long-term debt (IMF, 2005a). Inflation increased at two moments, during the balance-of-payments crisis of 1991 and during the 1997 Asian crisis (Figure 4.19). It should be stressed that inflation rate has been reduced while domestic interest rate has also declined.

4.3.4   China

The performance of the Chinese economy has been impressive: the average real GDP growth was 9.8 per cent from 1990 to 2006 (Figure 4.20), the same growth as 1980–89, which means that for more than 25 years China is growing on average by 10 per cent p.a.! Investment is the driving force of economic expansion: the investment rate has increased rapidly from 25 per cent of GDP in 1990 to more than 30 per cent after 1992 and since 2004 more than 40 per cent. Banking credit to business sector

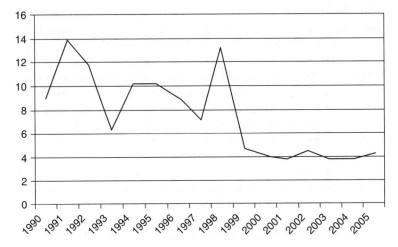

Figure 4.19   India – consumer price index (% p.a.)
Source: IMF.

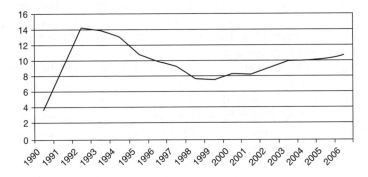

Figure 4.20   China – GDP real growth (% p.a.)
Source: IMF.

over GDP, under a bank-based system dominated by state-owned banks, has been almost double compared with OECD area (OECD, 2005, p. 42). Finally, the high growth performance is partly due to rapid growth in the export sector. This growth has been followed step-by-step by a remarkable expansion of China in the international trade: the country's share in world trade increased from 0.8 per cent to 7.7 per cent during 1988–2005 (Zhao, 2006, p. 4). Economic aperture in the Chinese experience has been gradual and incremental: reforms tend to be undertaken on an experimental basis in some localities or provinces before programmes are implemented on a nationwide basis; reforms started in the late 1970s, and in 1980 the first Special Economic Zones were created. From 1979 to 1986 China's policy towards FDI was characterized by the attitude that FDIs were welcome, but highly regulated; after 1986 China granted permission for the operation of wholly-owned foreign enterprises (Haihong, 2000, pp. 19–20). Major changes in the functioning of the economy were introduced in the 1990s, such as encouragement of foreign investment, reduction of effective tariffs on imported inputs,[25] the modernization of the public corporations, the abolition of multiple exchange rates, and the introduction of convertibility for current account transactions.

Since the end of the 1970s, exchange rate regime has changed sometimes: first it was centralized and still a fixed one; from 1986 to 1993 the exchange rate was dual, where the official rate, which was subject to periodic adjustments, coexisted with the market-determined rate in the swap centres[26] – the second rate was set at a relatively depreciated level compared with the official rate. In 1994 the official rate was devaluated and unified with the exchange rate at the swap centres, and a managed floating exchange regime was officially adopted. In practice, however, after a short period of some appreciation of nominal exchange rate, the *renminbi* (RMB), the domestic currency, also known as *yuan*, was de facto fixed to the US dollar from 1995 (Figure 4.19). Central bank's intervention to maintain a stable exchange rate has been large scale, with reserves rising to more than 30 per cent of GDP by end 2004. In July 2005 the Chinese authorities announced a revaluation of the exchange rate against the dollar of 2.1 per cent, with the currency able to move daily in a narrow range of ±0.3 per cent.[27] In addition, the central rate for the RMB is determined by a basket of currencies the composition of which was not revealed. Again, in practice it has not resulted in greater changes in the modus operandi of Chinese exchange rate policy.

Popular Bank of China, the central bank, acts as a market marker in the foreign exchange market.[28] The management of a (semi) fixed exchange rate in China has been possible owing to the existence of widespread capital controls on both inflows and outflows, mainly through the use of prohibitions and quantitative limits. The objectives of the controls evolved over time, but generally have included: (i) to help channel external savings to desired uses; (ii) keeping monetary policy independent of the influence of international developments, within a context of a managed exchange rate regime; (iii) preventing firms and financial institutions from taking excessive external risks; (iv) maintaining balance of payments equilibrium and keeping exchange rate stability; and (v) to insulate the economy from foreign financial crises (Zhao, 2006, p. 8). Indeed, China has followed a pattern of financial liberalization in which

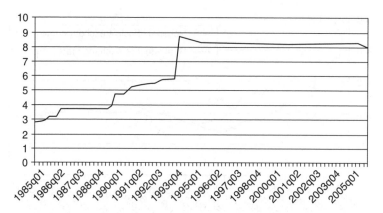

Figure 4.21 China – nominal exchange rate (% annual average)
Source: IMF.

the sequence starts with liberalizing the trade account, then relaxing foreign exchange restrictions, then the long-term capital account, and finally the short-term capital account (Epstein et al., 2005, pp. 33–4).

In 1996 China accepted the IMF Article VII, which resulted in the liberalization of foreign exchange controls related to current account transactions. Furthermore, since then controls over inflows and outflows by non-residents have been loosened, while maintaining strict but porous controls on inflows and outflows by residents. In fact, at the end of 1996 there were a lot of controls on foreign exchange transactions: (i) non-residents were forbidden to operate in the money market, stock market and derivative market; they could only buy some sort of shares; (ii) residents could only operate in these markets abroad with previous approval of the monetary authorities, while in some operations there were quantitative restrictions; (iii) prior approval was required for any foreign borrowing, foreign currency-denominated bond issues, and guarantees in foreign exchange (Haihong, 2000). Therefore, portfolio capitals were not welcome because of segregation among residents and non-residents in the stock markets, while restrictions on other types of external loans were pervasive and generally subject to strict ceilings – controls on foreign debt accumulation prevented the excessive accumulation of foreign debt by residents, controls on equity inflows prevented a speculative bubble in the stock market, while controls on outflows in general prevented devastating surges of capital flight.

The dynamic nature of the controls in China should be stressed, with the authorities tightening enforcement during crisis periods and then

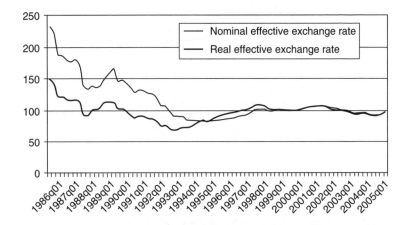

Figure 4.22   China – NEER and REER (period average, index number 2000 = 100)
Source: IMF.

loosening them when the crisis subsides (Epstein et al., 2005, p. 35). As can be seen in Table 4.4 and Figure 4.23, during 1997 Asian crisis, although current account remained in surplus and FDI remained strong, capital account deteriorated sharply. Under these circumstances, the authorities intensified enforcement of exchange and capital controls, and moved to reduce circumvention – including verification requirements on current account transactions to demonstrate that the transactions are in fact legitimate current transactions (Ariyoshi et al., 2000, p. 63). More recently some tight controls on foreign exchange transactions have been loosened, at the same time that tariffs and quotas on imports were reduced or eliminated. Such measures in general reduced the quantitative restrictions to the purchase of foreign currencies by residents, relaxing the restrictions on extending external guarantee, on issuing bonds in the international market and on foreign firms' borrowing in RMB.[29] Chinese authorities have attempted to alleviate recent appreciation pressures by easing controls on capital outflows.

The current level of exchange rate is considered devaluated in general. The real effective exchange rate, based on the consumer price index, had a lot of variations during the last 25 years: it depreciated sharply during the 1980s and beginning of the 1990s, due to frequent nominal exchange rate devaluations, and it appreciated for a short period until 1997, due to the increase in the inflation. Indeed, RMB was devaluated by 21 per cent in 1989, 9 per cent in 1990, and 14 per cent in 1994. Since 1997 real

Table 4.4 China – basic economic indicators

	1990	1991	1992	1993	1994	1995	1996	1997	1998	1999	2000	2001	2002	2003	2004	2005
GDP real growth (% p.a.)	3.8	9.2	14.2	13.9	13.1	10.9	10.0	9.3	7.8	7.6	8.4	8.3	9.1	10.0	10.1	10.2
Gross fixed capital formation (%GDP)	25.0	26.8	30.9	36.0	34.5	33.0	32.4	31.8	33.0	33.6	34.3	34.6	36.3	39.2	40.6	41.9
Consumer price index (% p.a.)	3.1	3.5	6.3	14.6	24.2	16.9	8.3	2.8	-0.8	-1.4	0.3	0.5	-0.8	1.2	4.0	1.8
Fiscal balance (% of GDP)	-3.7	-3.3	-2.6	-1.9	-1.9	-1.4	-1.2	-1.1	-1.5	-2.2	-2.8	-4.0	-2.6	-2.1	-1.3	-1.2
Public debt (% of GDP)	–	–	–	–	–	–	–	–	–	–	–	17.7	18.9	19.2	18.5	17.9
Exchange rate average (yuan/USD)	4.8	5.3	5.5	5.8	8.6	8.4	8.3	8.3	8.3	8.3	8.3	8.3	8.3	8.3	8.3	8.2
International reserves (excl.gold, USD million)	29 586	43 674	20 620	22 387	52 914	75 377	107 039	142 762	149 188	157 728	168 278	215 605	291 128	408 151	614 500	821 514
Current account (% of GDP)	3.2	2.2	1.3	-1.8	1.2	0.2	0.8	3.7	3.0	1.9	1.7	1.3	2.4	2.8	3.5	7.0
International reserves (% of imports)	57.3	70.1	27.1	22.7	46.9	58.4	78.6	102.3	109.4	97.0	76.0	89.9	100.2	100.1	110.3	124.9
External debt (% of GDP)	14.9	14.5	15.1	13.5	16.9	15.5	14.4	14.9	13.8	13.8	12.2	9.0	12.8	12.7	12.0	–
External debt/ exports ratio	1.07	1.02	1.04	1.14	0.98	0.92	0.85	0.80	0.78	0.78	0.58	0.69	0.57	0.48	0.42	–
Income debt (% of exports)	3.2	4.0	6.3	6.2	5.6	11.4	13.1	9.1	12.1	11.7	10.9	10.7	7.2	5.5	4.1	3.7
Long-term debt (% external debt)	82.3	82.1	81.0	82.2	82.6	81.1	80.3	78.6	88.0	90.0	91.0	69.5	64.6	57.7	52.8	–
Trade balance (USD million)	9165	8743	5183	-10654	7290	18050	19535	46222	46614	35982	34474	34017	44167	44652	58982	134189
Current account (USD million)	11997	13272	6401	-11609	6908	1618	7243	36963	31472	21115	20518	17401	35422	45875	68659	160818

Source: IMF – International Financial Statistics; Deutsche Bank Research (public debt); ADB (external debt).

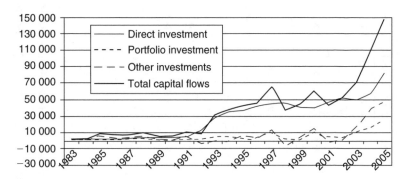

Figure 4.23   China – capital flows (liabilities, USD million)
Source: IMF.

effective exchange rate has had a stable trend, due to both low inflation and the stable nominal exchange rate (see Figures 4.21 and 4.25). The dramatic process of foreign reserves accumulation in China – reaching more than US$ 800 billion in 2005 (see Table 4.4) – started in the beginning of the 1990s, increasing in pace in particular since 2000, as a result of the deliberate foreign reserves accumulation policy in a context of increasing trade surplus and rising capital inflows, mainly FDI.

Considering the capital flows, it can be noted that there was a dramatic growth in the volume of capital flows in China during the 1990s, due mainly to the increase of FDI since 1993. Indeed, FDI increased dramatically during the 1990s, from US$ 4.3 billion in 1991 to US$ 44 billion in 1997, which made China the second largest recipient of FDI among all countries. FDI has been attracted by the long-term growth perspective of the Chinese economy (and increasing exports performance), and also by the fact that since the beginning of the reforms China sought to attract FDI. Foreign loans, however, had a low growth in the period, which is the result largely of the existence of restrictions on foreign debt. Therefore, at the same time that China has sought to attract FDI, it also has been very cautious about foreign loans and portfolio investments, although more recently such capital inflows have increased markedly, notably portfolio investments and other investments, such as loans, currency and deposits. The pick-up in export growth since 1995 came as a result of a set of factors, such as liberalization of the exports licensing system, the increasing productivity of industry, the cheap wages and the fall in the effective exchange rate. Overall, the current account surplus rose to more than 3 per cent of GDP since 2004 (see Table 4.4).

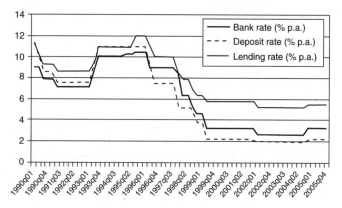

Figure 4.24 China – interest rate
Source: IMF.

As a consequence of the combination of the exceptional trade surplus, the dramatic increase of foreign reserves and the low level of external debt, the indexes of the external vulnerability of China show a very comfortable situation: the external debt-to-GDP ratio has been low and declining in the 1990–2004 period, reaching only 12.0 per cent in 2004. Further, the long-term debt over total external debt ratio had been higher than 70 per cent until 2000, evidence that the maturity structure of the debt is very healthy; more recently the ratio has declined due to the increase of external indebtedness, including short-term ones. Other indexes show additional evidence of a very good external situation: the external debt-to-exports ratio declined to less than 50 per cent in 2003, while reserve-to-imports ratio increased from 47 per cent on average in 1990–95 to 102 per cent in 1997 (Table 4.4).

After a short period of high inflation and high interest rates in the mid-1990s, China experienced low domestic rates and declining inflation and eventually even deflation (Figures 4.24 and 4.25). The combination of a stable exchange rate (and even real appreciation in 1994–98), strong labour productivity growth (as a result of strong investment rates), trade liberalization and declining commodity prices exerted significant downward pressure on inflation in 1996–2002, while demand factors played a smaller role (Prasad et al., 2004, p. 14). The reduction in inflation has been followed by expansionist monetary and fiscal policies during the period. China's fiscal position has been healthy due to the strong economic growth and low domestic interest rates, despite the fact that the primary fiscal position may appear weaker (Prasad et al., 2004, ch.V).

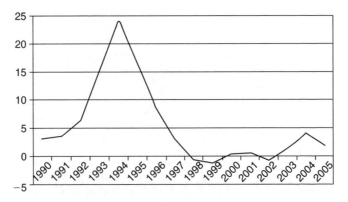

Figure 4.25   China – consumer price index (% p.a.)
Source: IMF.

More recently fiscal deficit over GDP has declined to 1.2 per cent in 2005. The Chinese authorities have attempted to isolate the domestic economy from the consequences of the combination of a fixed exchange rate and large capital inflows through sterilization. The sterilization of capital inflows has been facilitated by the fact that domestic interest rates have been lower than the interest rates of industrial country treasury bonds (Prasad et al., 2005, p. 12).

4.4 Conclusion

China and India, managing their exchange rate regimes with a restrictive capital account convertibility, have been successful cases of management of macroeconomic policy – in which the stability of exchange rate has a crucial role – that seek to create a stable environment for economic growth. China's and India's cases show how to implement gradual and careful management of capital account and policies oriented towards the reduction of external vulnerability. These experiences also show that capital controls can be helpful in protecting the economy against the destabilizing aspects of capital flows and helping to resolve certain types of policy dilemma, such as simultaneously managing exchange rate and the short-term interest rate.

Russia is an interesting case, as until 1998 the economy performed very badly, as a result of a chaotic transition process of liberalization to a market economy; since the 1998 crisis the economy has performed very well, due to both the increase in exports (mainly related to oil and gas) and the better management of macroeconomic policy, which has combined

Table 4.5 Exchange rate regime and capital account convertibility of BRICs countries

Country	Exchange rate regime	Monetary policy framework	Indicator of exchange rate	Capital account convertibility	Exchange rate volatility*
Brazil	Floating, with dirty floating	Inflation targeting	Nominal bilateral	High	High
China	Semi-fixed	Pegged exchange rate	Real effective	Partial, with many restrictions	Very low
India	Managed floating	Multiple indicators	Nominal bilateral and real effective	Partial, with many restrictions	Very low
Russia	Managed floating	Multiple indicators	Nominal bilateral	Partial, with some restrictions	Low

Source: Author's elaboration based on Mohanty and Scatigna (2005) and own data.
Note: *Exchange rate volatility related to 1999–2003, according to Mohanty and Scatigna (2005, Table A2).

a more active exchange rate policy and decreasing interest rates, in a context (at least until recently) of partial capital account convertibility. Brazil, on the other hand, has adopted a more liberal and orthodox economic policy, which includes a less interventionist approach related to exchange rate policy and a very open capital account, resulting in higher exchange rate volatility, higher interest rates, and a poorer economic performance. Table 4.5 shows a comparative synthesis of the analysis of the macroeconomic policy of each BRIC country.

Among the different factors that are important to the management of macroeconomic policy this chapter has stressed in particular the importance of reducing external vulnerability, which should be understood not only in terms of the external solvency of the country, but also in terms of its vulnerability to external shocks and changes in the market sentiment, in which the lower or higher degree of capital account convertibility can be an essential factor. In this particular concern, the recent experience of the BRICs countries shows the importance of having:

(a) a gradual and careful process of capital account liberalization;
(b) well-designed and dynamic capital management techniques in the sense that policy makers need to retain the ability to implement a variety of management techniques and alter as circumstances

warrant, but most importantly that they are coherent and consistent with the overall aims of the economic policy regime;

(c) a surplus balance in the current account or a deficit in low level, financed by external capital with the predominance of long-term capital;

(d) The accumulation of exchange reserves by central banks, in order to avoid speculative attacks on domestic currency and also to allow that the monetary authorities enhance their capability to influence the real effective exchange rate and to reduce the volatility of nominal exchange rate;

(e) A managed floating exchange regime, according to the specificities of each country, which aims for the preservation of a competitive and stable real exchange rate as an intermediate target of macroeconomic policies oriented to employment and growth objectives.

Notes

1. This chapter is the result of the author's research at the Centre for Brazilian Studies, University of Oxford. I am very grateful for CNPq financial support and to Fabio Barcelos for his generous research support.

2. For the purpose of this chapter, we define macroeconomic stability as a broader concept than just price stabilization, as it aims to reduce the uncertainties intrinsic to the business world in order to provide a favourable environment for investment and production decisions. Macroeconomic stability can also be defined as a situation of sustained economic growth with financial stability, that is, with inflation under control and with low likelihood of financial/currency crises. See more on this subject in Oreiro and Paula (2007, section 2).

3. Mohanty and Scatigna (2005, p. 19), using the IMF's de facto classification of exchange rate regimes report that the number of emerging countries opting for a flexible exchange rate has risen from a little above 15% in 1990 to about one half at the end of 2001, while the share of hard peg regimes increased moderately from under 10% at little above 15% during the same period, and intermediate regime has fallen from over three quarters to less than 35%. Reinhart and Rogoff (2002), however, using another classification based on parallel exchange market activity and other special features, concluded that many emerging economies have in effect crawling peg regimes.

4. According to Frenkel (2006, p. 579), 'a competitive RER [real exchange rate] involves the distortion of domestic relative prices in favor of tradable activities against nontradable activities: the combination of higher protection for local activities that compete with imports with a higher competitiveness for export activities. Consequently, the RER affects the employment growth rate in the long run due to its influence on the output growth rate, through its incentive on investment in tradable activities that accelerates productivity growth and generates positive externalities in other sectors'.

5. Cost of sterilization is calculated as the spread between the domestic and the US one-year Treasury bill rate, applied to the total outstanding stock of foreign exchange reserves in domestic currency.

6. Prudential controls can include: (i) to limit the opportunities for residents to borrow in foreign currency and to monitor them when they do, and (ii) to keep very tight constraints on banks' ability to have open foreign exchange positions or indirect exposure through foreign exchange loans.

7. Criticism on capital controls are partially related to the possible benefits of capital account liberalization, which are: increased opportunities for risk diversification, a higher efficiency of global allocation of savings, and external discipline on domestic macroeconomic policies (Fischer, 1998). However, empirical evidence of capital account liberalization upon economic performance is ambiguous while their links with financial crises are quite evident. IMF economists (Prasad et al., 2003, p. 3) resume the empirical findings of the literature: 'a systematic examination of the evidence suggests that is difficult to establish a robust causal relationship between the degree of financial integration and output growth performance'.

8. Real effective exchange rate index (REER) is defined as a nominal effective rate index (index of the period average exchange rate of the currency in question to a weighted average of exchange rates for the currencies of selected countries) adjusted for relative movements in national price of home country and selected countries. It should be stressed that REER in Brazil and other Latin American countries is calculated differently from the more conventional way, that is, REER is calculated by multiplying the nominal exchange rate by the inflation rate of home country and dividing by that of a partner country, while more frequently (as in case of China, India and Russia in this chapter) REER is calculated by multiplying the nominal exchange rate by the inflation rate of a partner country and dividing by that of home country. As a result, in the case of Brazil, when REER increases this means undervaluation and when it declines it means overvaluation.

9. Fiscal primary surplus (the budget surplus excluding interest payments) rose from 0.0% of GDP in 1998 to 3.2% in the following year, reaching 4.4 in 2003 and almost 5.0% in 2005.

10. Inflation targets were 4.0% in 2001, 3.5% in 2002, and 3.5% in 2003 (later it was changed to a maximum limit of 8.5%), with tolerance intervals of ±2%; the consumer price index (IPCA) was 7.7%, 12.5% and 9.3%, respectively in 2001, 2002 and 2003 (Figure 4.6).

11. Goldfajn and Minella (2005) report the norms on capital controls in Brazil.

12. The financial transaction tax was from 5% to 9% to Foreign Funds on Securities in October 1994.

13. According Ariyoshi et al. (2000) these capital controls were not effective in Brazil as capitals inflows increased a great deal and the sophistication of the financial system enabled participants to circumvent most controls.

14. In March 2005, Central Bank of Brazil authorized individuals and corporates to make transfer of resources abroad through their own bank accounts, a simplification in the norms that meant the end of CC-5 account.

15. Souza and Hoff (2006), using Calvo–Reinhart's fear of floating indicators, show that from January 1999 to December 2005 the frequency that monthly variation of exchange rate exceeded the band of ±2.5% was 52% in Brazil,

compared to 27% in other emerging countries of Latin America, and to 19% in Asian emerging countries (Indonesia, Singapore, Thailand, and South Korea).

16. 'Other investments', according to IMF's definition, include short-and long term trade credits, loans, currency and deposits (transferable and other), etc.

17. Unemployment rate increased quickly to more than 10% in 1997.

18. Non-residents were allowed to open special rouble-denominated bank accounts with which to buy government securities in either the primary or secondary markets. See more in Ariyoshi et al. (2000, Ch 2).

19. Several econometric studies conclude that monetary policy has tended to focus on an implicit exchange rate target since the late 1990s. See, among others, Esanov et al. (2005).

20. For more details on exchange restrictions in Russia, see IMF (2006a).

21. There are some concerns about this announcement, although Russian domestic interest rate settings have remained below those available in other emerging countries, which should reduce speculation related to interest rate arbitrage.

22. The Oil Stabilization Fund (OIF) was created in 2004 with the objective of reducing the impact of fluctuations of oil prices on the resources available to the budget. 'Surplus' revenues resulting from relatively high oil prices are accumulated in the Fund automatically: 95% of the income from the natural resource extraction tax and 100% of the crude oil export duty above that which would accrue at an oil price of $27/bbl (Urals) is automatically transferred to the Fund. Until the Fund accumulates a total of RUB 500 billion, Stabilization Fund may spend only to finance the federal deficit arising as a result of oil prices below the cut-off price of $27 for Urals crude (OECD, 2006, Ch 2).

23. For instance, mutual funds in India are now permitted to invest up to US$ 1 billion abroad.

24. India has had an increasing trade deficit due to the higher imports growth than exports growth. Although India has managed to diversify its exports towards higher value added goods, the country's export performance has lagged behind that of Asia with its share of global exports remaining low (IMF, 2006b, ch. II).

25. Average import customs duty was reduced from 45% in 1992 to 17.5% in 2000 (Ariff and Khalid, 2005, p. 88).

26. In the swap centres, exporters, importers, and other parties with foreign exchange supply or needs could transact at a market-determined exchange rate. By 1991 all residents were allowed to sell foreign exchange at the swap rate at the designed bank branches. In December 1998 swap centres were closed and all exchange payments were bought into the banking settlement system.

27. In May 2007 the range was enlarged to ±0.5%.

28. State Administration of Foreign Exchange (SAFE) is responsible for controlling and monitoring cross-border exchange flows and all businesses in foreign currency.

29. Liberalization of cross-border foreign exchange transactions include: authorization for purchase of foreign exchange for investments abroad in strategic projects (2001); introduction of the Qualified Foreign Investor Initiative (QFII) permitting non-residents to invest in the domestic stock market

(A shares), subject to some restrictions (2002); registration with the government to repay loan principal is no longer required for residents wishing to borrow foreign exchange from domestic Chinese financial institutions (2003); the ceilings on residents' foreign exchange for purposes of tourism and overseas study were raised from US$ 2000 to US$ 3000 or US$ 5000 (2003). See more in Prasad et al. (2005).

References

ADB (Asian Development Bank), *ADB Indicators*, various numbers.
Arida, P. (2004), 'Aspectos macroeconomicos da conversibilidade: uma discussao do caso brasileiro', unpublished manuscript.
Ariff, M. and Khalid, A. (2005), *Liberalization and Growth in Asia*. Cheltenham: Edward Elgar.
Ariyoshi, A. et al. (2000), 'Capital controls: country experiences with their use and liberalization'. *Occasional Paper* N.190. Washington: IMF.
Berengaut, J. and Elborgh-Woytek, K. (2005), 'Who is still haunted by the specter of communism? Explaining relative output contractions under transition'. *IMF Working Paper* 05/68, April.
Calvo, G. and Reinhart, C. (2002), 'Fear of floating'. *Quarterly Journal of Economics*, CXVII (2):379–408.
Deutsche Bank Research (2007), http://www.dbresearch.com, accessed in May.
ECLAC (2000), *Foreign Investment in Latin America and the Caribbean – 1999 Report*. Santiago: Chile.
Epstein, G., Grabel, I. and Jomo, K.S. (2003), 'Capital management techniques in developing countries', *Working Paper Series* No.56, University of Massachusetts.
Fischer, S. (1998), 'Capital Account Liberalization and the Role of the IMF', in *Essays in International Finance* No. 207, Princeton University, May.
Fischer, S. (2001), 'Exchange rate regimes: is the bipolar view correct?', *Journal of Economic Perspectives*, 15(2):3–24.
Frenkel, R. (2006), 'An alternative to inflation targeting in Latin America: macroeconomic policies focused on employment'. *Journal of Post Keynesian Economics* 28(4):573–91.
Goldfajn, I. and Minella, A. (2005), 'Capital flows and controls in Brazil: What have we learned?', *NBER Working Paper Series* No. 11640, September.
Grenville, S. (2000), 'Exchange rate regime for emerging countries'. *Reserve Bank of Australia Bulletin*, November.
Habermeier, K. (2000), 'India's experience with the liberalization of capital flows since 1991', in Arioyshi et al. (2000), op.cit.
Haihong, G. (2000), 'Liberalising China's capital account: lessons drawn from Thailand's experience', *Visiting Researchers Series* N.6. Institute of Southeast Asian Studies, February.
Hausmann, R., Pritchett, L. and Rodrik, D. (2004), 'Growth accelerations', *NBER Working Paper Series* No. 10566, June.
Ho, C. and McCauley, R. (2003), 'Living with flexible exchange rates: issues and recent experience in inflation targeting emerging market economies', *BIS Working Paper* No.130, February.
IMF (International Monetary Fund), *International Financial Statistics*, various numbers.

IMF (2001), 'India: Recent Economic Developments and Selected Issues', *IMF Country Report* No. 01/191, October.

IMF (2003), 'Russia: Staff Report for the 2003 Article IV Consultation, *IMF Country Report*. No. 03/144, May.

IMF (2004), 'Russia: Staff Report for the 2004 Article IV Consultation', *IMF Country Report*. No. 04/314, September.

IMF (2005), 'India: Staff Report for the 2004 Article IV Consultation', *IMF Country Report*. No. 05/86, March.

IMF (2006a), *Annual Report on Exchange Arrangements and Exchange Restrictions – 2006*. Washington: IMF.

IMF (2006b), 'India: Selected Issues', *IMF Country Report*. No.06/56, February.

Kholi. R. (2005), *Liberalizing Capital Flows*, New Delhi: Oxford University Press.

Magud, N. and Reinhart, C. (2006), 'Capital controls: an evaluation', *NBER Working Paper* No. 11973, January.

Mohanty, M. and Scatigna, M. (2005), 'Has globalization reduced monetary policy independence?', *BIS Papers* No. 23.

Mohanty, M. and Turner, P. (2006), 'Foreign exchange reserves in emerging countries', *BIS Quarterly Review* 24:39–42.

Moreno, R. (2005), 'Motives for intervention', *BIS Papers* No. 24, May.

Nayyar, D. (2002), 'Capital controls and the World Financial Authority: what can we learn from the Indian experience?', In Eatwell, J. and Taylor, L. (ed.). *International Capital Markets: Systems in Transition*, Oxford: Oxford University Press.

OECD (2005), 'China', *OECD Economic Surveys* vol. 2005/13, September.

OECD (2006), 'Russian Federation', *OECD Economic Surveys* vol. 2006/17, November.

Ono, F.H., Silva, G.J., Oreiro, J.L., and Paula, L.F. (2005), 'Conversibilidade da conta de capital, taxa de juros e crescimento econômico: uma avaliação da proposta de plena conversibilidade do Real', *Revista de Economia Contemporânea* 9(2): 231–61.

Oreiro, J.L. and Paula, L.F. (2007), 'Strategy for economic growth in Brazil: a Post Keynesian approach', in Arestis, P., Baddeley, M. and McCombie, J. (eds), *Economic Growth: New Directions in Theory and Policy*. Cheltenham, Edward Elgar.

Owen, D. and Robinson, D. (ed.) (2003), *Russia Rebounds*. Washington: IMF.

Paula, L.F. and Alves, Jr, A.J. (2000). 'External financial fragility and the 1998–1999 Brazilian currency crisis', *Journal of Post Keynesian Economics*, 22(4):589–617.

Prasad, E., Rogoff, K., Wei, S. and Kose, M. (2003), 'Effects of financial globalization on developing countries: some empirical evidence', http://www.imf.org/external/np/apd/seminars/2003/newdelhi/prasad.pdf.

Prasad, E. (2004), 'China's growth and integration into the world economy', *Occasional Paper* No. 232. Washington: IMF.

Prasad, E. and Wei, S.J. (2005), 'The Chinese approach to capital inflows: patterns and possible explanations', *NBER Working Paper Series*, No. 11306, April.

Purushothaman, R. and Wilson, D. (2003), 'Dreaming with BRICs: the path to 2050', http://www.gs.com, *Global Economics Paper*, No. 99, October.

Reinhart, C. and Rogoff, K. (2002), 'The modern history of exchange rate arrangements: a reinterpretation', *NBER Working Paper Series*, No. 8963, June.

Souza, F.E. and Hoff, C. (2006), 'O regime cambial brasileiro: 7 anos de flutuação', http://www.ie.ufrj.br/conjuntura/pdfs/TextoRedeMercosul.pdf.

Zhao, M. (2006), 'External liberalization and the evolution of China's exchange system', World Bank Beijing Office, http://siteresources.worldbank.org.

5
The Liberalization of Capital Outflows in Brazil, India and South Africa since the early 1990s

Ricardo Gottschalk and Cecilia Azevedo Sodré

5.1 Introduction

During the 1990s, a number of developing countries took major steps towards liberalizing their capital accounts. In a context of increasing availability of international capital, the liberalization process resulted in these countries attracting large amounts of capital flows. In the second half of the 1990s these countries faced major capital flow reversals which in many cases resulted in deep financial crises. Because liberalization was associated with so many crises, a great deal of work has been done on the topic.[1]

The literature has mainly analysed the liberalization of capital inflows, and has extensively discussed the use of capital controls aimed either at slowing down the inflows in times of capital surges, or at avoiding major capital reversals in times of international financial instability and crises.[2] However, much less has been done to examine the liberalization of capital outflows by residents.

This chapter aims to contribute to the literature on capital account liberalization (CAL) by focusing on the liberalization of capital outflows by residents, which, in our view, is a dimension of the liberalization process that has been overlooked. To this end, it examines the experience with the liberalization of capital outflows in Brazil, India and South Africa, in which similarities and differences are highlighted. Examining CAL in Brazil, India and South Africa is particularly pertinent for two reasons.

First, the process of capital account opening in these countries has gone furthest on the inflows side, which is a pattern of liberalization also observed in many other developing countries. Many of this larger group of countries face the challenge now of how to manage the process regarding the opening of the capital account for outflows (see for example Gottschalk, 2002). In analysing the experience of Brazil, India and South Africa, which are among those countries that have partially liberalized capital outflows, it is possible to draw lessons and offer recommendations for countries that have not liberalized such flows yet on how to do so in a sustainable manner.

Second, nowadays India along with China is seen as an emerging power in the world economy. The country has experienced rapid GDP growth in the past decade or so, and has accumulated large amounts of international reserves. All these facts have generated the expectations that India may take major steps towards further liberalization of its capital account, mainly on the outflows side. This, if confirmed, would imply breaking with the past when a rather cautious approach was followed. More broadly, the so-called BRICS countries – Brazil, Russia, India, China and South Africa – are becoming important (and sometimes allied) players in the world economy as a reflection of their growing combined economic power. In connection with this, a debate seems to be emerging on whether these countries' growing economic power might (or should) be matched by fuller capital account convertibility (CAC). We believe that examining the past CAL experience in these countries and exploring their intentions on possible further liberalization in the future can help inform the debate.

In addition, the chapter discusses the current strengths and weaknesses of the three countries, and addresses the questions: what are the main sources of vulnerability that governments should take into account before taking further CAL; and is full CAL appropriate even in the event that all remaining vulnerabilities have been eliminated?

The chapter shows that, among the countries discussed – Brazil, India and South Africa – Brazil has been the one that has liberalized furthest its capital outflows; also, it has been the country that has suffered most from the international financial instability, both in the 1990s and early this century. The chapter thus suggests the existence of causal links between the degree of liberalization of capital outflows and foreign exchange instability. In particular it suggests that, in Brazil, the capital that has flown out through legal channels has had an important role in the currency instability experienced by the country since CAL took place in the early 1990s. Both India and South Africa, in turn, have adopted a more cautious liberalization strategy, which can be seen among the factors that explain why these two countries have been far less affected by the various international turbulences in the recent past.

The chapter is organized in six sections. Section 5.2 describes the various measures undertaken regarding the liberalization of capital outflows in Brazil. Section 5.3 discusses the experience of South Africa, and section 5.4, India's experience. Section 5.5 provides a comparative analysis of the countries' experiences and is followed by conclusions.

5.2 The liberalization of capital outflows in Brazil

During the Collor government of 1990–92, Brazil took major liberalization steps, especially on the side of capital inflows.[3] On the outflows side, which is our interest here, in early 1992 the government permitted foreign banks to hold bank accounts in Brazil through which they could acquire dollars in the floating rate segment of the foreign exchange market, and send these abroad. Holding these bank accounts whereby such transactions could take place was made possible through a mechanism called Carta-Circular no 5 – hereafter CC-5. The liberalization of capital outflows took further steps in 1994 with the creation of the special investment funds abroad, known as Fiex (nowadays called *Fundos de Divida Externa*).[4] In addition, in 1996 Brazilian investors were permitted to acquire Brazilian Depositary Receipts (BDRs) from foreign corporates. In what follows we discuss the CC-5, the Fiex and the BDRs, which between their creation and early 2005 (when further liberalization was undertaken) were the main mechanisms through which residents could send capital abroad through legal means.

5.2.1 The CC-5

The CC-5 was until very recently the main way through which residents could invest abroad. It was created in 1969 to allow non-residents with business in Brazil to send money abroad.[5] Specifically, the CC-5 established that non-residents could only use national currency to buy foreign currency and send these abroad if the resources in domestic currency were the result of previous conversion from foreign currency brought by the non-resident to the country.

In February 1992, the Brazilian government deepened the liberalization process by creating a sub-account that foreign banks could draw upon to send dollars abroad without the need of previous internalization of equivalent amount of resources.[6] But the additional relevant element was that corporates and individual residents in Brazil could use these sub-accounts to make a direct investment abroad or to send money to their own account abroad. It was a de facto convertibility of domestic currency deposited in the CC-5 accounts that belonged to foreign banks (Van Der Laan et al., 2006).

In the case of individuals, there was no limit, at that point in time, to send resources abroad, nor restrictions as to how such resources could be used or invested. For those transactions involving values above R$ 10 thousand or more, individuals were expected to provide information on origin, destiny and aim of the transaction. Moreover, the operations had to be registered with the Central Bank.[7] Individuals then made use of this mechanism to send resources to their own accounts abroad, aiming to acquire real estate and/or invest directly in stocks or through an investment fund.

For corporates, investments above US$ 5 million required previous authorization from the Central Bank. These agents reportedly sent resources abroad as investment in fixed capital and for lending to other corporates.[8]

The importance of the CC-5 accounts lies in the fact that it was through them that most of the capital owned by residents left the country in periods of crises. For instance, US$ 1.4 billion was transferred abroad in December 2001, as a result of the uncertainties generated by the crisis in neighbouring Argentina towards the end of that year. In 2002, when the Lula presidential candidacy generated high uncertainty among investors, US$ 1.6 billion and US$ 2.2 billion left the country in August and October that year. Over the whole year, outflows reached US$ 9.1 billion, a 50 per cent increase in relation to the previous year, an outflow that resulted in strong pressure over the foreign exchange market. The largest outflows – US$ 24.8 billion – occurred in 1998 as a result of the contagion effects of the Russian crisis, a process that culminated in the large currency devaluation in January 1999. Sicsú (2005) points out that net outflows through CC-5 accounts were above US$ 113 billion between 1993 and 2004.

The increase in outflows in times of heightened expectations around exchange rate devaluation was to a considerable extent explained by the transfer by corporates of resources to meet external commitments in advance. In response to this, in 2004 the government authorized corporates to make payments relative to external commitments in advance if they so wished. Until then, debt obligations could be met only at the due dates. The aim was to reduce the use of the CC-5 for that purpose.

In March 2005 the CC-5, as a major mechanism for transfer abroad by residents, came to an end. By then, the Central Bank took the step of authorizing individuals and corporates to make transfer of resources abroad through their own bank accounts. Moreover, they can now obtain foreign exchange through foreign exchange contracts with authorized dealers, and face no quantitative limits to do so. The only remaining restriction faced by residents is to specify the purpose of the transfer. This measure took place together with the merging of the foreign exchange markets, which until then were split into the free-rate market and the floating rate segment.

In September 2006 further liberalization for residents took place. Corporates and individuals have been allowed to send resources abroad through the foreign exchange market to acquire stocks, derivatives and other investments (such as in investment and pension funds) in the international capital markets. Until then, residents could only acquire stocks from Mercosur countries, and securities issued by Brazilian corporates abroad (e.g. ADRs), by foreign corporates domestically (BDRs), or through the Fiex – see below.

The new measures of March 2005 and September 2006 could be interpreted as providing more transparent mechanisms for a de facto situation. But in removing an important bureaucratic barrier, it in fact represents a major liberalization step of the capital account, as the ease with each resources can be sent abroad has increased significantly.

5.2.2   The special investment funds abroad (Fiex)

The Fiex (or *Fundos de Divida Externa* as noted earlier) is a special investment fund created in 1994 which domestic institutional investors, financial institutions, non-financial corporates and individuals could use to invest abroad. The rules that initially governed the fund were that at least 60 per cent of the total resources had to be invested in Brazilian foreign debt, with the remaining being permitted to be invested in other securities, derivatives or held in the form of bank deposits abroad.[9] For monitoring purposes, all investments made via the Fiex had to take place through financial institutions authorized to operate in the foreign exchange market and all operations had to be registered with the Central Bank. The fund clearly represented an additional mechanism through which resources could be sent abroad; and perhaps even more importantly, it constituted a new institutional framework that challenged the notion that national savings had to remain within national borders.

Following the currency crisis of January 1999, the Brazilian authorities increased the minimum limit for investing in Brazil's external debt, from 60 per cent to 80 per cent. This measure was undertaken in February that year. In March, a further restrictive measure was adopted – of forbidding financial institutions to invest in the Fiex. But for individuals and non-financial corporates, Fiex became an important vehicle for their portfolio diversification.

Institutional investors were also permitted to invest in the Fiex, as mentioned above. However, they could only invest 10 per cent of their total resources in it. This limit applied for pension funds as well as insurance companies, among other institutional investors. According to a major pension fund in Brazil, pension funds did not invest abroad in spite of being able to do so through the Fiex, because it would imply losing fiscal exemptions that are valid only for domestic investments.

Restrictions on foreign investment by pension funds is publicly justified to ensure prudential investment patterns, but an alternative explanation is that it is felt to be necessary to protect the country from the possible occurrence of major capital outflows (Carvalho, 2004), which could have major destabilizing effects over the foreign exchange markets. From the country's perspective, this sort of legal restriction is important not only to avoid major currency instability, but also to ensure that national savings held by institutional investors are used for long-term investments within the country, and to support the mortgage and capital markets.[10]

5.2.3   Brazilian Depositary Receipts (BDRs)

In addition to CC-5 and Fiex, residents could invest abroad through acquiring Depositary Receipts (DRs) of Brazilian corporates, as well as Brazilian Depositary Receipts (BDRs) of foreign corporates. As is known, DRs are securities that represent shares of Brazilian corporates that can be transacted in international markets, while BDRs are securities representing shares issued by foreign public corporates.[11] Of course, from a micro perspective, DRs constitute an investment abroad, but also and in equivalent terms external borrowing by domestic public corporates; therefore, DRs are neutral from a balance of payments perspective. The BDRs represent an outright outflow of resources, although when the investment comes to an end, resources cannot be used for another investment modality abroad, thus returning to the country instead.

5.2.4   Comments on Brazil's experience

Brazil liberalized first, and in a major way, outflows by corporates and individuals (via changes in the CC-5 in 1992). More recently, the new measures brought the CC-5 to an end as a vehicle for capital outflows by residents, by permitting non-financial corporates and individuals to buy and sell foreign currency through their own bank accounts. While beforehand all such operations occurred in the floating segment of the foreign exchange markets, nowadays these take place in the unified foreign exchange market. These changes represent further reduction of barriers to capital outflows. At the same time, they give the Central Bank greater capacity to monitor the operations and check their legality. The liberalization of capital outflows by institutional investors, however, has been more limited, with the imposition of quantitative and other restrictions.

The liberalization of capital outflows in Brazil has occurred simultaneously with efforts to adopt prudent macroeconomic policies, especially after the implementation of the Real Plan in 1994. However, despite such efforts, the liberalization process contributed to increased macroeconomic volatility and currency crisis. After witnessing a currency crisis in early 1999, and a fairly long period of decline in the net flows of capital and poor growth performance, capital started to flow back in increasing amounts and the Brazilian economy began to recover in a more sustainable fashion at the end of 2003. Brazil's new cabinet – which took office at the beginning of 2003 – maintained the macroeconomic orientation that prevailed in the previous government. This included floating exchange rate regime, fiscal austerity and an inflation targeting framework.

Since then, some positive macroeconomic trends have been observed: inflation has converged towards the official target of 4.5 per cent, and the external indicators have improved considerably, with growing trade balance and a surplus in the current account emerging after many years of continued deficit (from a deficit of approximately 4.25 per cent of GDP in 1998, the current account registered a surplus of 1.75 per cent of GDP in 2005; IMF, 2006a; Paiva, 2006).

The external debt also has been brought down, with the total debt service ratio (in per cent of exports of goods and services) declining from 136.5 per cent in 2000 to 68.9 per cent in 2005 (IMF, 2006a). At the same time, international reserves have shown a moderate increase, reaching about US$ 75 billion in October 2006. On the fiscal front, Brazil's nonfinancial public sector primary surplus reached 4.8 per cent of GDP in 2005 – above the target of 4.25 per cent – and net public debt declined from 54.3 per cent of GDP at end-2004 to around 51.8 per cent in 2005, reflecting the combined effects of the primary surplus and exchange rate appreciation (Paiva, 2006).

However, these positive trends should be tempered. The currency has appreciated in the recent past thus undermining future export performance, reserves have not grown as much as it could have (to protect the economy from possible future shocks such as a decline in international commodity prices and higher international interest rates following possible sharp adjustment in the US economy); and on the fiscal side, both overall public deficit and debt are still very high. These are key indicators that should throw caution on plans for future CAL.

Despite these areas of remaining vulnerability, there is an ongoing debate in Brazil as to whether the country should adopt full capital account convertibility or not. Those in favour argue that capital controls can be circumvented by domestic investors fairly easily. A more elaborate argument that has been put forward is that full capital account convertibility would increase investors' confidence in the country's currency and that this would permit lower risk premium on Brazil's debt (see Arida, 2003). This argument is, however, contested. Oreiro et al. (2004) for example test this claim econometrically and find no relationship between capital controls and country risk-premium for Brazil.

A main concern among those that defend caution towards CAL is with the macroeconomic volatility and macroeconomic management challenges a fully convertible capital account creates, the loss of autonomy in macroeconomic policy formulation, and the risk of full-blown crises caused by sudden capital flow reversals, which can be very costly both in economic and social terms. A further current concern in Brazil is with the related liberalization steps in the current account, such as the recent permission granted to exporters to hold their export revenues in external accounts up to one year. This increases the unpredictability of foreign exchange flows and in times of heightened uncertainty greater potential for speculative actions in the foreign exchange market.

In what follows, we discuss liberalization in South Africa where, contrary to Brazil (and India as will be seen further below), outflows by institutional investors has been given priority over other resident investors.

5.3 The South African experience

Since 1994, when the South African economy was reintegrated into the world economy, the country's authorities promoted the liberalization of the capital account in two phases. First, they liberalized capital flows for non-residents in March 1995, and in July of the same year they initiated a liberalization process on the side of capital flows by residents.

The first phase, on liberalization of capital flows by non-residents, took place very rapidly during March 1995 when restrictions on non-residents in the foreign exchange market were removed with the unification of the foreign exchange (Wesso, 2001). The liberalization was adopted for all forms of flows, including short-term capital.

In relation to the second phase, which was focused on residents, the liberalization of capital flows has been gradual and sequenced.

Starting in mid-1995, institutional investors were granted permission to invest abroad via an asset-swap mechanism, amounting to 5 per cent of their total assets. According to this mechanism, the resident investor had to find an external counterpart interested in investing in South Africa's financial assets, and this investment had to be equivalent in value to the financial investment of the South African investor abroad. The aim was to ensure balance of payments neutrality (National Treasury, 2001). The 5 per cent limit was increased to 10 per cent in 1996, coupled with the requirement that investors could transfer resources abroad amounting to 3 per cent of the net inflows of funds during the previous year. Moreover, corporations were allowed to expand their offshore investments, provided that these were financed from profits generated or financed abroad.

Since then, significant steps have been taken regarding the liberalization of capital outflows. The limit on institutional investors' external assets was increased to 15 per cent of total assets in 1999, with the limit of foreign exchange purchase increasing from 3 to 5 per cent of the net inflows of fund during the previous year. In 2001, the asset-swap mechanism was eliminated, as well as restrictions relative to annual inflows. This applied for long-term insurers, pension funds and fund managers. Unit trusts could hold external assets up to 20 per cent of their total assets, subject to the upper limit of 10 per cent of annual net inflows in the previous period (IMF, 2002; National Treasury, 2001; Hviding, 2005).

Corporations and individuals are also permitted to hold financial assets abroad, although the limits they face were initially more restrictive, especially for individuals. Corporations have permission to invest in fixed capital abroad, but there is no specification for financial investments. As for individuals, initially they could invest up to 750 thousand rands, and maintain foreign-earned income abroad. Nowadays, they are allowed to invest up to 2 million rands abroad. In addition to the above, there are remaining restrictions on the transfer of funds abroad by emigrants (denominated 'blocked funds'), and the investment of currency proceeds from exports (they must be repatriated within 180 days).[12] Finally, in 2004 South Africa gave permission for residents to hold foreign instruments listed on South African exchanges (bond exchange South Africa and JSE Securities Exchange South Africa; IMF, 2005).

We can thus see that liberalization of capital outflows (not inflows) has been not only in a gradual fashion, but also sequenced, as institutional investors have been subjected to fewer restrictions to invest abroad than corporates and individuals. As we can see, this order of liberalization is opposite to that followed in Brazil, where liberalization took place first and more extensively for corporates and individuals.

It could be said that South Africa meets a number of the pre-conditions to broaden the liberalization of capital account. First, the government has pursued prudent macroeconomic policies, reforms in the financial sector and tax policy reforms. In the macroeconomic area, the fiscal deficit has declined gradually over time and inflation has been progressively lowered to about 3 per cent in mid-2005, after reaching between 10 and 15 per cent in the early 1990s (Nowak, 2005), despite periods of sharp exchange rate depreciation. In the fiscal area, improvements have taken place related to tax collection, facilitated by the creation of the South African Revenue Service (SARS); moreover, the government implemented the Public Finance Management Act (1999), designed to better monitor and control public spending, and also to provide safeguards against waste in government.

However, important areas of concern remain. First, since the change in the political regime in 1994, growth has accelerated, but from a very low level, up to an average of less than 3 per cent, although it has accelerated more recently, reaching nearly 5 per cent in 2005 (IMF, 2006c). Sluggish growth for most of the period can to a significant extent be explained by the macroeconomic policy responses adopted in South Africa. These have taken the form of high interest rates that South African policy makers adopted to deal with the successive external shocks that hit South Africa during the second half of the 1990s and early this century, to which the economy was vulnerable due to a fairly open capital account. Moreover, under a regime of fully flexible exchange rate, adopted by South Africa at the end of Apartheid (a policy option that was made in part due to the country's very low levels of international reserves at the time), economic growth has been hindered even during periods of capital surges, as these caused sharp exchange rate appreciation, which in turn undermined the competitiveness of the export activities.

A more worrying trend, however, can be observed in the current account deficit more recently. After reaching 1.3 per cent of GDP, it increased to 4.2 per cent of GDP in 2005 and to 6.4 per cent of GDP in the first quarter of 2006 (IMF, 2006b). The widening of the current account deficit has reflected the increasing deficit in the trade balance (from a surplus of US$ 4.1 billion in 2002 it reached a deficit of US$ 3.5 billion in 2005) and large dividend payments to foreign shareholders. The growing trade deficit is a particularly worrying trend because it has happened at a time of a primary commodity export boom. This deficit has been financed by FDI and portfolio flows,[13] enabling the country to increase its gross international reserves (from US$ 7.4 billion to US$ 24.1 billion between end-1999 and May 2006; IMF, 2006b).

Until now, South Africa has escaped financial crises because it has a relatively strong and sophisticated financial system, and a floating exchange rate regime. But the costs to external shocks have been high in terms of high macroeconomic volatility, sluggish economic growth, high unemployment rates and increased income inequalities (see Leite et al., 2006).

Although the international environment is relatively benign at present, it can deteriorate very rapidly, and cause rapid outflows of capital, with destabilizing effects. The full liberalization of capital outflows by residents would only reinforce these effects. Also, it should be emphasized that although some (not all) of the country's external indicators are favourable at present, they could deteriorate very quickly. Despite the increase in international reserves, which are a key economic indicator, they are not as high as could be. Considering this, the best course of action would be to be caution towards further CAL.

More generally, despite the relative political stability after the end of Apartheid, structural weaknesses of the South African economy that limited diversification and stifled investment may contribute to capital flight. Liberalizing further outflows by residents would just ease the process. This should be avoided, as domestic investors tend to be the first to pull out of the country when things are not going well, thereby triggering a crisis, as the crisis experiences in other countries have shown.

Of course, the argument that the effectiveness of restrictions is limited should not be dismissed. Domestic savers often find a way around restrictions to invest their capital in foreign assets. This is true, but only to a certain extent. While many capital holders in fact succeed in sending their capital abroad, this is done at a price. Most importantly, restrictions help reduce major outflows by banks, institutional investors and brokers, who are under strict supervision by the country's supervisory bodies, when these are in place.[14] Liberalization of outflows could have certain benefits, like those of diversification of risk for residents, but the risks associated with it are enormous (Gottschalk, 2002).

In what follows, we discuss India's case, which will show that, of the three countries here analyzed, it is the one that has adopted the slowest liberalization strategy, and where it furthermore signals that it intends to maintain this strategy despite increased expectations and mounting pressure to speed up liberalization for capital outflows.

5.4   The experience of India

India has taken non-trivial steps towards CAL since June 1997 when the Tarapore Committee recommended a timetable for implementing it (Reserve Bank of India, 2000). Until then, India's capital account was fairly restricted, as a result of a very slow liberalization process that had started back in the early 1990s.

According to the proposed timetable by the Tarapore Committee I, the capital account in India would be liberalized gradually, in three phases covering a total of three years: 1997–98 (phase 1); 1998–99 (phase 2); and 1999–2000 (phase 3). The proposed liberalization included both capital inflows and outflows. Thus, an important feature was the concomitant liberalization of these flows, though at different speeds.

As regards capital outflows, which are the focus of this chapter, the proposal made by the committee involved the following categories of residents:

1. Corporates
2. The Security Exchange Board of India (SEBI), which registers Indian investors (including mutual funds)
3. Individuals.

Corporates would initially be permitted to make transfers of financial capital abroad up to US$ 25 thousand. Later this limit would be raised to US$ 50 thousand and US$ 100 thousand in the second and third phases of the proposed liberalization.[15] Banks, in their turn, would be permitted to invest up to US$ 10 million in overseas money markets, mutual funds and/or debt instruments. This limit was increased to US$ 25 million in November 2002.

For the Security Exchange Board of India (SEBI), the Tarapore Committee I proposed, from an initial situation in which no investment abroad was permitted, that investors be permitted to invest in overseas financial markets, subject to an overall ceiling of US$ 500 million in the first phase, US$ 1 billion in the second phase and US$ 2 billion in the third phase. The Committee observed that it was important to ensure that the total amount was not met by just a few large-sized funds.

Similarly to institutional investors, until 1997 individuals were not permitted to invest abroad. The Tarapore Committee changed it by proposing that individuals be able to invest in financial markets and/or hold deposits abroad up to US$ 25 thousand per annum in the first phase, US$ 50 thousand in the second phase and US$ 100 thousand in the third phase. (The same limits were given to Indian non-residents regarding their non-repatriable assets in India.) They were also permitted to invest without any limits in overseas corporates listed on a stock exchange and which had a shareholding of at least 10 per cent in an Indian company listed on a local stock exchange, as well as in rated bonds/fixed income securities.

Among institutional investors, in practical terms there was no liberalization of capital outflows for pension funds and insurance companies, as these are nearly all public and therefore controlled and/or managed by the government.

At the time of the announcement of the report, it was believed that the liberalization of capital outflows would represent a strong commitment to CAL. Moreover, it was hoped that liberalizing outflows would work as an important instrument to compensate at least partially for surges of capital inflows that India was expecting to face with the liberalization of capital inflows, thereby contributing to attenuate pressures on the country's exchange rate towards appreciation of the rupee as well as on the monetary aggregates.

The recommendations for the liberalization of the capital account by the Tarapore Committee were made on the back of positive macroeconomic indicators for India. These included average annual economic growth of 7 per cent, a declining fiscal deficit from 8 per cent in 1990–91 to 5 per cent in 1996–97, an inflation rate below 6 per cent, a current account deficit of only 1 per cent in 1996–97, a debt to GDP ratio of 29 per cent in 1995–96 and a debt service ratio of 25.7 per cent in 1995–96 (Reserve Bank of India, 2000).

However, the Committee recognized that India still exhibited some weaknesses. These were mainly related to the financial system, by then still partially repressed (with administered interest rates and high levels of cash reserve requirements). Moreover, the country had a large quasi-fiscal deficit owing to a high level of public sector debt.

In view of these weaknesses, the Tarapore Committee made the implementation of the liberalization steps conditional on the country meeting certain preconditions. These were: bringing the fiscal deficit from 4.5 per cent in 1997–98 to 3.5 per cent in 1999–2000; maintaining inflation between 3 per cent and 5 per cent between 1997 and 2000; reducing the non-performing assets of the public sector banking system from 13.7 per cent to 5 per cent in 2000; reducing the cash reserve requirements from 9 per cent to 3 per cent; implementing a band system for the exchange rate, with a +/− 5 per cent band around a neutral real effective exchange rate, and finally reducing the debt service ratio from 25 per cent to 20 per cent (Indian Investment Center, 1997). In addition to these preconditions, the Tarapore Committee placed a great deal of importance on the level of international reserves.

Of all these preconditions, it was recognized that the most important was the need to strengthen the domestic financial system which, together with the public debt, were seen as the two major sources of vulnerability of the Indian economy. These vulnerabilities were perceived as the major obstacles for a successful capital account liberalization. In fact, the weakness of the country's financial system, and the fact that it remained largely repressed during the 1990s, was the main reason why India adopted a very cautious liberalization path for the capital account.

It is widely known that the timetable proposed by the 1997 Tarapore Committee was not fully implemented. Admittedly the main reason for this was the fact that the East Asian crisis occurred just after the Tarapore report was released. However, even if the East Asian crisis had not occurred, the recommendations still probably would not have been adopted in full owing to the failure to meet some of the above-mentioned preconditions.

Having said that, as the macroeconomic conditions in India have improved in the recent years and the financial system has become less repressed and stronger, the country has in certain areas undertaken liberalization steps beyond what has been proposed by the Tarapore Committee. Nowadays, international reserves have reached a comfortable position of US$ 151.6 billion in 2005–06 which correspond to about 11.6 months of imports. In terms of total external liabilities (which include portfolio stock), India's reserves cover over one half of such liabilities. This high level of reserves is a fact that has given the country the confidence to move further in the liberalization process.

Reflecting this, a new Tarapore Committee (called Tarapore Committee II) on CAL was set up in March 2006 and a report was made public at the end of July 2006. It recommended a phased increase in the ceilings on outward transfer of resources by the different types of investors. Moreover, this report proposed the roadmap for capital account convertibility (CAC), which will be briefly discussed in this section.

Like the previous report, the Tarapore II recommended a three-phased approach over a five-year period for further CAL in India: 2006–07 (phase 1); 2007–09 (phase 2); 2009–11 (phase 3). As established in Tarapore Committee I, the latest report has included further liberalization of outflows for corporates, Security Exchange Board of India (SEBI) and individuals.

1. Corporates: these will initially be permitted to invest up to 25 per cent of their net worth in overseas corporates having at least

10 per cent shareholding in listed Indian corporates and in rated bonds/fixed income securities. This restriction should be abolished at the end of phase 1. Banks should maintain the same limits observed previously in Tarapore I without any changes.

2. SEBI registered Indian investors (including mutual funds): the Tarapore II proposed that investors should be allowed to invest from an overall ceiling of US$ 2 billion to US$ 3 billion in the first phase. An overall ceiling of US$ 4 billion is expected to be observed in the second phase and of US$ 5 billion in the third phase.

3. Individuals: the committee changed the annual limits of transfers of money abroad by individuals. It should be raised to US$ 50 thousand in the first phase from the existing US$ 25 thousand per annum; to US$ 100 thousand in the second phase and to US$ 200 thousand in the third phase. The present rule regarding investments without any limit in overseas corporates listed on a stock exchange (and having a shareholding of at least 10 per cent in an Indian company) should be banned in the context of the large increase in the limits mentioned above. It is expected the committee will review this scheme in case of difficulties in managing it.

As was the case with the CAL recommendations made by the Tarapore Committee in 1997, the 2006 recommendations were made in a context of positive macroeconomic indicators for the Indian economy. These include average annual GDP growth of 8.1 per cent in 2005–06; an annual inflation rate below 5 per cent at the time the Tarapore II was announced; a debt service ratio of 10.2 for 2005–06, against 25.7 per cent back in 1995–96. The fiscal deficit as a proportion of the GDP declined from 8 per cent in 1990–91 to 5 per cent in 1996–97 and to 4.1 per cent in 2005–06 (Reserve Bank of India, 2000; Reserve Bank of India, 2006).

While the Indian government claims to have made significant efforts at fiscal consolidation and fiscal transparency, some weaknesses still exist. The domestic liabilities of the central government as a percentage of GDP grew from 45.4 per cent in 1996–97 to 60.3 per cent in 2005–06.

The committee's report also suggests a road map for Fuller Capital Account Convertibility (FCAC) – which does not necessarily mean zero capital restrictions. The report addresses some important implications of FCAC for monetary and exchange rate management, the financial system, and for fiscal revenues and fiscal deficit of both the central government and Indian states. It also addresses the need for strengthening the financial sector, which is still not sufficiently developed in India.

In view of such weaknesses, the Tarapore Committee II indicates that there is a need to set out a broad framework for designing the sequencing and timing of further capital account liberalization. For this purpose, the report believes it is important that India meets certain pre-conditions. These are: reducing the fiscal deficit to 3 per cent of GDP by 31 March, 2009;[16] bringing inflation rates down towards international levels; setting out the objectives of monetary policy; restructuring and strengthening the banking system[17] and developing segments of financial markets like foreign exchange, money and government securities. In addition, the government should monitor the current account deficit which increased in 2004–06, after reaching a surplus in the preceding three years (2001–04); it should maintain the existing band system for the exchange rate, with a +/– 5 per cent band around a neutral real effective exchange rate. However, if the current account deficit persists beyond 3 per cent of GDP, the exchange rate policy should be reviewed (see Reserve Bank of India, 2006).

Of all these preconditions, it was once more recognized that the most important is the need to strengthen the domestic financial system. This and the large public debt remain as two major sources of vulnerabilities in the Indian economy. These vulnerabilities are still perceived as major obstacles to a successful CAL or to a FCAC as intended by the government. Particularly in regard to the financial sector, the committee's view is that the Indian banking system is weak and fragmented, which cannot co-exist with an opened and liberalized system. In addition, a gradual increase in the presence of foreign banks is expected after 2009, thereby contributing to exposing domestic banks to intense competition from large global banks.

In sum, the Tarapore II report has proposed further liberalization steps regarding capital outflows by granting corporates in particular more freedom to invest abroad.[18] However, there are still some concerns related to the liberalization of outflows especially for individuals because of fears of waves of capital flight. Reflecting this, the increase of the limits for individuals' investments abroad has been moderate. For some analysts this however appears to be a move backwards, if one takes the recommendations of Tarapore I as a benchmark. What the Indian resident may be allowed to transfer abroad by 2008/09, that is US$ 100 thousand, was in fact supposed to be reached fully by 1999/2000 and it is about 30 per cent less in real terms than was recommended at that time.[19]

Moving briefly towards the issue of capital account convertibility in India, the Tarapore II report reflects some doubts related to the alleged benefits of CAC, which have been intensively debated among academics. It transpires from the debate that it is still not clear that capital account convertibility results in rapid growth especially in developing countries.

It may well be the case that being on the side of caution brings more benefits than costs. Panagariya and Mukerji (2006) offer some reasons why India should not rush into full convertibility of capital account. First, they argue that persuasive empirical evidence on the benefits resulting from full CAC is lacking. On the fiscal side, despite the high average growth rate during 2003–06, the fiscal deficit will become even higher if the GDP growth rate turns down after 2006–07. Besides, convertibility could hurt export growth by causing appreciation of the exchange rate and by making it more volatile.

For those who are in favour of speeding up the convertibility process, the adoption of CAC will improve the reforms, especially in the financial sector. As a result, corporations and individuals will have full access to the international financial markets, which may bring pressure on the domestic banks to become more competitive. An additional argument is that FCAC could reduce the cost of capital which the economy badly needs to sustain its high growth rates (*The Economist*, 2006).

Another argument in favour of FCAC is that it could help India turn into a major financial centre in Asia, which might be possible due to the country's high skilled labour force as well as its developed ICT industry. However, as observed by Panagariya and Mukerji (2006), a question can be raised: how could India, which has a financial sector heavily dominated by the public sector, be turned into an international financial centre without privatizing what is still a largely public owned system? It seems that the Indian government has no intention of promoting a broad privatization programme for the financial sector; the authorities may encourage the setting up of new private sector banks instead.

The setting up of two Tarapore committees over the years shows that, in India, a consultative process preceding a decision-making process provides in-built mechanisms to ensure prudence; moreover, Tarapore II indicates that prudence will continue to be the case despite government intentions to broaden liberalization. Having said that, Tarapore I and II are reports that endeavour to provide clear guidelines for when and how to liberalize the capital account, but policy makers are not strictly bound by it and therefore may have some flexibility in how to conduct the process.

5.5   Brief comparative analysis

It is interesting to observe the contrasting liberalization experiences between South Africa, on the one hand, and India and Brazil, on the other. While South Africa has prioritized liberalization of financial

Table 5.1 Liberalization of financial outflows by residents: limits/restrictions

	Institutional investors	Corporates	Individuals
Brazil	Investment funds have no limits to invest abroad; end-use restrictions. Pension funds can invest abroad up to 10% of total assets; end-use restrictions.	Until 2005, investment through CC-5 accounts beyond US$ 5 million required previous authorization from the Central Bank. Since then, transfer can be made directly, and restrictions have been removed. Need to specify purpose of transfers.	Until 2005, transfers could be made through CC-5 accounts. Since then, transfers can be made directly, with no limits. Need to specify purpose of transfer.
India	Aggregate limit of US$ 2 billion per annum set by Tarapore I. Recommended by Tarapore II to be increased to US$ 5 billion by 2009–11. This is in practice valid for investment funds, but not pension funds or insurers, which are mainly public-owned.	Restrictive quantitative limits. Tarapore II indicates they will be permitted to invest up to 25% of their net worth in overseas companies having at least 10% shareholding in listed Indian companies and in rated bonds/fixed income securities.	Current limit of US$ 25 thousand per annum to be increased to US$ 50 thousand, US$ 100 thousand and US$ 200 thousand by 2006–07, 2007–09 and 2009–11, as recommended by Tarapore II. Existing permission to invest without limits in overseas

South Africa	Pension funds, insurers and mutual funds permitted to invest abroad subject to the aggregate limit of 15% of total assets (20% for unit trust industry). Limits of up to 5% of total net inflows in the previous year (but removed since 2001, except for unit trusts, which still face a higher limit, of up to 10%).	In 2002, Banks permitted to invest up to US$ 25 million.	N/a	companies listed on a stock exchange, and having a at least 10% shareholding in an Indian company should be banned. Upper limit of R750 thousand, later increased to R2 million; they can also maintain abroad foreign-earned income. Residents permitted to invest in foreign instruments listed on South African exchanges (Bond Exchange South Africa and JSE Securities Exchange South Africa).

outflows by all institutional investors, India and especially Brazil to a greater extent have liberalized outflows by corporations and individuals. As regards financial outflows by institutional investors, Brazil and India have both have maintained some restrictions, including end-use restriction in the case of Brazil. In India, mutual funds face overall upper limits to investing abroad; while institutional investors such as pension funds are public-owned investing mainly in domestic assets and the insurance industry is almost totally public-owned, being subject to reforms involving privatization only very recently.[20]

In Brazil, individuals and corporates were fully liberalized at a time the country was witnessing large capital inflows, and this measure was not reversed during the periods of international financial instability that followed. India started to liberalize first financial outflows by corporations and individuals and investment funds, but this process was set to be gradual and conditioned on meeting clearly established macroeconomic targets. South Africa has prioritized liberalization for institutional investors, apparently in response to strong pressures by such investors. But it has restricted liberalization for corporates and individuals because of fear that a sudden and large outflow could happen due to lack of confidence in the country, which could cause strong exchange rate instability.

As a result of a more cautious approach and as noted earlier, unlike Brazil, India escaped unscathed from the various financial crises of the late 1990s. Although South Africa did not suffer a currency crisis like Brazil, it did witness sharp currency volatility, and its growth performance has been for many years rather poor, in part because of the monetary and fiscal policies pursued in response to the contagion effects the country suffered from the various financial crises since 1994/95.

Nowadays, all three countries are either signalling or effectively undertaking further liberalization steps. Brazil has concretely done so in the recent past, and India is proposing a timetable to further the process. The arguments backing these new liberalization initiatives are varied, and include signalling to external investors that the country is committed to financial liberalization and that it has confidence in its own currency system. Moreover, it is recurrently raised the argument that controls over outflows are largely ineffective and that therefore it is better to create legal mechanisms for something that already occurs in reality. A related argument is that maintaining restrictions on outflows when inflows are largely liberalized in countries with fairly developed financial systems – the cases of Brazil and South Africa – would only make economic agents find alternative ways to send financial resources abroad.

However, the premise that outflows take place anyway regardless of restrictions is, in our view, exaggerated. It is true that some capital is sent abroad through illegal means, and that these may achieve large amounts in periods of heightened uncertainty or in instances where the country face chronic confidence deficit. But the bulk of national domestic financial capital is held by institutional investors and others who do not have the flexibility to send resources abroad, are not prepared to take risks and do not want to face the costs associated with it.

5.6 Conclusions

The experiences with the liberalization of capital outflows show that these have occurred in diverse ways among the three countries under analysis.

Brazil took first the step towards liberalizing the capital outflows in the early 1990s when it granted permission for foreign banks to hold accounts – in the form of sub-accounts within the CC-5 – in the country, through which they could purchase dollars in the floating segment of the foreign exchange market and send these abroad. Still in the first half of the 1990s, the Brazilian government created another outflow channel by permitting the acquisition by domestic investors of Brazil's external debt via the Fiex. This investment channel was opened to corporations, individuals and institutional investors. As we highlighted above, these funds became important instruments through which both individuals and non-financial corporates could diversify their investment portfolios. This however did not occur among pension funds and insurers, which have faced quantitative restrictions to invest abroad.

South Africa was considerably more cautious than Brazil concerning the liberalization of capital outflows. Starting in 1995 when the country fully liberalized the capital account for inflows, it kept strong restrictions for outflows by corporations and individuals, but provided somewhat greater openness for institutional investors.

India has been among the three countries the one that adopted the slowest liberalization process for capital outflows. In the 1990s, the government of India established quantitative limits for outflows by individuals and corporations. At the same time, overall quantitative limits have been imposed on SEBI investors. As regards institutional investors, such as pension funds and insurance corporates, practically no investments abroad took place, as these are controlled by the State. Overall, liberalization in India has been linked to meeting macroeconomic preconditions and to the need of a strengthened financial system; these factors constituted important elements to explain why liberalization has been gradual and, in fact, slower than proposed by the Tarapore Committee. This together with a similarly gradual liberalization for capital inflows, seem to have contributed to the country's reduced external vulnerability.

The Brazilian experience with capital outflows seems to have been the one that went furthest in the past 15 years or so. Of the three experiences, Brazil was the only one that suffered currency crises in the past few years. It seems there is no doubt that rapid and deep liberalization for capital inflows was among the most important factors in explaining the country's external vulnerability which resulted in the 1999 currency crisis and in the large depreciation of the Real in the second semester of 2002. However, the large liberalization of capital outflows by corporations and individuals appears to have contributed to external instability as well, as it permitted such agents to send resources abroad easily and safely, in response to growing uncertainties regarding the government's capacity to defend the exchange rate (in the second half of 1998) and to honour its financial commitments (during 2002).

In South Africa, a currency crisis has only been averted since liberalization in 1995 despite contagion effects due to the adoption of a fully flexible exchange rate regime. However, notwithstanding the fact the country did not suffer a currency crisis in a strict sense, it suffered a great deal of exchange rate volatility caused by the mobility of capital that could flow in and out of the country freely due to total liberalization of capital flows by non-residents.

At present, Brazil, India and South Africa are proposing and/or undertaking further liberalization steps for capital outflows, which at least for Brazil and South Africa, is in practical terms the last area to be fully liberalized. However, the relatively benign international environment these countries are facing at present may come to an end soon and abruptly if adjustments to the current global financial imbalances are not addressed in an organized, co-ordinated fashion. A strong adjustment in the global economy will probably have an immediate effect on the three countries' key macroeconomic variables, but the Indian liberalization process is the only one that provides safeguards in case that happens.

The recent past has shown that India and other countries that have adopted a gradual liberalization approach have escaped full blown crises and that therefore this approach seems more appropriate for countries that have not truly achieved macroeconomic stability in a sustainable manner, have relatively low levels of domestic savings and whose financial system is not sufficiently developed.

But even if these conditions are met in Brazil, India and South Africa in the near future, would full capital account convertibility still be appropriate?

All three countries are regional powers and, in the case of India, a world power-house seems to be emerging. They therefore have at least regional ambitions. South Africa, for example, clearly has the aim of turning itself into an important international financial centre with a dominant role in the African continent for the provision of sophisticated financial services. However, all three countries still face striking levels of poverty, high unemployment rates (especially in South Africa) and highly unequal income distribution (or not so large in India though becoming so rapidly). These shortcomings are partly historical, but partly a by-product of the unbalanced growth these countries are experiencing at present. Their development challenges are therefore huge. Full CAC might possibly bring some benefits, though these are very uncertain. It is more likely, however, that it will just accentuate the existing imbalances and increase the possibility of future financial crises.

Notes

1. See, *inter alia*, Fischer and Reisen (1992); Mathieson & Rojas-Suarez (1993); Eichengreen & Mussa (1998); Rodrik (1998); Radelet & Sachs (1998); Ariyoshi et al. (2000); Griffith-Jones et al. (2003).
2. Chile's unremunerated reserve requirements (URR) is a classical example of the literature on controls to reduce the amount of capital flowing to a country; and Malaysia's capital controls has been widely debated as a mechanism to stem capital outflows in times of crisis – see, for example, Le Fort and Lehmann (2000) and Ariyoshi et al. (2000) on Chile's and Malaysia's experiences respectively.
3. These steps included further opening of the domestic capital markets to foreign portfolio investment (involving both the stock and derivative markets and fixed income) following limited opening in 1987, and permission given to Brazilian companies to issue different types of securities abroad (Prates, 1998).
4. Fiex is the acronym for *Fundos de Investimento no Exterior*, which we translate into English as special investment funds abroad. *Fundos de Divida Externa* can be translated as External Debt Funds.
5. See Carta-Circular No 5, of 27 February 1969.
6. Cartas-Circulares 2.242 of 7 October 1992.
7. Resolution 1.846 of 29 July 1992 and Carta-Circular 2.242/92.
8. Information obtained from interviews with foreign banks in Brazil.

9. See Circular of the Central Bank of Brazil No 2.111 of 22 September 1994 and Circular No 2.714 of 28 August 1996.
10. Interview material.
11. In the case of DRs, see Resolution No. 1.848 of 10 August 1991, later replaced with 1.927 of 18 May 1992. In the case of BDRs, see Resolution No. 2.318 of 25 September 1996.
12. The transfer of blocked funds over 2 million rands for individuals and 4 million rands for families is allowed, provided it pays 10 per cent exit levy. Dividends and interest payments on these funds are freely transferable abroad and travel allowances can be augmented if documented (IMF, 2006b).
13. These inflows have recently been dominated by equity flows and in 2005 included a large foreign direct investment transaction when Barclays Bank acquired one of the four largest South African banks.
14. This point is made by Cooper (1998) in his analysis of capital account convertibility.
15. Of course, the proposed upper limits for FDI abroad were much higher. For FDI in the form of joint venture and/or wholly-owned subsidiaries these were proposed to be raised from US$ 4 million to US$ 50 million per annum. In the 2002/03 budget, this limit was in fact raised again to US$ 100 million.
16. The Twelfth Finance Commission (TFC) recommended that the States should eliminate their revenue deficits by 2008–09 and their fiscal deficits should be reduced to 3 per cent of GDP.
17. For achieving this purpose, the Tarapore Committee II recommended some measures as follows: establishing a single Banking Legislation which, in practice, will abolish separate frameworks for groups of public sector banks; decreasing the minimum share of government/RBI in the capital of public sector banks from 51 per cent to 33 per cent, following the Narasimham Committee on Banking Sector and Reforms (1998). The committee also recommended putting on hold the proposed transfer of ownership of SBI (State Bank of India) from the Reserve Bank of India to government, due to the necessity of strengthening the capital of banks in the context of Basel II and FCAC. Finally it proposed to revisit the issue of investments by foreign banks in Indian banking system. For more details see Report of the Committee on Fuller Capital Account Convertibility, Reserve Bank of India (2006).
18. It can be expected that in a full capital account convertibility environment the existing limits on corporates and individuals' acquisitions of financial assets and other capital assets abroad will be banned. This will probably be positively appraised especially by companies that intend to leverage acquisitions overseas broadening their position in the global market.
19. This point was made by Surjit S. Bhalla, who is a member of the Tarapore Committee. See Bhalla (2006).
20. Interview material.

References

Arida, P. (2003), 'Ainda sobre a Conversibilidade', *Revista de Economia Politica*, 23(3): 135–42.

Ariyoshi, A. et al. (2000), 'Capital Controls: Country Experiences with Their Use and Liberalization', *IMF Occasional Paper* No. 190, May 17.

Banco Central (1993), *O Regime cambial brasileiro. Evolução recente e perspectivas.* Brasília, D.F.: Banco Central do Brasil.

Bhalla, S.S. (2006), 'Dissent Note on the Report on Fuller Capital Account Convertibility', in Reserve Bank of India (2006). 'Report of the Committee on Fuller Capital Account Convertibility', 31 July, http://www.rbi.org.

Carvalho, F.J.C. (2004), 'Controles de Capitais: uma agenda de pesquisa' Série Seminários de Pesquisa, Universidade Federal do Rio de Janeiro, Instituto de Economia, TD no. 001/2004.

Cooper, R. (1998), 'Should Capital-Account Convertibility Be a World Objective?', in Fischer, S. (ed.) *Should the IMF Pursue Capital-Account Convertibility?*, Essays in International Finance, no. 207, May.

The Economist (2006), 'Slowly does it', 9 September, p. 87.

Eichengreen, B. and Mussa, M. (1998), 'Capital account liberalization: Theoretical and empirical aspects', *IMF Occasional Papers*, No. 172, International Monetary Fund.

Fischer, B. and Reisen, H. (1992), 'Towards Capital Account Convertibility', OECD *Development Centre Policy Brief*, no. 4.

Gottschalk, R. (2002), 'Capital Account Liberalization: The International Experience and Lessons for South Africa', report prepared for the South African National Treasury, December.

Griffith-Jones, S., Gottschalk, R. and Cailloux, J. (2003), *International Capital Flows in Calm and Turbulent Times: The Need for New International Architecture*, University of Michigan Press: Ann Arbor.

Hviding, K. (2005), 'Liberalizing Trade and Capital Transactions: An Overview', in Nowak, M. and Ricci, L.A. (eds) *Post-Apartheid South Africa. The First Ten Years After Apartheid*, International Monetary Fund.

IMF (2002), International Financial Statistics, July.

IMF (2005), 'Annual Report on Exchange Arrangements and Exchange Restrictions', IMF, August.

IMF (2006a), 'Article IV Consultation with Brazil', Public Information Notice (PIN) No. 06/69, June 19.

IMF (2006b), 'South Africa: 2006 Article IV Consultation – Staff Report', *Country Report* no. 06/237, September.

IMF (2006c), 'South Africa: Selected Issues', *IMF Country Report* No. 06/328, September.

Indian Investment Centre (1997), 'Recommendations of Tarapore Committee on Capital Account Convertibility', in: Highlights of India's Economic Policies, http://iic.nic.in/vsiic/iic3_j.htm.

Le Fort, G. and Lehmann, S. (2000), 'El Encaje, los Flujos de Capitales y el Gasto: una Evaluacion empirica', *Working Paper of Central Bank of Chile* no. 64, Santiago, February.

Leite, P.G. et al. (2006), 'The Post-Apartheid Evolution of Earnings Inequality in South Africa, 1995–2004', United Nations Development Programme. *Working Paper* no. 32, October 2006.

Mathieson, D. and Rojas-Suarez, L. (1993), 'Liberalization of the Capital Account: Experiences and Issues', *Occasional Paper*, 103, IMF, Washington DC, March.

National Treasury (2001), 'The Role of the National Treasury in the Economy', mimeo, South African National Treasury.

Nowak, M. (2005), 'The First Ten Years After Apartheid: An Overview of the South African Economy', in Nowak, M. and Ricci, L.A. *Post-Apartheid South Africa. The First Ten Years After Apartheid*, International Monetary Fund.

Oreiro, J.L., Paula, L.F. and Silva, G.J. (2004), Por uma moeda parcialmente conversível: uma crítica a Arida e Bacha. *Revista de Economia Política*, 24(2): 223–37.

Paiva, C. (2006), 'External Adjustment and Equilibrium Exchange Rate in Brazil', IMF Working Paper, WP/06/221, October.

Panagariya, A. and Mukerji, P. (2006), 'Don't rush into full convertibility', *Economic Times*, 26 July.

Prates, D.M. (1998), 'Investimentos de Portfolio no Mercado Financeiro Domestico', in: Fundap, *Abertura Externa e Sistema Financeiro*. Relatorio Final, chapter 1, Sao Paulo, May.

Radelet, S. and Sachs, J. (1998), 'The onset of the East Asian crisis', mimeo, Harvard University.

Reserve Bank of India (2000), 'Recommendations of Tarapore Committee on Capital Account Convertibility', http:www.rbi.org.in/index/dl...001&secid=21/0/0&archivemode=0.

Reserve Bank of India (2006), 'Report of the Committee on Fuller Capital Account Convertibility', 31 July, http://www.rbi.org.

Rezende, F. and Tafner, P (eds) (2005), 'Brazil: The State of the Nation', Institute for Applied Economic Research (IPEA) and UNDP, International Poverty Centre.

Rodrik, D. (1998), 'Who Needs Capital-Account Convertibility', in Fischer, S. (ed.) *Should the IMF Pursue Capital-Account Convertibility? Essays in International Finance*, no. 207, May.

Sicsú, J. (2005), 'Um passo liberalizante: comentários sobre as novas normas cambiais'. Texto para Discussão UFRJ, Instituto de Economia, Versão de 11 de março, http://www.ie.ufrj.br/moeda/textos_para_discussao.php.

Van Der Laan, C.R., Cunha, A.M., Lélis, M. and Bichara, J. (2006), 'Los efectos de la globalización financiera en los países en desarrollo: la experiencia de Brasil a partir de los años 90', VIII Reunión de Economía Mundial, Alicante, 20–22 April.

Wesso, G.R. (2001), 'The dynamics of capital flows in South Africa: an empirical investigation', *Quarterly Bulletin*, SA Reserve Bank, June, pp. 59–77.

6
Financial Liberalization in Brazil and Argentina

Fernando J. Cardim de Carvalho

6.1 Introduction

Debating the results of financial liberalization processes in countries like Brazil or Argentina is not an easy task. Except in the improbable world of textbooks, a financial liberalization process rarely comes alone. Practically everywhere, it was implemented as an element of a much wider liberalization strategy that touched a large numbers of sectors of the economy more or less simultaneously. Its effects are hard to isolate from the impacts caused by other liberalization processes or even from the general change in world view that gave it its initial push. In addition, as Stallings and Studart (2006) warn us, the concept usually conflates two different, although to some extent interdependent, processes. On the one hand, a large part of the literature takes it to mean the process of domestic financial liberalization through which the burden of regulation over domestic financial institutions and markets is alleviated. Ceilings on interest rates are eliminated, forced market segmentation is attenuated, strict rules of behaviour for institutions are softened or have their nature transformed, financial supervisors as well as monetary policy makers adopt market-friendly instruments to implement decisions. All these changes are elements of the liberal approach according to which government policy has to act through incentives to desired private action, not through proscription of undesired behaviours.

But a second process usually accompanies domestic liberalization albeit obeying a different logic: external financial liberalization or capital account liberalization. In this case, obstacles to the free circulation of financial flows into and out of the country are totally or partially removed, moving towards what the IMF calls capital account convertibility. Capital and/or exchange controls are dismantled so that private agents can freely decide the currency in which they prefer to hold their assets.

With the exception of Chile, which began liberalizing its economy right after the 1973 military coup, most middle-income countries in Latin America initiated a liberalization process in the aftermath of the debt crisis of the early 1980s. Although external pressures were certainly not the only factors to explain the engagement of these countries in the liberalization processes, one cannot neglect the fact that the IMF played an important role in the protracted process whereby a solution for the debt crisis was worked out and that that institution pushed strongly for capital account liberalization, at least until the Asian crises of the late 1990s. Be that as it may, the choice of the liberalization path has shown itself to be surprisingly durable. Deep crises in the 1990s and the election of left-leaning leaders all over the region have not substantially thwarted these countries from the liberal path nor have they reversed some or most of the major characteristics of the financial regimes created in the liberalization process. The resilience of liberal choices in view of the problems the economies of Argentina and Brazil went through in the 1990s and 2000s is a puzzle that demands careful investigation. We certainly do not aspire to explain this resilience in this chapter but we want to try to speculate about some of its possible causes.

Domestic and external financial liberalization respond to different stimuli and address different difficulties and either one of the two can certainly go a long way without the other. In the cases of Brazil and Argentina, however, as in many others, they developed more or less simultaneously, in part as elements of a long-term stabilization programme, but also because of another common cause: the identification of previous modes of state intervention with the authoritarianism of military regimes that reigned in the region between the 1960s and the 1980s.

Financial liberalization, at its dawn, fed great expectations that these economies would be able to unleash their entrepreneurial energies and reach a sustained high growth path supported by external savings. In this chapter we will try to examine the extent to which these expectations were confirmed or disappointed. To do so, we begin, in the next section, by examining what was expected from financial liberalization, domestic and external. Section 6.3 will summarily describe the main steps in the financial liberalization process undergone by Brazil and Argentina. Section 6.4 supplies statistical information to help evaluate how far financial liberalization was successful in fulfilling the hopes it generated. Section 6.5 concludes the chapter.

6.2 Reasons for financial liberalization

Theoretically, domestic financial liberalization is defended to combat financial repression and the problems it creates. Financial repression manifests itself mostly in the form of negative (or below equilibrium) real interest rates causing households to avoid saving and atrophying financial intermediaries. Societies where financial repression prevails, therefore, should exhibit low savings, low financial intermediation, with undeveloped banking systems and shallow, if any, capital markets.[1] Liberalization means first and foremost to liberalize interest rate formation. As a result, in the aftermath of liberalization interest rates should increase. However, this should not penalize investments. Under financial repression, investments would be stimulated by low interest rates but could not materialize because there would be insufficient finance to support them. In fact, some of these desired investments would represent potential overinvestment, since they would only be justified by interest rates that were unsustainably low. When these rates increase, after liberalization, some of the investment plans will be sacrificed, but these are the investments that should be cut anyway. In contrast, those investments that *should* be realized, because their rate of return would equal the rate of discount of future consumption with respect to present consumption, would find the necessary saving available in the financial system.

Therefore, one should find that ending *domestic* financial repression would increase savings *and* investment, and at the same time it would also improve the efficiency of the financial system, with more diversification and financial deepening.[2] Welfare should increase, even if the economy as a whole did not grow, because a better, more diversified financial system would allocate resources more efficiently between present and future consumption. Of course, one should expect that higher investments would bring about higher income growth rates.

External financial liberalization should also stimulate financial diversification and deepening. Its impact on interest rates, however, should be the opposite of domestic liberalization, at least in developing countries. While domestic liberalization would increase domestic interest rates, external liberalization should reduce them. *Ceteris paribus*, dismantling the obstacles to the free circulation of financial flows would allow capital to flow from countries where it is abundant (and therefore earns a low rate of return) to those where it is scarce (and therefore enjoys higher rates of return).[3] The increasing supply of financial capital in developing countries should thus reduce domestic interest rates, by reducing local scarcity of capital. If liberalization of capital flows is accompanied by liberalization of entry of foreign financial institutions, it is also expected that banks and other intermediaries from developed countries would upgrade the operation of local financial markets in developing countries. Foreign banks are supposed to bring to developing countries better technologies, better operational practices and better risk analysis systems. In addition, it was usually said that a large presence of foreign banks in a developing country would reduce its vulnerability to financial distress because the local subsidiaries could always appeal to the deep pockets of their headquarters.[4]

In sum, the standard arguments in favour of full, domestic and external, liberalization included greater efficiency of the financial system, with greater financial deepening and diversification, stronger inducements to save and, thus, to finance investments, greater supply of capital and less external vulnerability. A welcome by-product of financial liberalization was supposed to be the imposition of tougher market discipline on governments that are always assumed to be short-sighted and willing to sacrifice long-term permanent gains to short-term temporary benefits. Governments and democratic methods are always suspicious in the eyes of orthodox economic theory. When one is dealing with developing countries, the situation is automatically assumed to be worse, so tougher market discipline would represent a greater gain for developing than for developed countries. Therefore, the enthusiasts of financial liberalization would not lament the loss of government autonomy that would result from the process: quite the opposite.

This kind of reasoning helped to anchor the financial liberalization process in the attempts to eliminate the high inflation regimes that lasted more than 20 years in Brazil and Argentina. For those who believed that inflation resulted from continuing irresponsible and short-sighted policy making, financial markets discipline would help to control governments once the pace of price increase was broken. In fact, the assumption that governments are inherently inflationary helped to influence the sentiment of the population in favour of liberalization.

There were additional reasons for Brazilians and Argentineans to expect a positive role for financial liberalization. In the mid-1980s when liberalization was initiated both countries had for some time already been going through a period of stagnation and high inflation attributed by liberal critics to the state-intensive import substitution process developed in the postwar period. Policymaking was characterized as chaotic, incompetent and corrupt. Governments were not just unable to control the main scourge of these societies, high and accelerating inflation, their decisions were also seen as actually *causing* crises, culminating with the bankruptcy of the two countries in the early 1980s.

Finally, another association was made in the period that was to work as a powerful lever in favour of liberalization. In the minds of a large fraction of the population, state interventionism came to be associated with military authoritarianism. It was a great victory for liberal ideologues that the defeat of the military regimes in the region and the restoration of political democracy came also to be identified with economic liberalization.

In sum, the shift toward liberalization was motivated at the very least as much by high expectations as to the ability of private agents to respond to the challenges placed by a freer market economy as it was by the disillusionment with the performance of government. This disillusionment was a particularly strong element in persuading the population to accept a large privatization initiative in the 1990s. State-owned companies were seen as dominated by special interests, squandering public resources to the benefit of a few *crony* capitalists and other minor and less than legitimate interests.[5] It helped liberal critics that many of these companies were effectively unable to offer the expected services, as was the case most visibly with the telecommunications companies in Brazil.[6] Even though not all state firms were in the same situation, the state control of firms had few defenders in the 1990s, let alone the nationalization of new ones.

6.3   The process of financial liberalization

Financial liberalization proceeded along parallel lines in Brazil and Argentina. Argentina, however, led the process in time and rooted it more deeply in the institutional structure of its economy than Brazil.

6.3.1   Argentina

The landmark of financial liberalization in Argentina was the Financial Entities Law of 1977 (Studart and Hermann, n.d.). This piece of legislation allowed the formation of universal banks, stimulating the formation of financial conglomerates. At the same time, the authorities gave incentives to increase the degree of concentration in the industry. It was expected that taking advantage of scale and scope economies would lead financial institutions to operate more efficiently, reducing the cost of capital to borrowers.

Argentina had embarked earlier in a process of external financial opening, conducted by Finance Minister Martinez de Oz during the military regime. Both liberalization processes were interwoven through the passing of legislation allowing domestic banks to seek resources with foreign investors. Accordingly, a second step in the process was the authorization, given in December 1978, for Argentinean banks to accept deposits by non-residents denominated in foreign currencies, as long as these resources remained in the country for at least one year. This latter requirement was gradually abandoned though, until it disappeared in 1979.

As is well known, this experiment with liberalization, and particularly with external financial liberalization ended in a large wave of capital flight and a huge crisis at the beginning of the 1980s. To this day the name of Martinez de Oz is associated in Argentina with the idea of irresponsible, possibly corrupt, policies of financial opening, capital flight and balance of payments crises. *Martinazo* became the Argentinean word for a balance of payments crisis induced by wrong-headed liberalization policies.

President Carlos Menem launched a new liberal offensive, after political democracy was restored, beginning in the late 1980s. Domestic and external liberalization were now elements of an explicit strategy to fight inflation which, after two hyperinflationary episodes, had become then by far the foremost economic problem for Argentinean society. Studart and Hermann (n.d.) listed the main initiatives in this offensive:

- In August 1989, an Economic Emergency Law was passed according to which foreign direct investment would enjoy the same legal status recognized to domestic investment.
- Also in August 1989, a State Reform Law determined ways and rules for the privatization of public companies, including national and provincial banks, and conceding stimuli for the participation of foreign investors in the process.
- In July 1989, and again in March 1991, the Central Bank defined norms regulating deposit-taking and loan-making activities in US dollars by Argentinean banks.
- In December 1989, and again in April 1991, the Central Bank issued instructions liberalizing exchange market operations.
- In November 1991, the Deregulating Securities Markets Decree eliminated taxes and other restrictions on securities transactions.
- In September 1992, a new statute was adopted by the Central Bank, giving it independence and practically eliminating its role as lender of last resort.
- In 1994, decree 146 extended national treatment to foreign financial institutions.

Most of these measures, plus the permission for foreign financial institutions to freely enter the domestic market, were taken under the umbrella of the Cavallo stabilization plan, that created a quasi-currency board[7] and reduced inflation drastically in a short period of time. In fact, both sets of measures, the monetary reform and the domestic and external financial liberalization were largely seen as elements of the same strategy.

The tequila crisis of 1995 led to some new initiatives directed at increasing the resilience of the financial system in the absence of lender of last resort facilities. A facility to fund recapitalization of problem banks or to finance the purchase of problem banks by healthy ones was created in March 1995. In May, a Deposit Guarantee Fund, funded by banks themselves, was constituted, and the main clauses of the 1988 Basle Accord and its 1996 amendment were adopted. In addition, the Argentinean government negotiated with international banks the pre-establishment of credit lines in foreign currency to be used in emergency situations to allow the central bank to act as a lender of last resort without violating the currency board rules.

It is worth noting that, besides financial liberalization, the Argentinean government implemented a far-reaching privatization programme, selling practically everything, from the Post Office to the national airline, from banks to electric power generators. The liberal programme was sustained until the 2001 crisis.

6.3.2 Brazil

Financial liberalization in Brazil basically began with a banking reform in 1988. The reform itself represented little more than giving the government's blessing to changes that had been going on in the banking sector for quite a while. Officially, the financial sector was organized in 1988 as it was structured by the 1964 and 1965 reforms. Law segmented financial markets and financial institutions were constrained to operate only in a given segment or a small set of segments. The financial reform act of 1965 was largely inspired by the Glass/Steagal Act, which imposed segmentation and functional specialization in the United States. In the Brazilian case, however, many loopholes in the financial laws ended up allowing financial institutions to conglomerate and form universal banks all but in name. The 1988 reform just recognized this reality, allowing financial institutions to diversify and to organize themselves as universal banks (locally called *multiple banks*). The reforms also freed most interest rates and rationalized the monetary system by breaking the connections between Banco do Brasil (a federally-owned commercial bank) and the Central Bank that in practice allowed the former to literally create money.

In that time, under the first civilian administration after 21 years of military dictatorship, the notion of privatization was being tentatively advanced in the political arena. As it was (and still is) typical of Brazil, no ideological arguments were proposed to defend it. In fact, privatization was being proposed for pragmatic reasons: under high inflation, real government tax revenues were being eaten by the rapid rise in prices. The federal government was on the verge of bankruptcy and was thus unable to make the necessary investments in the sectors it controlled, such as telecommunications, railways, power generation, and so on. Privatization was not proposed because of an alleged superior entrepreneurial ability of private investors but because it would allow those sectors to survive the bankruptcy of the state.

The overall picture was also important in understanding the impact of financial liberalization. Inflation in Brazil had not destroyed the domestic financial system, quite the contrary. However, since the mid-1980s, domestic financial institutions (banks being by far the most important type of institution) were mostly dedicated to treasury operations with public debt. At the same time, banks' customers demanded more and more agile payments systems to deal with accelerating inflation. Domestic banks, private and public, were able to respond to these demands, developing very advanced payments systems technologies.

The permission to organize as universal banks allowed former commercial banks to develop their securities trading activities. Non-bank financial institutions, on the other hand, transformed themselves into universal banks in order to receive demand deposits to be able to participate in the public securities primary markets as well as to have access to liquidity finance in the interbank market and from the central bank. In other words, in a situation where dealing with public securities was practically the only business that was safe and profitable, universal banks were created not exactly to allow diversification of existing institutions into new lines of business. What the reform did was to increase the number of potential participants in the market for public debt. This was not an accident, since guaranteeing the existence of a permanent market for public securities was a major goal of the authorities running a government starved of tax revenues.

The point just made is, in fact, more general. It is an important feature of Brazilian political culture that few decisions are ever made because of ideological reasons. Even major choices, such as those pertaining to the role of the state in the economy, can be better understood as expedients to solve short, or medium, term problems than as the result of a firm commitment to a strategic view. A telling example of the validity of this proposition relates to the opening of the Brazilian domestic banking market to foreign banks.[8]

In 1995, in the aftermath of the *Real* Stabilization Plan,[9] the Brazilian banking sector was subjected to strong pressures. Banks were adapted to the high inflation regime and to giving priority to treasury operations. As a result, all the leading banks had a large network of branches spread throughout the country in order to capture as many deposits as possible in order to finance the purchase of public securities and receive the large remuneration offered by these assets. 'Inflation revenues' generated by the payment of generous overnight interest rates on banks' securities portfolios represented more than 40 per cent of banks' revenues before the Real Plan. After stabilization, with the pace of price increases falling dramatically, banks expected that the buyers' market for public securities would quickly disappear. They had to shift their strategic focus to supplying credit to the private sector to remain profitable. However, without many skills in this area and under the high interest rates that were maintained as part of the effort to control inflation, many banks quickly ran into problems in 1995. After two among the ten largest private banks had to be put under intervention, with a third under serious threat, the risk of a large-scale banking crisis was real. The monetary authorities decided then to create a programme to finance, under very generous terms, the absorption of problem banks by healthy ones, known by the acronym PROER. It was also decided to stimulate mergers and acquisitions to strengthen the remaining banks.

It was in this general picture that the decision was made to allow new foreign banks to enter the domestic market. This decision was taken to avoid having the largest domestic banks taking over the weak ones and increasing the already significant degree of concentration to unacceptable levels. The domestic market, however, was never really opened, though. Foreign banks had to obtain specific authorizations from the authorities and these authorizations were only conceded while there was the need to guarantee the stability of the banking system. From 1997 on, when the distress had already dissipated, no new authorizations were issued.

This episode dramatically illustrates the difference in approaches to financial liberalization that characterized the Argentinean and the Brazilian cases. Argentina made a bet on liberalization to overcome the persistent difficulties that prevented the country to control inflation and recover its ability to grow. Liberalizing reforms were deep and wide. Brazil never committed to liberalization to the same extent. Most of the reforms, including privatization and financial liberalization, were implemented because (and to the extent that) they could solve some problem at some point in time. Once the problem was solved, the programmes were interrupted. A telling example relates to the financial sector itself. Privatization of public banks owned by state governments was strongly stimulated because such banks created difficulties for the federal government. They lent money to governments, and when these loans didn't perform, the central bank had to extend credit lines to the banks to avoid distressing the banking market. Thus, state banks prevented both fiscal and monetary policies from being effectively run by the federal government. For this reason, almost all banks owned by the states were privatized. However, no federal bank was privatized or was even considered for privatization. Not even President Cardoso's conservative administrations went that far.[10]

A significant exception to the proposed rule about the unimportance of ideology in Brazilian policy-making, however, relates to external financial liberalization. Until the 1970s, Brazil maintained extensive capital controls, over both in and outflows. Controls over capital inflows were imposed on an on-and-off basis, whenever excess liquidity prevailed in international financial markets. Controls on outflows by residents were permanent. In 1996, they were weakened by an arguably illegal initiative of the Central Bank.[11] Since then controls on outflows have been continuously weakened being nowadays practically ineffective.[12]

Dismantling capital controls did not respond to any particular emergency demand but it obviously agreed with very definite interests of financial investors, a social group that was strengthened in the 1990s and 2000s by the policies of Presidents Cardoso and Lula. The process of capital account liberalization in fact is still moving forward under specific pressures of investors, exporters, banks, and so on.

Many institutional reforms were introduced in the 1990s and 2000s to stimulate growth and diversification in the financial sector. In particular, initiatives to support growth of capital markets abounded although their efficacy was always very low because of the negative impact of the high interest rates paid by the federal government on its debt. A new electronic payment system among banks was introduced to improve systemic safety. Specific legal provisions stimulated securitization processes. The 1988 Basle agreement was introduced in the country in 1994, and there is already a chronogram to introduce Basle II until 2011. An active process of reform has been unfolding but it is not clear if it should be construed as financial liberalization as such. Of course, they are market friendly reforms but it is unclear the extent to which they really alter the balance between state activities and private activities as conceived by liberalization proponents.

6.3.3 The present state of financial liberalization

Around the turn of the millennium, Brazil and Argentina parted ways. Argentina, which had committed herself to a radical process of liberalization, suffered a catastrophic crisis at the end of 2001. The crisis led to a steep fall in GDP and to deep political instability. A measure of control was recovered with the implementation of exceptional policy measures, such as the 'corralito', which interrupted a bank run by forcing banks to stay closed or to make only low value operations. The imposition of controls on bank activities served also as capital controls, since the public could not access their cash balances to move resources away from Argentina. Most importantly, the Argentinean government decided to default on its debt and opened a process of renegotiation of its terms.

By 2003 the Argentinean economy began a process of recovery which turned into a growth process that has been proceeding at 'Chinese' rates. Some of the liberalizing reforms of the 1990s have been rolled back. Presently, controls on capital inflows are in force and the authorities monitor capital outflows.[13] As a consequence of the restructuring of public debt, the Central Bank has been able to maintain low interest rates. At the same time, the currency board of the 1990s was replaced by a dirty floating exchange rates regime through which exchange rate overvaluation has been successfully prevented. As a result, Argentina is experiencing its fourth year of intense growth, with consumption, investment and exports growing at high rates.[14]

Brazil, on the other hand, was spared a crisis of Argentinean magnitude but this does not mean that liberalization has been costless. The exchange regime was changed in 1999 to a floating exchange rate regime, with eventual interventions by the Central Bank. The permanence of the public debt overhang contributes to keeping interest rates too high to allow private investments to grow. At the same time, servicing public debt strangles the ability of the government to invest. With low levels of private and public investment, growth rates have been among the lowest among emerging economies.

The World Bank calculates a financial liberalization index that tries to capture the direction and intensity of liberalization processes among member countries. The index is broken down into three components: domestic financial liberalization, capital account liberalization and stock market liberalization. Figures 6.1 and 6.2 show the evolution of these indices for Argentina and Brazil, respectively, since 1990. The values of the index range from 1 to 3 (3 meaning complete liberalization). One can see from Figure 6.1 that Argentina, after experimenting with a radical liberalization process, retracted to a more controlled environment with the crisis of the early 2000s. Brazil, on the other hand, moved more slowly toward liberalization, reaching the highest possible value by the end of the period.

The series was interrupted in 2002, so we cannot follow the indices after that year. It is at the very least intriguing, in any case, that growth has accelerated in Argentina after she significantly moved away from full liberalization (at least as measured by the World Bank), while Brazil has been unable to grow more rapidly while fully liberalizing its financial system.

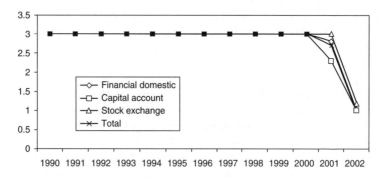

Figure 6.1   Financial liberalization index – Argentina

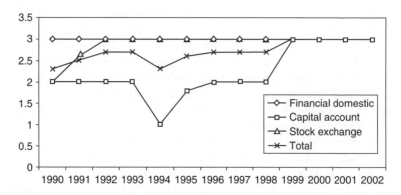

Figure 6.2   Financial liberalization index – Brazil

6.4 An evaluation

As was pointed out in the introduction, it is extremely difficult to make a precise evaluation of the results of the financial liberalization process because, in the case of both Argentina and Brazil, it was enmeshed in at least two larger movements: the overall process of economic liberalization inspired by a rejection of the activist state of the past; and the fight for price stabilization. Many steps on the way to liberalization were actually taken because of these other concerns. But, in the same sense, liberalization processes may have been cut short because of concerns with other sectors of the economy or because liberalization, at least in the Brazilian case, was rarely a goal in itself but an instrument to reach something else.

If we take the two most important macroeconomic variables, output and prices, the results of the liberalization process are certainly ambiguous. The fight against inflation was extremely successful in both countries (see Table 6.1). Not only the process of ever-accelerating inflation was broken but, in fact, price stability has been very resilient, resisting important pressures, particularly supply shocks. The price stabilization process was so successful that we cannot in the same figure draw the trajectory of prices or of rates of growth of prices before and after the 1991 stabilization plan in Argentina and the 1994 plan in Brazil.

The output criterion, on the other hand, has been more than just disappointing. Economic growth in Brazil has been less than mediocre even if we only consider the post debt-crisis years, after the late 1980s. In particular, if we contrast the liberal years since the 1990s with the

Table 6.1 Inflation rates in Argentina and Brazil
Annual rates of change in consumer prices (%)

Year	Argentina	Brazil
1995	1.6	22.4
1996	0.1	9.6
1997	0.3	5.2
1998	0.7	1.7
1999	−1.8	8.9
2000	−0.7	6
2001	−1.5	7.7
2002	41	12.5
2003	3.7	9.3

Source: CEPAL data base.

preceding period, as shown in Figure 6.3, the poverty of the liberal alternative is even more visible. Argentina, on the other hand, has followed
a path that was even more volatile. Figure 6.4 shows, however, that the
liberal 1990s were also disappointing. Price stabilization in 1991 apparently gave a strong push forward to the Argentinean economy, but this
push was strongly helped by the overvaluation of the Brazilian currency
and did not survive the devaluation of the Brazilian real in 1999. It was
only after the 2001 crisis, when many of the liberal reforms were rolled
back that Argentina reached very high rates of growth.

Of course, we cannot attribute either the success in the fight against
inflation or the failure to revive growth to financial liberalization alone.
Monetary policies, exchange rate regimes, and fiscal policies adopted
under duress (first with the debt crisis of the early 1980s and the tutorship
of the IMF in the years that followed, later under the crises of the 1990s)

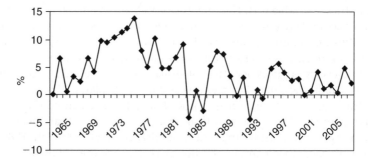

Figure 6.3   Growth rate of per capita GDP – Brazil

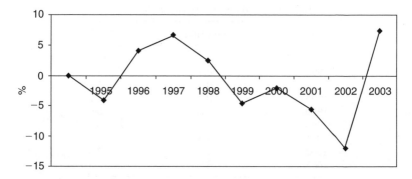

Figure 6.4   Growth rate of per capita GDP – Argentina

certainly contributed decisively for both positive and negative results. Trade opening was also a decisive element to keep prices down but also to push towards deindustrialization in both countries. But financial liberalization, particularly in relation to the capital account of the balance of payments, was a central element of the price stabilization strategy of the 1990s at the price of intensifying output volatility in the period. On the other hand, the hopes that financial liberalization would stimulate investment and growth were widely dashed. Investment as a fraction of GDP remained low during all the relevant period in both countries, as is shown in Table 6.2.

Foreign savings, defined as the current account deficit in the balance of payments did grow in both countries in the 1990s (see Table 6.3). Far from having the positive effect on growth expected by the conventional theory, though, the capital inflows necessary to cover current account deficits led to an accumulation of foreign debt that was a strong factor in the exchange crises suffered by both countries by the end of the decade.

Proponents of financial liberalization also expected an increase in the supply of credit to the private sector and an increase in financial deepening. The supply of credit did grow in the period, although it started from very low levels (see Table 6.4). As a result, after more than a decade of price stabilization, financial deepening indicators in both countries still exhibit below-average numbers (Figure 6.5).

One should also point out that financial liberalization, domestic and external, did not reduce the vulnerability to bank crises. In particular, the expected effect of an increasing participation of foreign banks in domestic markets, that is, that international banks would support their

Table 6.2 Investment/GDP ratio

Year	Argentina	Brazil
1995	18.5	22.3
1996	19.6	20.9
1997	20.9	21.5
1998	21	21.1
1999	17.9	20.2
2000	17.5	21.5
2001	15.6	21.2
2002	10.8	19.8
2003	14.2	20.1

Source: CEPAL database.

Table 6.3 Foreign savings and gross foreign debt
As shares of GDP (%)

Year	Argentina		Brazil	
	Foreign saving	Foreign debt	Foreign saving	Foreign debt
1995	2	38.2	2.8	23.5
1996	2.5	40.6	3.1	24.1
1997	4.2	42.7	4.1	25.8
1998	4.9	47.5	4.3	32
1999	4.2	51.2	4.7	45
2000	3.2	51.5	4.2	39.2
2001	1.7	52.2	4.5	44.5
2002	−8.7	131.5	1.1	49.4
2003	−5.7	112.2	−0.8	47.8

Source: CEPAL data base.

Table 6.4 Credit supply in Argentina and Brazil
Total credit supply directed to the private sector

Year	Argentina*	Brazil**
1990	10.753	4.493
1991	22.770	25.737
1992	35.005	431.107
1993	43.244	13.570
1994	52.029	179.705
1995	51.505	226.475
1996	54.939	236.488
1997	64.234	266.642
1998	72.206	311.725
1999	70.578	331.922
2000	67.910	381.941
2001	56.006	410.676

Notes: *Millions of Pesos; **Millions of Reals.
Source: IMF, International Financial Statistics, May 1997, December 2002.

local subsidiaries in moment of crises, was grossly falsified by the Argentinean crisis of 2001. Brazil does not confirm the conventional thesis but neither can it be cited to disprove it since entry of foreign banks was kept under strict control.

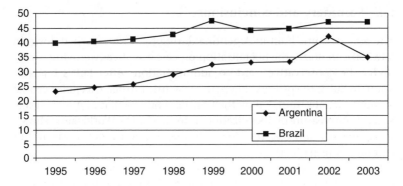

Figure 6.5 Total credit supply/GDP ratio

Finally, one has to examine the impact of financial liberalization on the operation of domestic financial systems. Again, we have to keep in mind that the financial liberalization process did not happen in a vacuum. The effect on interest rates, for instance, cannot be examined without explicitly taking into consideration that liberalization took place during the implementation of stabilization plans. This adds two complications to an already complex picture. First, it is extremely difficult to compare interest rates, and especially real interest rates, before and after liberalization given the difficulty of comparing interest rates before and after price stabilization. Second, high interest rates were instrumental in pushing inflation down after the adoption of price stabilization plans in 1991 in Argentina and 1994 in Brazil.

If one turns to operational efficiency, the data are still ambiguous. The presence of foreign banks in domestic markets should exert pressures to make domestic banks more efficient and more focused on supplying credit to the private sector. The Brazilian experience amply falsified these expectations.[15] Foreign banks were not instrumental in changing the mode of operation of domestic banks in Brazil. In fact, the opposite happened. Foreign banks do not seem to exhibit any particular advantage or any different behaviour from that exhibited by local banks. There are some important differences in behaviour between private (domestic and foreign) and public banks, but not between domestic and foreign institutions.

One can always argue, correctly, that these processes take longer than we are allowing for. Be that as it may, there is still no evidence that, at least in the Brazilian case, any change of substance will come out of the entry of foreign banks in local markets.

6.5   Summary and conclusions

The policy regime built in Argentina during the 1990s crashed down in late 2001. In Brazil, the liberalization process was already moving slowly under the conservative Cardoso administration. After Lula's inauguration, in 2003, the process slowed down a little further, except for capital account liberalization, led by the Central Bank. Be that as it may, if one accepts the measure of liberalization proposed by the World Bank, shown in Figures 6.1 and 6.2, the financial liberalization process was all but complete already in 1999.

Financial liberalization was promoted in Argentina and Brazil as part of an overall attempt to reduce the role of the state in the economy, which was in itself an element of the attempt to reduce the perceived influence of the state on the lives of people. The activist state was successfully associated with liberal circles close to the military state that eliminated political as well as economic liberties. Authoritarianism, corruption and incompetence became widely accepted characteristics of the activist state, so that economic liberalization came to be seen as a necessary parallel to political liberalization, that is, as equally needed to build democratic ways of decision-making.

The ideological view of the state as an obstacle to freedom took deeper roots in Argentina than in Brazil.[16] Accordingly, liberalization processes in general, and financial liberalization in particular, were taken much further in Argentina than in Brazil. The expectations surrounding financial liberalization, however, were similar in the two countries. One expected more efficient financial systems, more savings, more investment and more growth, all of it with price stability. Price stabilization was indeed achieved and it has so far proven more durable than even the more optimistic analysts would have expected when the stabilization plans were adopted in the two countries. The expectations related to investment and growth, however, have been largely disappointed.

It may not be possible to measure the actual impact of financial liberalization per se on the efficiency and growth capabilities of both economies. It may very well be the case that financial liberalization did contribute positively to growth but that these effects were counterbalanced by the negative influences of contractionary monetary and fiscal policies, overvalued exchange rates, political instability and so forth. The available data so far, however, does not warrant such optimism. Financial repression is long gone, although some remnants remain in the form of, for instance, required destinations of a fraction of the credit supply still practised in Brazil. Capital markets grew and diversified but private investors still display a strong resistance to invest in anything other than short-term public securities. Year after year growth has been disappointing, even though it is always possible to find ad hoc explanations for each failure episode. Argentina is growing strongly, but the country has reneged on many of its liberal reforms.

Currently, there is no significant constituency fighting for a reinstatement of controls over domestic financial systems (although an important debate remains about whether capital controls should be recreated or not). But there is an important school of opinion that suggests that activist states and liberalized financial systems can co-exist if only adequate ways to decide and implement policies can be found. This may very well be wishful thinking. But the failure of Brazil in reviving growth and the recent success of Argentina in recovering from its deep 2001 crisis suggest that this may be the best bet.

Notes

1. A classical, if not original, reference to financial repression is given by Fry (1988). A presentation and critique of the concept is also given in Studart (1995), chapter 2.
2. Without financial repression, savings would grow and financial institutions would compete to capture them, by offering new instruments to fit the diversity of profiles among savers.
3. For a discussion and critique of the expected advantages of external financial liberalization, see Carvalho and Sicsú (2004).
4. 'A banking system with an internationally diversified asset base is less likely to be destabilized by adverse domestic conditions and in turn to worsen them into crises. Domestic branches of foreign banks effectively possess their own private lender of last resort in the form of the foreign head office, and the latter has potential access to last-resort lending by the central bank of the country in which the home office resides, typically one of the mature markets.' (IMF, 1998, p. 76). Most of these expectations were actually falsified both by the Argentinean and the Brazilian experience. On Argentina, cf. Vanoli (2007). On Brazil, see Carvalho (2000) and (2002).
5. In Brazil state companies were usually called 'jobs cloth-hangers', meaning that politicians used them to give favours to their constituents.
6. Home telephones were such rare commodities that taxpayers were supposed to declare in their income tax returns whether they had one, informing their market values. Private firms worked as telephone exchanges where telephone lines could be bought and sold at 'free' market prices. In fact, buying a phone line was a normal 'investment' opportunity considered by private investors.
7. See O'Connel (2005).
8. The following paragraphs are based on Carvalho (1998).

9. *Real* is the name of the new currency created with the launching of the plan.
10. It is interesting to note that in the 2006 presidential campaign neither the incumbent President Lula, nor his main opponent from former president Cardoso's party, PSDB, proposed further privatizations. The latter, in fact, stated emphatically that he would not privatize anything, making a point of appearing in public with badges of Banco do Brazil, the oil company, Petrobrás, and the National Savings Bank (Caixa Econômica Federal) stuck to his shirt.
11. A paper by two former directors of the Brazilian Central Bank practically admits this much. See Franco and Pinho Neto (2004).
12. For an exhaustive list of measures of liberalization, see Sicsu (2006).
13. I thank Diego Bastourre and Roberto Frenkel for directing me to the Comunicado 48633, dated 10 October, 2006, issued by the Central Bank of the Argentine Republic, listing the present regulations in force in the exchange market.
14. Argentina has already moved from a cyclical recovery stage to a growth phase. In the first quarter of 2006, GDP reached a level 9.2% higher than the pre-crisis peak reached in the second quarter of 1998. See graph 1 in CEP (2006). For an examination of the policies that led to Argentina's recovery and rapid growth, see Frenkel and Rapetti (2007).
15. See Carvalho (2002).
16. Which may not be an accident given the fact that military regimes in post-1966 Argentina were much more bloody than those in post-1964 Brazil.

References

Carvalho, F. (1998), 'The Real Stabilization Plan and the Banking Sector in Brazil', *Banca Nazionale del Lavoro Quarterly Review*, 51 (206), September.

Carvalho, F. (2000), 'New competitive strategies of foreign banks in large emerging economies: the case of Brazil', *Banca Nazionale del Lavoro Quarterly Review*, 53 (213), June.

Carvalho, F. (2002), 'The recent expansion of foreign banks in Brazil: first results', *Latin American Business Review*, 3 (4).

Carvalho, F. and Sicsu, J. (2004), 'Controversias recentes sobre controles de capitais', *Brazilian Journal of Political Economy*, 24 (2), April/June.

CEP (Centro de Estudios para la Producción, Ministério de Economia y Producción, Argentina)(2006), *Sintesis de la Economia Real*, n. 52, Buenos Aires, July.

Franco, G. and Pinho Neto, D. (2004), 'A desregulamentação da conta de capitais: limitações macroeconômicas e regulatorias', manuscript, www.econ.puc-rio.br/gfranco/BMF_desregulamentação_cambial.htm.

Frenkel, R. and Rapetti, M. (2007), 'Argentina's monetary and exchange rate policies after the convertibility regime collapse', PERI/CEPR working paper.

Fry, M. (1988), *Money, Interest, and Banking in Economic Development*, Baltimore: Johns Hopkins University Press.

International Monetary Fund (1998), *International Capital Markets*, Washington: IMF.

O'Connel, A. (2005), 'The recent crisis – and recovery – of the Argentine economy: some elements and background', in G. Epstein (ed), *Financialization and the World Economy*, Cheltenham: Edward Elgar.

Sicsu, J. (2006), 'A liberalização financeira brasileira no periodo 1988/2002', in J. Sicsu and F. Ferrari Filho (eds), *Cambio e Controles de Capitais*, Rio de Janeiro: Campus/Elsevier.

Stallings, B. and Studart, R. (2006), *Finance for Development. Latin America in Comparative Perspective*, Washington: Brookings Institutions.

Studart, R. (1995), *Investment Finance in Economic Development*, London: Routledge.

Studart, R. and Hermann, J. (n.d.), *Sistemas Financeiros Argentino e Brasileiro*, manuscript.

Vanoli, A. (2007), 'Basel II: systemic consequences – a study of its implementation in the Argentinean financial system', manuscript.

7
Capital Controls and Economic Development in China

Hansjörg Herr

7.1 Introduction

The People's Republic of China is one of most successful developing countries in recent decades.[1] However, it is not a showcase for policies recommended by mainstream neoclassical thinking and international institutions, especially the International Monetary Fund (IMF). China did not follow the policies of the so-called Washington Consensus.[2] Showcases for such policies, from Argentina to Mongolia, did not perform very well. Often China is considered as a very special case not transferable to other countries. This is not true; other developing countries can learn from China.

In the second section economic development since the start of reforms in China is sketched. The third section gives an overview of capital flow regulations in China. It follows with an empirical analyses of capital flows in section four and a discussion of the high Chinese official reserves in section five. Section six evaluates the Chinese development. The last section raises the question what other countries can learn from China.

7.2 Chinese economic transition

Since economic reforms were introduced in 1978, China has experienced over 25 years rapid GDP growth of around 9 per cent per year. Growth in the 1980s was high and slowed down a bit at the end of the decade. Then it increased again until it was slightly reduced after the Asian crisis in 1997. In 2002 a new strong growth wave began (see Table 7.1). Taking one US dollar a day as a measure, China is the country with the biggest absolute reduction in poverty. This shows that China has not only been able to bring about overall economic prosperity, but has also reduced

142

Table 7.1 Basic macroeconomic data for China 1990–2005

	Annual real GDP growth*	GDP* per capita growth	Gross capital formation in % of GDP	Final consumption expenditure in % of GDP	Exports of goods and services in % of GDP	Inflation rate (CPI)*	Overall budget balance in % of GDP	Current account balance in % of GDP
1990	3.8	2.3	34.7	62.1	17.5	3.1	n.a	3.1
1991	9.2	7.7	34.8	61.9	19.4	3.4	n.a	3.3
1992	14.3	12.8	36.2	62.3	19.5	6.4	n.a	1.3
1993	13.5	12.2	43.3	58.2	17.1	14.7	n.a	-2.0
1994	12.8	11.3	41.2	56.9	25.3	24.1	n.a	1.4
1995	10.5	9.3	40.8	56.9	23.9	17.1	n.a	0.2
1996	9.6	8.5	39.6	58.3	21.0	8.3	n.a	0.9
1997	8.8	7.7	38.2	57.0	23.1	2.8	-1.9	3.8
1998	7.8	6.8	37.7	57.7	21.9	-0.8	-3.0	3.3
1999	7.1	6.1	37.7	59.9	22.3	-1.4	-4.0	1.6
2000	8.0	7.2	36.3	60.1	28.9	0.4	-3.6	1.9
2001	7.5	6.7	38.5	59.1	25.5	0.7	-3.1	1.5
2002	8.3	7.6	40.4	56.6	28.9	-0.8	-3.3	2.8
2003	9.3	8.6	44.4	53.1	34.3	1.2	-2.8	3.2
2004	9.5	8.8	44.9	n.a	40.2	3.9	-1.7	4.2
2005	8.5	8.0	n.a	n.a	n.a	3.0	n.a	4.1

Note: * GDP in constant local currency or constant USD; change to previous year.
Source: World Bank, World Development Indicators 2005, IMF World Economic Outlook, September 2006.

poverty substantially in spite of the more unequal income distribution today than at the beginning of the reform period (Priewe and Herr, 2005).

China did not follow a big-bang strategy. Instead, a gradual strategy of reform was chosen with far-reaching government intervention. For example, in the sequence of transition, privatization was put at the end and property rights remained rather unclear. Prices were also liberalized gradually as well as the foreign trade. International capital flows were strictly controlled (see section 2). China grew slowly out of the plan (Naughton, 1994). As one pillar of development state-owned enterprises stimulated development and were used for keeping investment high and for industrial policy. As a second pillar small- and medium-sized market based enterprises were allowed to grow and were also supported. In many cases small enterprises were organized as collectives and later became ordinary private firms. Over the years the share of state-owned enterprises in producing Chinese GDP became smaller but in industrial production it is still around 30 per cent.

In looking at the different demand elements it becomes clear that growth in China is driven by high investment demand. Growth rates in gross capital formation as well as the proportion of gross capital formation in per cent of GDP have been high (see Table 7.1). During the high growth in the 1980s foreign direct investment (FDI) was very low. From the early 1990s on FDI increased sharply and added to investment demand. However, more important is that part of FDI was a way of importing technology and management skills and open export channels. For a developing country inflation rates in China were rather low. There was an inflationary wave at the end of the 1980s with inflation rates in two years of nearly 20 per cent. In 1990 inflation was reduced along with a fall in growth rates. The following strong upswing brought an inflation rate of over 20 per cent in 1994 – the year with the highest inflation rate since the start of reforms. The inflation could be reduced without a drastic fall in GDP growth. After the Asian crisis in 1997, China fell into mild deflation with lower GDP-growth rates. Expansionary fiscal policy together with the investment of state-owned enterprise were the main policy instruments used to stabilize demand and output and to control deflation. By 2003 deflation had been overcome and growth rates increased again, leading to a strong economic upswing. This overall good performance as far as inflation rates and GDP growth is concerned led to high confidence in the domestic currency, which never eroded as in the case of many other developing countries. Of course currencies like the US dollar are more attractive than the renminbi (RMB), but China never had to fight in a fundamental way against cumulative capital flight and dollarization both of which were widespread in many other developing countries.

Development in China would not have been possible without the financial system supporting and even pushing investment. The backbone of the financial system are the four big state-owned commercial banks, which up to the present day cover two-thirds of deposit collection and bank credits given. Until the late 1990s there had been a credit plan with credit ceilings and politically influenced credit allocation. The People's Bank of China, the central bank, sets deposits and lending rates and uses moral persuasion to control credit volumes. The financial system and especially the nexus of state-owned banks and state-owned enterprises has been the demand-side backbone of the Chinese economy (Herr and Priewe, 1999). It stimulated permanently high investment with all of its multiplier effects for the other sectors of the economy. Due to a high savings rate, large increases in income led to high savings and not the other way round. There is paramount evidence that China has managed to create a Schumpeterian–Keynesian credit-investment-income-creation process which has led to economic prosperity.[3]

In 1994 China changed from a system of several exchange rates, which was typical for planned economies, to a system with only one exchange rate. Before that year the RMB had been weak and had devalued frequently. In 1994 the official exchange rate was adjusted close to the black market exchange rate and the RMB was unofficially pegged to the US dollar allowing only minimal fluctuations around the central rate.[4] In spite of depreciation pressures after the Asian Crisis in 1997 and appreciation pressures later on, the RMB–US-dollar peg was kept until July 2005. Then China changed to a managed floating exchange rate system pegging to a basket of currencies the composition of which was not made public. Floating was limited to 0.3 per cent around the central rate. The step led to a 2.1 per cent appreciation and then a permanent further small appreciation against the US dollar (Federal Reserve Bank of Dallas 2005). The stable nominal exchange rate anchor vis-à-vis the US dollar plus the appreciation pressure of the RMB undoubtedly increased the reputation of the Chinese currency.

China has been integrating into the world economy at top speed. In 1980, it realized one per cent of total world exports. In 2003 (first half of the year) it reached 5.8 per cent, compared with Germany 9.2 per cent, Japan 6.4 per cent, NIEs (Hong Kong, Korea, Singapore, Taiwan) 8.8 per cent and the United States 10.4 per cent. China became competitive in low-tech industrial production, but step-by-step increased its technological know-how (Rumbaugh and Blancher, 2004). China's trade openness (the value of exports and imports divided by GDP) reached 76 per cent in 2004, compared with about 25 per cent in Japan or the USA or 39 per cent in India, although Malaysia realized 221 per cent in 2004, Vietnam 142 per cent and Thailand 135 per cent (World Bank 2005). For a large economy, Chinese openness is high. It is a success because of the strong link to the international division of labour, but it is also a problem because it makes development in China dependent on the world market. This point is even more conspicuous as the less developed parts of the Chinese economy are largely excluded from the export boom, so economic integration into the world market adds to the regional problems in China.

From the beginning of reforms until the mid-1990s, China realized an overall balanced current account with a deficit in some years and a surplus in others. Since the mid-1990s China became one of the big surplus countries in the world. With an estimated current account surplus of US 184 billion dollars in 2006 China joined the group of countries with traditionally the largest surpluses in the world: Japan with a surplus of US 167 billion dollars and Germany of US 121 billion dollars. These figures correspond to an estimated US current account deficit of 869 billion in 2006 (IMF 2006a). China realizes a large proportion of its surplus vis-à-vis the United States. As Japan and other Asian countries realize current account surpluses vis-à-vis China, it became a wheel for trade and a growth locomotive for many Asian countries (Rumbaugh and Blancher, 2004).

China obviously did not follow a strategy of import-led development. It never had the aim of attracting net-capital imports to achieve a deficit in the current account and net resource inflow. It was very reluctant to take foreign credits as it did not want to become dependent on foreign creditors including foreign governments and international institutions. China does not fit the traditional World Bank model (Chenery and Strout, 1966) based on the assumption that developing countries have a lack of domestic savings and of a physical capital stock, and that foreign savings and a deficit in the current account should augment domestic savings and increase the domestic capital stock. This fact has become even clearer since the second half of the 1990s when China realized high current account surpluses (see Table 7.1).

China managed to establish an ideal macroeconomic constellation for development as it combined high domestic investment with current account surpluses, the two growth drivers, with FDI inflows, one of the technology drivers, and a stable nominal exchange rate, one of the drivers to create confidence in the RMB. Such a constellation stimulates domestic demand, avoids foreign indebtedness, relies on a mostly positive type of capital inflow and at the same time improves the reputation of the domestic currency. It is clear that without capital import controls to influence the structure and the volume of capital flow and central bank interventions such a constellation is difficult to achieve over a long period of time.

7.3 The capital control regime in China

China used in the past and still uses a comprehensive system of capital controls. This system is mainly based on administrative approval and quantitative limitation. Market-based instruments to regulate capital flows have not been developed as yet (Icard, 2003, p. 20).

Using the IMF country table matrix in the 'Annual Reports on Exchange Arrangements and Exchange Restrictions' (AREAER), the situation of China's capital account controls at the end of 2005 is listed in Table 7.2. According to this table, at the end of 2005 among the 41 categories of cross-border financial transactions defined by the IMF, 27 are partially convertible, 10 are not convertible and four are without information. The table reveals that China is indeed a country with some integration in the international financial markets, albeit without a very high degree of capital account liberalization. The high number of partially open cross-border transactions shows that China is following a gradual strategy of capital account liberalization. The table also makes clear that capital account convertibility for non-residents has been realized to a large extent. On the other hand, many cross-border transactions in the capital account are prohibited or partly prohibited for residents.

7.3.1 Institutions of control

Controls on cross-border capital flows are imposed by several government departments like the State Development and Planning Commission, the People's Bank of China, the China Security Regulation Commission or the Ministry of Commerce (before March 2003, the Ministry of Foreign Trade and Economic Cooperation, MOFTEC).[5] A large administrative body, entitled State Administration of Foreign Exchange (SAFE), is the key institution, which carries out controls, enforces the rules and makes discretionary decisions in many areas. The role and function of SAFE is also to draft policies concerning RMB capital account convertibility, to oversee statistics on capital and financial transactions and to provide warning signals concerning the external sector.

Table 7.2 Overview of China's capital account convertibility, end 2005

Capital market securities

Shares		Bonds	
Purchase locally by non-residents	Partially convertible	Purchase locally by non-residents	Partially convertible*
Sale or issue locally by non-residents	Partially convertible	Sale or issue locally by non-residents	Partially convertible**
Purchase abroad by residents	Partially convertible	Purchase abroad by residents	Partially convertible
Sale or issue abroad by residents	Partially convertible	Sale or issue abroad by residents	Partially convertible

Money market securities

Purchase locally by non-residents	Non-convertible
Sale or issue locally by non-residents	Non-convertible
Purchase abroad by residents	Partially convertible
Sale or issue abroad by residents	Partially convertible

Collective investment securities

Purchase locally by non-residents	Non-convertible
Sale or issue locally by non-residents	Non-convertible
Purchase abroad by residents	Partially convertible
Sale or issue abroad by residents	Partially convertible

Derivatives and other instruments

Purchase locally by non-residents	Non-convertible
Sale or issue locally by non-residents	Non-convertible
Purchase abroad by residents	Partially convertible
Sale or issue abroad by residents	Partially convertible

Real estate

Purchase locally by non-residents	Non-convertible
Sale locally by non-residents	Partially convertible
Purchase abroad by residents	Non-convertible

Commercial credits

By residents to non-residents	Partially convertible
To residents from non-residents	Partially convertible

Financial credits

By residents to non-residents	Partially convertible
To residents from non-residents	Partially convertible

Guarantees, sureties, and financial backup facilities

By residents to non-residents	Partially convertible
To residents non-residents	Partially convertible

Direct investment

Outward direct investment	Partially convertible
Inward direct investment	Partially convertible

Loans

By residents to non-residents	Partially convertible
To residents from non-residents	Partially convertible

Personal capital transactions

Transfer of assets	Partially convertible
Transfer abroad by emigrants	Information not available
Transfer into the country by immigrants	Information not available
Transfer of gambling and prize earnings	
Transfer out	Partially convertible
Transfer in	Information not available

Personal capital transactions

Loans

By residents to non-residents	Non-convertible
To residents from non-residents	Non-convertible

Gifts, endowments, inheritance and legacies

By residents to non-residents	Partially convertible
To residents from non-residents	Partially convertible

Liquidation of direct investment

Of inward direct investment	Partially convertible
Of outward direct investment	Information not available

Notes: * According to the People's Bank of China public notice No. 28 of 30 April 2005 the Pacific Asian Index Fund (PAIF), which is a qualified foreign institutional investor, is allowed to transact in the domestic inter-bank bond market with an approved quota of US 0.18 billion dollars.
** According to the Provisional Administrative Rules on International Development Institutions' Issuance of RMB Bonds on 18 February 2005, international financial institutions lending or investing for development purposes may issue RMB denominated bonds in China.
Source: IMF Annual Reports on AREAER and People's Bank of China documents.

It sets up and carries out rules and regulations to manage and supervise cross-border capital and financial transactions and foreign exchange transactions. SAFE also drafts domestic foreign exchange market management regulations; supervises domestic foreign exchange market operations, initiates and coordinates anti-laundering activities, examines the execution of foreign exchange management regulation by financial institutions, and effects punishment to those who violate the regulations.

7.3.2 Current account transactions

At the end of 1996 full current account convertibility was realized. In spite of this to control cross-border capital flows in a comprehensive way it is necessary to control current account transactions. Otherwise exporters for example could keep their revenues abroad and export and import prices could be declared wrongly to transfer capital.

From 1953 to 1978, under the planned economy, foreign exchange was monopolized by the state. Import and export were conducted by the state through designated state-owned companies and were totally controlled. From 1979 to 1993, a so-called retaining system was implemented. Under such a system, entities (foreign-funded enterprises excluded) could retain certain foreign currency revenues in their foreign exchange account. The ratio was determined by the foreign currency received, according to different entities and districts, and overall state policy. The remaining foreign exchange receipt had to be sold to the state through the Bank of China, one of the four big state-owned commercial banks. From 1994 to the present, a system called 'purchasing and surrendering' has been implemented. Under this system, Chinese-funded enterprises or organizations must change foreign exchange receipts into RMB (except the foreign exchange receipts which are allowed to be kept in designated banks). But all foreign currency needed to pay for imports can be bought from designated banks with effective contracts and commercial documents, such as a commercial invoice or payment notice. Foreign-funded enterprises have been incorporated in the purchasing and surrendering system. For both Chinese and foreign-funded enterprises, there is a limit to foreign currency accounts, although different for the two types of enterprises. For instance, to those Chinese-funded enterprises, which satisfy certain requirements for international trading volume and registered capital and financial position set by SAFE, the limit is 15 per cent of the previous year's import plus export volume. Foreign exchange receipts within the limit can be kept in the foreign currency account, or sold to designated banks. For foreign-funded enterprises, the limit is higher.

7.3.3 Foreign direct investment

In the last 25 years, the Chinese government has gradually eased restrictions and encouraged inward FDI. Encouragement included setting up special economic zones, preferential tax treatment, preferential arrangement of land use rights, and the release of profit remittance requirements, and so on. Now there are no restrictions with regard to inward FDI except that they follow the industrial guidance for investment set by the Chinese government. The Chinese government began to allow and regulate FDI outflows in 1991. FDI outflows at that time had to be approved by MOFTEC and registered by SAFE. In 2001 the purchase of foreign exchange was authorized for investment abroad in strategic foreign projects approved by the State Council, projects that entail especially imports of natural resources and technology. In 2003 some provinces and regions raised the limits on individual outward direct investment from US 1 million dollar to US 3 million dollar. Looking at FDI, China is a very open country and much more open than for example the United States, which shelters a large part of its industry to prevent military and high-tech knowledge spreading to other countries.[6]

7.3.4 Cross-border credit relations

Before 1979 external debt in China was prohibited. After 1979 it was allowed under a national plan and regulations were later frequently modified. According to these laws, the state manages the country's foreign debt completely. The National Development and Reform Commission (before its existence, its predecessor), the Ministry of Finance and SAFE are in charge of controlling national foreign debt. The National Development and Reform Commission, together with related authorities, are in charge of setting up a national foreign debt plan, including the total volume and the structure of debt, based on the situation of the national economy, social development, balance of payment status, and national solvency. For this purpose quantitative controls are executed. Specifically, medium- and long-term foreign credits and annual development of external debt are regulated. The allocation of external debt to industries and regions, as well as arrangements of maturity and currency denomination of foreign debt is also decided by the commission. For Chinese-funded organizations, SAFE controls the outstanding balance of their foreign short-term borrowing, while the National Development and Reform Commission exercises quota management on medium- and long-term foreign loans according to the overall national plan.

Loans from international financial organizations and foreign governments must be conducted by the state. In particular, the National

Development and Reform Commission, together with the Ministry of Finance and other related authorities, set the list of loans, and then the Ministry of Finance organizes negotiation, signing and transferring to domestic debtors. Overseas bond issuance by the Ministry of Finance on behalf of the state requires approval from the State Council, and the scale must be incorporated into the national foreign debt plan. For foreign enterprises there are special regulations. For them the sum of foreign debt should not exceed the gap between the total project investment and the registered capital. Within the gap, foreign-funded enterprises are free of any restrictions on raising short-, medium-, and long-term debt in foreign markets.

All domestic entities including foreign-funded enterprises (except for the Ministry of Finance overseas bonds issuance) must get approval from the National Development and Reform Commission, SAFE and the State Council, if they want to issue bonds in overseas markets. With the establishment of 'Qualified Foreign Institutional Investors' in 2002 foreign institutions were allowed to take part in the Chinese bond market to a limited extent.

Capital outflows in the form of credits are also strictly controlled. As for bonds, only banks authorized by the People's Bank of China may purchase foreign bonds but must use their own foreign exchange funds and are not permitted to purchase foreign exchange for this purpose. Concerning derivatives and other instruments, only financial institutions approved by the People's Bank of China and those that carry out foreign exchange trading operations for their own account or on behalf of customers are allowed to purchase derivative instruments without prior SAFE approval.

7.3.5   Cross-border portfolio investment in stocks

China strictly controls portfolio investment in the form of buying and selling shares. At the end of the 1980s/early 1990s stock markets in China were opened in Shenzhen and Shanghai. Stocks – so-called A-shares – could be sold and bought by Chinese citizens and firms in domestic currency. In 1992 B-shares were offered, providing foreign investors with a legal channel of investment in China's equity market. B-shares had to be bought in foreign currency. Since 27 February 2001, B-shares were opened to individual Chinese investors. However, like foreigners they have to use foreign currency to buy shares. Apart from B-shares with the approval of SAFE, domestic corporations are allowed to issue H-shares in Hong Kong, N-shares in New York, and S-shares in Singapore. Foreign portfolio investment in China in shares has been small and was not very attractive for foreigners. This is not surprising. Only state-owned enterprises issued shares, only minority ownership was possible, equity was not well protected, there was insider trading and a lack of transparency, and so on.

In 2002 there was a further opening of the stock market. According to the 'Qualified Foreign Institutional Investors Regulation' overseas investors were allowed to invest in Chinese A-shares (as well as in bonds traded).[7] Foreign funds, insurance companies and other asset management institutions have to run through a strict application process to get investment quotas and are forced to follow a certain settlement mechanism and reporting process to take part in the Chinese capital market. Shares held by each 'qualified foreign institutional investor' in one listed company should not exceed 10 per cent of the total outstanding shares of the company; total shares held by all 'qualified foreign institutional investors' in one listed company should not exceed 20 per cent of the total outstanding shares of the company. The China Securities Regulatory Commission has the right to adjust the percentage according to the development of the securities market.[8] In addition from the same year domestic companies listed overseas and China-held foreign listed companies have been allowed to sell shares abroad with prior approval by the China Securities Regulatory Commission.

Concerning capital outflows, the listing of overseas companies in the Shanghai or Shenzhen Stock Exchange is not permitted. Individual residents are forbidden to invest in overseas stock markets. Since 2004 the Chinese government has begun to smooth and enlarge the channels for capital outflow. Insurance companies are allowed to invest in equities in overseas securities markets within approved investment quotas. The establishment of 'Qualified Domestic Institutional Investors' will further stimulate controlled capital outflow in the field of stocks in China in future.

7.3.6 RMB offshore market

In China there is no relevant offshore currency market, which in many developing countries played a destabilizing role and has no other function than to help tax evasion, money laundering and other criminal activities. Such markets need domestic deposits held by offshore banks as well as free capital in- and outflow in the form of taking foreign credit and investing domestic deposits abroad. None of these conditions exist in China.

7.3.7   Dollarization

In the past Chinese exporting enterprises have been and still are allowed to keep part of their export revenues in foreign currency. This is one of the sources of deposit dollarization in China. Over time regulations made it easier to hold foreign currency deposits. For example, in 1996 individuals were allowed to hold foreign currency deposits and sell them to designated banks, and they were allowed to purchase foreign currency through designated banks within a set limit. Domestic credits in foreign currency are restricted. In 2002 it was allowed that under certain conditions large and medium-sized domestic state-owned enterprises issue foreign currency bonds to Chinese investors.

7.4   The empirical development

Not taking into account central bank interventions, FDI flows dominated net capital flows in China (see Figure 7.1). FDI inflows were small in the 1980s but jumped to high levels after Deng Xiaoping announced the new opening of China in the early 1990s. Since the mid 1990s net FDI inflows have been high and stable at a level of around 40 billion US dollar. Most FDI, more than 40 per cent, over the whole period came from Hong Kong and the Virgin Islands. Two explanations are possible. First, there might be substantial legal and illegal 'round-tripping' from mainland China to Hong Kong or the Virgin Islands and back to exploit

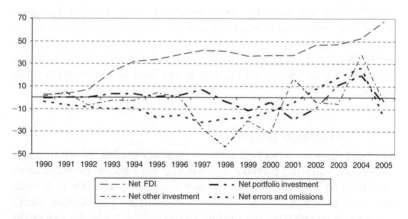

Figure 7.1 Net FDI, portfolio investment, 'other investment' and errors and omissions in US billion dollars 1990–2005 – China
Source: IMF, International Financial Statistics 2006.

preferential tax treatment, subsidies from local governments, etc. which do not exist for domestic investment. Taking 'round-tripping' into consideration, the actual FDI flows to China may be much smaller than statistically reported. Secondly, Hong Kong and the Virgin Islands may be used by investors from Europe, Japan, the United States, Taiwan, etc. to evade tax payments and other regulations in their home countries. In contrast to the general assumption most FDI-flows to China did not come from the industrial centres (United States, Japan, or the European Union). China, rather, became a host country for FDI from its neighbouring countries. This is the case even if it is assumed that a large part of FDI from Hong Kong and the Virgin Islands comes from industrial centres. Most FDI-inflows (from 2000 to 2004, more than 60 per cent) went into the manufacturing sector and were concentrated in coastal regions. During the last few years the share of electronics and communication equipment was increased substantially (Prasad and Wei, 2005).

Not all FDI flows are good. For example, part of FDI-inflows especially form neighbouring countries went to export-processing involving backward technology and very poor working conditions. FDI-inflows in the real estate sectors were about 10 per cent of total FDI-inflows during recent years and added to the real estate bubble which developed in the coastal regions in China. Last but not least foreign-owned firms were given many channels to export and import capital.

Although foreign debt transactions were strictly controlled, China did not fully suppress foreign credits. Until the mid-1990s foreign borrowing stayed low. Looking at 'net other investment', mainly credit relations, after the Asian crisis in 1997 outflows increased up to US 43 billion dollars in 1998. Then in 2001 there was a net inflow of around US 17 billion dollars. The following years' net flows became low again (see Figure 7.1). Due to capital controls Chinese foreign debt is relatively low. From 1979 to 1982, the volume of Chinese foreign borrowing was US 10.7 billion dollars and until 1987 increased only by US 26.5 billion dollars (Tian 2004). In the 1990s foreign debt increased faster and reached according to SAFE around US 300 billion dollars in September 2006.[9] Since the mid-1990s the stock of foreign debt has been around 15 per cent of GDP. This is less than 50 per cent of the average debt quota of emerging markets and developing countries.[10] Compared with the Chinese official reserves of over US 900 billion dollars in 2006 foreign debt is relatively low.

International net portfolio investment in China has been small. Until the Asian crises in 1997 it was usually positive. However, after the Asian crises it turned negative with the highest outflow of nearly US 20 billion dollars in 2001. Then it became positive again.

There is no doubt that capital controls in China successfully shaped the structure of capital flows away from portfolio investment and bank credits towards FDI. FDI flows clearly dominated legal capital flows in China. This is a big difference to other developing countries, which showed much higher percentages of portfolio investment and 'other investment' to aggregate cross-border flows (see Table 7.3). FDI flows together with portfolio investment in the form of shares have a fundamental advantage in that they do not create foreign debt. Foreign debt of developing countries is always denominated in foreign currency. In such a case depreciation increases the debt burden of domestic debtors. In a long list of countries this effect led to twin-crises – a simultaneous currency and domestic liquidity or even solvency crises. In case of FDI the exchange rate risk is on the side of the foreign investor. Indeed, China never had a foreign debt crisis with its disastrous effects.

FDI is not automatically positive for a country but it is usually the most stable type of capital flow. Portfolio investment is short-term oriented and increases the volatility of international capital flows. The same is the case for short-term credit, which also increases the volatility of international capital flows. Owing to the large share of FDI flows China has overall a relatively low volatility of international capital flows.[11] 'Net other investment' and portfolio investment were not stable in China. They became negative after the Asian crisis in 1997 when it was expected that contagion would spread to China and the RMB would devalue substantially. Then half a decade later appreciation pressure of RMB led to reducing capital outflows and later to increasing capital inflows.

Capital controls never work perfectly. Thus illegal capital flows, first among all outflows, in China are not surprising. The explanation can be found in the motives of portfolio diversification, higher returns abroad, tax evasion and as a camouflage of criminal activities. As capital controls were comprehensive in the 1980s, illegal capital movements in that period were very small in China. However, beginning in the early 1990s with the new wave of opening in China new channels of illegal capital flows were opened, too. Errors and omissions in the balance of payment statistics can be taken as a rough indicator of illegal capital flows. In the first half of the 1990s errors and omissions showed small but increasing illegal capital outflows. In 1997, the year of the outbreak of the Asian crisis, errors and omissions signalled the highest illegal outflow of around US 22 billion dollars. However, in per cent of GDP the volume was moderate and far below 0.5 per cent. Later outflows became smaller and in 2003 strong pressure to appreciate the Chinese currency reversed illegal capital flows and 'hot' money was imported illegally (see Figure 7.1).

Table 7.3 FDI, portfolio investment and 'other investment' for selected countries 1990–2005
Percentage (%) of total inflows and outflows of the aggregate of the three types of capital flows

	Brazil	Hong Kong	Singapore	South Africa	Chile	Malaysia	Russia	Argentina	China
FDI									
1990	19.3	n.a.	65.2	3.7	23.3	81.0	n.a.	16.9	73.7
1991	14.4	n.a.	48.8	14.1	27.9	71.1	n.a.	11.1	48.7
1992	17.0	n.a.	19.8	40.9	29.1	47.2	n.a.	48.4	64.9
1993	8.6	n.a.	20.7	16.6	36.3	35.5	n.a.	6.3	82.2
1994	4.4	n.a.	34.6	28.5	43.0	51.7	3.1	20.5	83.7
1995	16.6	n.a.	39.6	35.2	82.3	49.1	26.8	23.7	84.4
1996	28.7	n.a.	30.4	17.0	59.9	50.7	9.3	28.4	88.7
1997	52.2	n.a.	20.9	23.5	54.3	43.2	15.7	30.9	43.7
1998	42.3	9.6	27.1	10.2	39.4	27.1	13.7	34.7	49.4
1999	53.5	16.8	35.4	11.3	47.8	37.2	22.5	69.1	50.7
2000	65.8	48.6	33.4	15.4	67.3	41.8	14.8	64.5	34.4
2001	69.5	19.8	66.9	46.4	57.6	15.6	54.9	11.8	52.3
2002	51.9	19.5	25.0	24.5	31.9	39.4	40.3	10.2	74.3
2003	33.6	17.7	19.8	13.6	40.3	36.2	28.5	12.7	53.3
2004	70.9	36.7	31.5	15.9	46.5	21.8	35.5	25.8	49.6
2005	59.0	41.1	23.3	31.9	47.4	39.2	23.5	40.6	39.0
Portfolio investment									
1990	7.5	n.a.	18.7	24.0	12.6	8.8	n.a.	12.4	4.0
1991	25.9	n.a.	8.2	31.3	5.6	3.0	n.a.	74.9	8.3
1992	56.8	n.a.	14.0	40.9	10.0	10.2	n.a.	41.2	3.6
1993	65.0	n.a.	32.5	41.3	22.5	5.0	n.a.	66.0	10.9
1994	54.3	n.a.	20.9	52.4	19.8	19.6	0.7	49.9	10.1
1995	29.6	n.a.	15.4	31.8	1.4	5.1	24.5	25.4	1.8
1996	52.6	n.a.	24.3	58.8	14.1	2.7	12.6	48.1	6.3
1997	27.0	n.a.	12.8	60.8	29.1	2.1	35.1	32.0	8.2

(Continued)

Table 7.3 (Continued)

	Brazil	Hong Kong	Singapore	South Africa	Chile	Malaysia	Russia	Argentina	China
1998	24.0	8.7	32.2	72.3	26.8	3.5	22.2	45.4	4.2
1999	6.7	32.1	22.0	69.2	35.3	7.2	8.8	18.2	14.0
2000	19.4	27.5	21.8	67.5	6.8	18.2	33.7	14.7	16.3
2001	4.7	23.3	27.2	35.7	28.9	17.4	8.0	50.3	22.4
2002	13.9	27.9	35.9	28.7	47.5	10.8	26.2	20.6	19.8
2003	17.2	34.0	31.3	10.2	45.2	12.9	7.3	40.5	12.9
2004	12.2	21.7	21.7	66.0	31.0	29.9	10.0	48.4	17.2
2005	28.1	33.8	20.7	30.0	29.4	20.9	10.0	22.5	20.5
Other investment									
1990	73.2	n.a.	16.1	72.3	64.2	10.2	n.a.	70.8	22.2
1991	59.7	n.a.	43.0	54.6	66.5	25.8	n.a.	13.9	43.0
1992	26.2	n.a.	66.2	18.2	60.8	42.6	n.a.	10.4	31.5
1993	26.5	n.a.	46.8	42.0	41.2	59.4	n.a.	27.7	6.9
1994	41.4	n.a.	44.5	19.1	37.2	28.7	96.2	29.6	6.3
1995	53.7	n.a.	45.0	33.1	16.3	45.8	48.7	50.9	13.8
1996	18.7	n.a.	45.3	24.2	25.9	46.6	78.1	23.5	5.0
1997	20.8	n.a.	66.3	15.7	16.6	54.8	48.7	37.1	48.2
1998	33.7	81.7	40.7	17.5	33.9	69.4	64.2	19.9	46.5
1999	39.8	51.0	42.6	19.5	16.9	55.6	68.3	12.6	35.3
2000	14.8	23.9	44.7	17.1	25.9	40.0	51.4	20.8	49.2
2001	25.8	57.0	5.9	17.9	13.6	67.0	39.7	37.9	25.3
2002	34.1	52.6	39.0	46.8	20.6	49.8	33.4	69.2	5.9
2003	49.2	48.3	48.8	76.3	14.4	50.9	64.3	46.9	33.8
2004	16.9	41.6	46.8	18.1	22.5	48.3	54.5	25.8	33.2
2005	12.9	25.1	55.9	38.1	23.2	39.8	66.5	36.9	40.5

Source: IMF, International Financial Statistics 2006, own calculations.

Illegal flows follow to a large extent the same incentives as legal flows. This is also the case in China. Taking legal and illegal flows together after the Asian crisis China experienced aggregate outflows of portfolio investment, 'other investment' and errors and omissions of yearly US 40 to 50 billion dollars with the peak in 1998 at about US 60 billion dollars. Without the stabilizing effect of high FDI inflows of around US 40 billion dollars the RMB foreign value may have come under severe pressure during these years. There is no guarantee that FDI inflows are stable. To a certain extent China was lucky that FDI flows were not affected by the Asian crisis.

There are a number of investigations about Chinese capital flows, which follow market incentives like exchange rate expectations and interest rate differentials. Some of these flows are illegal; others use legal channels but follow market incentives. The different estimates of market based capital flows show two important results (Zhu et al., 2005; Wu and Tang 2000; Song 1999; Gunter 2004; Chen 2003). First, there were always capital outflows. This signals that there is a strong incentive for Chinese wealth holders to keep foreign currency assets abroad as part of portfolio diversification and to keep wealth in superior currencies like the US dollar and to a smaller extent the euro or yen. A sudden deregulation of capital exports would most likely lead to high and sudden capital exports. Secondly, all the estimates show that such flows in China were low in the 1980s but picked up throughout the 1990s. In the second half of the 1990s especially some of the estimates show outflows of a yearly volume of about US 100 billion dollars, especially in the years of the Asian crisis in 1997 and 1998. However, most estimates arrived at figures of about US 20 to 30 billion dollars or less. After 1998 such capital outflows dropped substantially, reflecting that depreciation expectations had disappeared and later changed into appreciation expectations of the RMB. Thus the Chinese capital account cannot be considered closed, and under certain constellations strong purely market-based flows are obviously possible. However, the quantitative volume of these capital flows was relatively low compared with the overall constellation. Without capital controls China would have been severely hit by the Asian crisis and inflows of 'hot' money also would have been much higher in the period of RMB strength.[12]

Compared with other developing countries dollarization in China is relatively low. Deposit dollarization in the period 1992–2001 for which data are available was between 8 and 15 per cent of domestic deposits and mostly in the form of dollar deposits.[13] Domestic foreign currency credits (credit dollarization) in China were lower, fluctuating between 6 and 12 per cent of domestic bank credits in the same period (People's Bank of China, 2006). The difference can be explained by restrictions of domestic credits in foreign currency. Ma and McCauley (2003) showed that interest rate differentials, exchange rate expectations and deregulation steps explain a large part of changes in foreign currency holdings especially by households. These holdings increased substantially after the Asian crisis as many market participants expected a devaluation of RMB. Chinese foreign currency deposits also reacted to interest rate differentials between onshore dollar deposits and RMB deposits. When the B-share market was opened for Chinese citizens in February 2001, foreign currency deposits dropped by US 2.5 billion dollars within a few months as Chinese investors with dollar deposits bought B-shares; they 'snapped them up' (Ma and McCauley, 2003, p. 28).

7.5 Chinese foreign reserves

In China during the 1980s the current account was more or less balanced. Since the 1990s except the year 1993, the year before the large RMB depreciation, Chinese current account has been in surplus and has become bigger and bigger. At the same time high net capital inflows, mainly caused by FDI inflows but also increasingly caused by other flows, caused a surplus in the capital balance. Of course such a constellation is only possible if the central bank intervenes in the foreign exchange market. The double surplus in the balance of payments led to an explosion of central bank interventions by the People's Bank of China (see Figure 7.2). With over US 900 billion dollar at end-2006 China (without

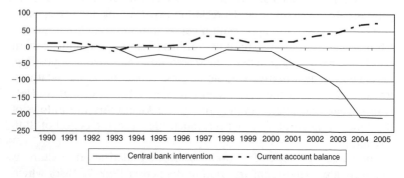

Figure 7.2 Current account balance and central bank interventions in US billion dollar from 1990–2005 – China

Source: IMF International Financial Statistics 2006, IMF World Economic Outlook September 2006.

Taiwan) kept the highest official reserves in the world. The Bank of Japan, traditionally the central bank with the highest reserves, is now in second place also close to US 900 billion dollar (IMF, 2006). Using any indicator of foreign reserves requirements (level of short-tem debt, import needs, etc.) China owns reserves in abundance. There are no official publications about the currency composition of Chinese reserves. However, it is known that China holds a substantial part of US treasury bonds and also US government's debt-securities with longer maturity. During recent years it seems that China has started to invest more in corporate bonds and slowly increases, as other central banks, its share of the euro in its official reserves (Galati and Wooldridge 2006).

Foreign exchange interventions are sterilized by issuing central bank bills to reduce the liquidity created. So far the People's Bank of China has had no serous difficulties sterilizing the huge foreign exchange interventions. For some central banks, however, sterilization is costly as interest rates offered are higher than interest rates earned by invested reserves abroad. However, because of the low interest rates in China the People's Bank of China does not suffer from this effect (Prasad and Wei, 2005, p. 13). But sterilization costs are of secondary importance. The paramount aim of such interventions is to prevent an appreciation of the RMB to guarantee surpluses in the current account. Thus, the People's Bank of China defends the market constellation of export-supported growth, which has been so beneficial for China. The benefits for China of such a constellation by far outweigh the potential sterilization costs. In any event central banks are not profit maximizing institutions. Nobody, for example, would argue that the European Central Bank should increase interest rates as high as possible to earn a high profit.

In recent years and especially after the Asian crisis in 1997 central banks in many developing countries intervened in foreign exchange markets to prevent the appreciation of their currencies and defend current account surpluses or prevent increases in current account deficits. These countries obviously do not want to be pushed again into dangerous current account deficits and a constellation of high foreign debt. Foreign exchange interventions stabilize the situation of these countries and reduce the danger of twin crises. The German 'miracle' of the 1950s and 1960s, which was based on export-led growth, would not have been possible without foreign exchange interventions by the German Bundesbank. Many countries in the group of the NIEs, and other examples, have been characterized by the same policy: Japan has been doing it for decades.

The explosion of international reserves held by central banks led to the speculation that the world economy has implicitly fallen back to a revived Bretton Woods system with the US dollar in the centre and developing countries like China and developed countries like Japan on the periphery (Dooley et al., 2003). The new system, so says the argument, is of mutual interest and can last for decades as the periphery can follow export-led growth and the United States can realize high welfare gains due to their overvalued currency. The hypothesis of a revived Bretton Woods system is not very convincing (Palley, 2006; Eichengreen, 2004). The higher foreign US debt and foreign official reserves in US dollars (measured as percentage of US GDP), the more likely trust in the US dollar erodes. The longer the present system prevails the more fragile the situation becomes. The so-called revived Bretton Woods system is not based on an international treaty. It is rather a kind of private cartel to stabilize the exchange rate of the US dollar. The European Monetary Union with the euro, the most important competitor of the US dollar, takes no part in the system. Only the first central bank switching from US dollar to euro or other currencies avoids losses in case the external value of the US dollar collapses. As the number of countries in the revived Bretton Woods system is large the private cartel can break down any time. And even if central banks stick to the cartel the millions of international wealth holders keeping huge sums of monetary wealth in US dollars may change their expectations and switch to other currencies. There is the likelihood that the present system violently breaks down and adds to worldwide instability. For the United States the present system is of mixed blessing. It increases without doubt domestic consumption. And more important, the United States has the privilege of having foreign debt dominated in domestic currency and the sweetness of building up foreign debt will not turn into the bitterness of a twin crisis when the US dollar devalues. However, the present system reduces domestic growth and employment in the United States and sooner or later may create a big disadvantage for the USA.

The accumulation of foreign reserves in China and other countries with the huge US current account deficit as the other side of the coin reflects the failure of international institutions and the leading industrial nations to develop a suitable international reserve medium. The Special Drawing Rights, created as international reserves in the 1960s, are quantitatively unimportant and were not developed further. The world is lacking an international reserve medium like the 'bancor' suggested by Keynes (1942) or the 'global greenback' brought into discussion by Stiglitz (2006). In the present unstable world economy central bank interventions and high official reserves are a legitimate instrument in protecting developing countries form unstable international capital flows, current account deficit and high foreign debt. In addition they function as a buffer against world market shocks. It can be discussed whether for the sake of world market equilibrium the appreciation of RMB could have been stronger over the last years and the Chinese current account surplus smaller. But there are no good arguments to blame China that it prevented the high capital inflows destroying its current account surplus and overall positive market constellation.

7.6 Evaluation of capital controls and foreign exchange interventions in China

Capital controls and foreign exchange interventions have been creating a number of positive effects for China and are an important part of the Chinese economic success story.

First, capital controls in China had the function of preventing boom–bust cycles which in so many developing countries led to temporary high net capital inflows, pushed countries into current account deficits and a constellation of high foreign debt before sudden destabilizing capital outflows resulted in destructive currency and banking crises. Capital controls together with foreign exchange interventions by the People's Bank of China have been safeguarding China against disastrous and unsustainable capital inflows and high foreign debt. Since China started its reform in 1978 it has never experienced a currency crisis, which in many countries in the world led to deep crises and even long-term stagnation. China has never had to go to the IMF, which definitely demanded a transitions strategy not wanted by the Chinese government and which most likely would have produced the same bad results as in many other countries following the spirit of the Washington Consensus (Stiglitz, 2006).

Secondly, due to capital controls the People's Bank of China could use monetary policy more or less entirely for domestic purposes, both in periods of inflationary pressure and in periods of a slowdown in economic growth. Nominal deposit and lending rates, which were fixed by the People's Bank of China were regulated at a level which guaranteed slightly positive real rates. This is in deep contrast to the very high real interest rates in many other developing countries, which opened their capital account. It is self-evident that low interest rates are good for investment and economic growth. Without capital controls such a policy would not have been possible. The Chinese way of supporting investment and the industrial sector, keeping interest rates low as well as politically influencing credit allocation is not unique. It was the backbone of the south-east Asian miracle after the Second World War (World Bank, 1993, Stiglitz and Uy, 1996).[14] Politically, in China and in many other successful Asian countries, holders of monetary wealth got their share of income. However, policies were geared towards economic growth and the development of industry (Wade, 2005).

Thirdly, China was able, as mentioned above, to trigger a domestically based Schumpeterian–Keynesian credit-investment-income-creation process which led to economic prosperity. Capital controls protected the domestic financial system; List's (1841) argument to protect infant industries was transferred to the financial system. The expansionary effect of the credit system in China becomes clear when the ratio between domestic bank credit to GDP in China is compared with other countries (see Table 7.4). Using this ratio China is in the group of developed countries and has a unique position for a developing country with comparable GDP per capita.[15]

How can the extraordinary credit expansion in China be explained? Let us analyse a typical economic expansion process in a developed country: Commercial banks give credit to firms in domestic currency and are refinanced by the central bank; firms invest the money and create demand for investment goods, intermediate goods etc.; production increases as well as employment; income is created and stimulates

Table 7.4   Domestic credit provided by the banking sector in per cent to GDP in 2003 (in domestic and foreign currency)

Low-income countries	45.31
Middle-income countries	85.35
High-income countries	181.89
China	177.80
India	57.32
Indonesia	55.70
Vietnam	52.47
Uganda	12.46
South Africa	15.82
Mozambique	11.03
Nigeria	23.38
Russian Federation	27.57
Belarus	21.22
Brazil	61.08

Source: World Bank, World Development Indicators 2005.

consumption demand which further stimulates aggregate demand, production and income; and saving will be created subsequently out of the new income to mach net investment. The act of giving credits in domestic currency by the commercial banking system creates deposits in domestic currency at the same time. The deposits created by the commercial banking system during the economic expansion are kept by private households and firms. They are partly restructured in other forms of monetary wealth like time deposits, bonds, and so on, but this is the only modification of the liability side of the balance sheets of financial institutions. What is important here is that credit expansion and creation of monetary wealth – both in domestic currency – takes place at the same time and the public is prepared to keep the domestic monetary wealth created. Central banks accommodate such a process, as there is no inflationary danger.

The key point is now that developing countries are confronted with a systematically tighter constraint for credit expansion. Let us assume that in a developing country 100 units of domestic monetary wealth is created. According to the preference of wealth owners a certain percentage of the newly created wealth will be exchanged in hard currencies. If wealth holders want to keep 50 per cent of their monetary wealth in hard currency inside (dollarization) and/or outside the country (capital exports) – a very conservative assumption for most developing countries – 50 units of domestic wealth will be exchanged in hard currency. Everything unchanged this leads to a depreciation of the domestic currency which can be accepted only to a limited extent by a central bank as it leads to an increase in the real burden of domestic debt, to inflationary developments, and so on. It follows that countries with low-quality currencies – more or less all developing countries – have a distorted financial system and are only to a very limited extent able to create a credit-investment-income-creating process which is the backbone of economic development. Capital controls and a low degree of dollarization allow a higher domestic credit expansion in developing countries than otherwise would be possible. And this happened in China.[16]

Some critiques argue that the Chinese credit expansion led to the accumulation of non-performing loans (Aziz and Duenwald, 2002). Indeed, parts of the credits were used to finance loss-making state-owned enterprises and probably not all investment projects financed were successful. The result was the increase of non-performing loans in the Chinese banking system. Despite several attempts to reduce non-performing loans it is estimated that nowadays at least 15 per cent of credits given by commercial banks are non-performing and most Chinese banks are not able to fulfil the eight per cent minimum capital adequacy ratio consistent with the Basel I international standard (Federal Reserve Bank of Dallas, 2005). Obviously the flow problem of non-performing loans is not yet sufficiently solved and creates a stock problem again and again. The banking system in China still takes over quasi-fiscal functions to keep loss-making enterprises alive and to slow down socially and politically costly restructuring. However, it should be noted that the non-performing loan problem in China is not out of control. Non-performing loans in per cent of GDP are not especially high in China and, more important, are denominated in domestic currency. As government debt to GDP in China is below 30 per cent there is room to reorganize the banking system. The huge foreign reserves held by the People's Bank of China can also be used (and were used) to control the problem. Recently foreign investors have been allowed to become minority shareholders of the four big commercial banks, which increased their equity. Finally it should not be forgotten that China is a fast growing country and this helps to reduce the problem. Overall non-performing loans in China can be controlled and despite their disadvantage they served a positive social purpose.

Capital controls in China were not without costs. There are not only the administrative costs for SAFE and other institutions to carry out supervision and controls, like any controls capital controls can become a source of corruption, injustice and income inequality. Capital controls can also lead to lower efficiency compared with 'optimal allocation of resources' in neoclassical static models. In China requirements of macroeconomic stability clearly dominated microeconomic efficiency. However, the protection of macroeconomic stability including the growth constellation in China stimulated productivity development in a dynamic way.[17] In the trade-off between costs and benefits of capital controls China is an exemplary case for a high net advantage of such controls.

In the past China followed a control system based on direct restrictions mainly with administrative approvals and quantitative restrictions. There is a lot of room to implement more market-based instruments to regulate cross-border capital flows. Market instruments reduce the possibility of rent seeking and corruption. Also banking supervision, for example to strictly control currency mismatches of domestic financial institutions and firms, could partly substitute capital controls. There is great demand from Chinese households to invest abroad and also from foreign investors to channel capital to China. In a regulated way such flows can be combined with macroeconomic stability. The model of selected 'qualified institutionally investors' represents an innovative approach to partly liberalize international capital flows.

Which way China's future will develop remains unknown. It seems that full convertibility is one of the final aims of transition. Before the Asian crisis in 1997 China had planned to liberalize capital flows within a few years. Now Chinese government seems to be more cautious. However, it cannot be excluded that outside pressure and interests of groups inside China may lead to a quick liberalization of international capital flows. Such a development would be dangerous as China is still a developing country and the financial system and the economy as a whole needs protection form an unstable world financial market. Some channels of cross border capital flows are already too open. China should, for example, become more selective in allowing FDI-inflows. It is questionable whether China benefits from high FDI inflows in the real estate sector. Also some FDI inflows in labour intensive low-tech areas benefit from regulations in China which are more of a Manchester type of early capitalism including child labour than of a country still struggling for a social dimension in development. It is also questionable whether the opening up of the financial system to foreign financial institutions benefits China. There is no good argument to speed up deregulation of international capital flows. It is desirable, even if liberalization takes place, to keep all the instruments in place to use them again when needed.

7.7 What can we learn from China?

China's high growth is based on a stable macroeconomic constellation and a mix of clever government interventions and productively set market incentives (which cannot be discussed here (Rodrik 2005)). The Chinese macroeconomic constellation, which can be transferred to other countries, has been created and protected by

(a) capital controls shaping the structure of capital flows and controlling the volume of flows without isolating China from the international financial market;
(b) large central bank interventions and sterilization to keep the current account in surplus;
(c) exchange rate stability with elements of flexibility since 2005; and
(d) macroeconomic domestic stability, especially low inflation rates and manageable fiscal deficits, to avoid the erosion of the quality of the domestic currency.

Capital controls can be of different nature and strict banking supervision can especially help to prevent destabilizing capital inflows. International institutions like the IMF should help countries to create clever and efficient capital controls. Controls in developing countries should be supported by regulations in developed countries to prevent over-lending, which took place in the past.

Exchange rate stability does not mean fixed exchange rates. Different exchange rate regimes are possible including formally flexible exchange rates with central bank interventions and capital controls. Independent of the policy mix, current account deficits should be avoided to prevent high foreign debt with all its disastrous effects for developing countries. The higher the foreign debt is, the smaller the degree of freedom to use the exchange rate to keep the current account positive or at least balanced. The prevention of current account deficits is more important than absolute exchange rate stability. The idea developed here is close to Williamson's (2005) argument for an intermediate exchange rate regime. It may be argued that not all countries in the world can have current account surpluses. This is of course correct. But if there are current account deficits developed countries have to realize them to create a world market constellation, which stimulates development for all.[18]

Point d) has always to be achieved. Otherwise the domestic monetary system erodes and capital flight and dollarization lead to destructive exchange rate movements and economic chaos. Policies a) to c) can be followed by countries with different mixtures. China kept the exchange rate relatively stable and used capital controls and central bank interventions to stabilize its growth constellation. A mix of stricter capital controls, especially controlling FDI flows, and more exchange rate flexibility would probably have reduced the need for foreign exchange interventions. Other countries could follow a policy of a less stable exchange rate than China and combine this with capital controls and central bank interventions. Again other countries may manage external stability only with exchange rate adjustments and large central bank interventions and keep tough capital controls only for periods of high instability.[19]

Only ideological thinking posits a world of free capital movements, no central bank interventions and completely flexible exchange rates as ideals the world should strive for. Here a different vision is developed. Monetary policy should be allowed to use all instruments available. Foreign exchange interventions, sterilization, capital controls, exchange rate movements and interest rate policy should all be legitimate and normal policy instruments used by central banks to keep the economy stable and support sustainable growth and prosperity.

Notes

1. This chapter is based on the report 'Capital Account Regimes and Monetary Policy in Developing Countries – Liberalization with Regulation' written for the German Ministry for Economic Cooperation and Development in 2006 together with Jan Priewe.

2. 'Washington Consensus' became a catch word especially for IMF shock policies of privatization, deregulation of labour markets and other markets, free trade in developing countries, unregulated international capital flows, procyclical fiscal and tight monetary policy (for details see Herr and Priewe, 2005 and 2006). Williamson's (1990) summary of the Washington Consensus was in many aspects more differentiated and less market radical than actual IMF policies became. For a comprehensive critique of the Washington Consensus also see Stiglitz (2006).

3. Schumpeter (1934) argued that credit created ad hoc – out of nothing – has to be given to the entrepreneur to create development. Keynes (1937) also stressed the need to finance investment to trigger income creation and savings.

4. During the first period of reform, more than one exchange rate existed. In 1981 the exchange rate for imports and exports (2.8 yuan/US-dollar) was different from the official rate (1.5 yuan/US dollar) which was used for non-trade settlement. In 1985 a single rate (2.8 yuan/US dollar) was used for trade and non-trade settlement. In 1988, when the foreign exchange transferring market was established, again two parallel rates came into existence. For instance, at the end of 1993, the so-called official exchange rate was 5.72 yuan/US dollar while the so-called market rate was 8.72 yuan/US dollar.

5. Details of capital control regime in China are based on Fengjuan (2005).

6. 'One could even say that China has been more open to foreign direct investment (FDI) than some OECD economies, especially as it has lately encouraged outward FDI in natural resources and technology' (Icard 2004, p. 15).

7. Mainland China followed more or less the approach also used in Taiwan in the early 1990s to carefully liberalize stock and debt-security markets (Lu 2003).

8. By 30 June 2005, there were 26 foreign investors being approved as 'qualified foreign institutional investors' with a total investment quota of US 4 billion doller (www.safe.gov.cn).

9. See http://www.finanznachrichten.de/nachrichten-2006-12/artikel-7513085.asp

10. At the end of 2005 the total group of 'Other Emerging Market and Developing Countries' had a ratio of external debt to GDP of over 30 per cent (IMF, 2005). Behind the average there are many countries with substantially higher debt ratios.

11. Fengjuan and Kimball (2005) calculated the standard deviations of non-official capital flows in China, Malaysia, Brazil, Mexico, South Korea, Thailand, Chile, Argentina, Singapore and Hong Kong for the period 1996 to 2003. The calculation shows that the standard deviation for inflows, outflows and net flows in China is relatively low. From the ten countries, China's standard deviation of inflows is the lowest, for outflows it is the third lowest and for net flows it is the second lowest.

12. The last point is also stressed by Prasad and Wei, 2005, p. 10: 'It should nevertheless be noted that, given the apparent one-way bet on the renminbi; the fact that these inflows are not larger than they are suggests that capital controls may be at least partly effective.'

13. Ma and McCauley (2003) report that anecdotal evidence suggests that early in this decade about 90 per cent of foreign currency deposits were in US dollars.

14. Japan used this type of regulation until the mid-1980s, and only after abolishing it, did it slip into the asset price bubble during the second half of the 1980s and the deflation in the second half of the 1990s (Mikuni and Murphy 2002).

15. The development of the financial system fits to the World Bank's (2001) view of 'Finance for Growth'. In this book a long debate about finance and development is summarized. One of the key conclusions is that the development of financial indicators like the ratio of bank credits to GDP is a good indicator to explain economic development. The World Bank stresses the role of the financial sector to increase productivity and efficiency – factors like better corporate governance and intermediation of savings, improvements of the payment systems, better possibilities for risk sharing, etc. are stressed. We agree that such factors are important and play a role in the development process. However, we believe that a credit-investment-income-creation process is more important to explain the development for example in China (see Priewe and Herr 2005).

16. There is one possibility compatible with deregulated financial markets and a high credit expansion, at least for a while. If the country is able to create an inflow of hard currency, the process of domestic credit expansion can go on as hard currencies continuously flow into the pockets of wealth owners who can realize their desired structure of wealth holding without creating depreciation pressures. Hard currency inflows can be created by current account surpluses and/or by capital imports. The better and sustainable option is the creation of current account surpluses. The relative good performance of Russia during the last years is based on high current account surpluses largely created by high prices of natural resources. If hard currency inflows take the form of higher foreign indebtedness the process is dangerous. In such a scenario a credit expansion in domestic currency can continue as long as foreign capital is flowing into the country. However, as soon as capital inflows stop a strong depreciation becomes unavoidable and a deep twin crisis will result.

17. 'Optimal allocation of resources' implies a static efficiency measurement excluding the mechanisms to improve technology, create innovations, build-up human capital, develop research capabilities, etc. In a dynamic approach government interventions at many different levels in China look much more optimal than under a static perspective.

18. Very poor countries should get official transfers if resource inflows are needed.

19. Such a mixture could also be a model for developed countries.

References

Aziz, J. and Duenwald, C. (2002), 'Growth-Financial Intermediation Nexus in China', IMF *Working Paper*, 02/194, Washington DC.

Chen, G. (2003), 'The Scale and Reasons of China's Capital Flight', *Working Paper* No. C2003004, China Centre for Economic Research.

Chenery, H.B. and Strout, A.M. (1966), 'Foreign Assistance and Economic Development', *American Economic Review*, 56 (4) Part 1, pp. 679–733.

Dooley, M., Folkerts-Landau, D. and Garber, P. (2003), 'An Essay on the Revived Bretton Woods System', *NBER Working Paper* 9971, September.

Eichengreen, B. (2004), 'Global Imbalances and the Lessons of Bretton Woods', *NBER Working Paper* 10497.

Federal Reserve Bank of Dallas (2005), *Southwest Economy*, Issue 4, July/August 2005 (http://www.dallasfed.org/research/swe/2005/swe0504d.html).

Fengjuan, X. (2005), 'Capital Controls in China Since 1990', manuscript, Central University of Finance and Economics, Beijing, China.

Fengjuan, X. and Kimball, D. (2005), 'Effectiveness and Effects of China's Capital Controls', *Journal of China & World Economy*, Chinese Academy of Social Sciences, July–August.

Galati, G. and Wooldridge, P. (2006), 'The Euro as a Reserve Currency: A Challenge to the Pre-Eminence of the US Dollar?', BIS Working Paper, No. 218, Basel.

Gunter, F. (2004), 'Capital Flight from China: 1984–2001', *China Economic Review*, 15, pp. 63–85.

Herr, H. and Priewe, J. (1999), 'High Growth in China – Transition without a Transition Crisis?', *Intereconomics*, 34, pp. 303–16.

Herr, H. and Priewe, J. (2005), 'Development Strategies Beyond the Washington Consensus', *International Politics and Society*, No 2, pp. 72–97.

Herr, H. and Priewe, H. (2006), 'The Washington Consensus and (Non-) Development', in: L.R. Wray and M. Forstater (eds), *Money, Financial Instability and Stabilization Policy*, Cheltenham, UK and Northampton, MA: Edward Elgar, pp. 171–91.

Icard, A. (2003), 'Capital Account Liberalisation in China: International Perspectives', *BIS Papers* No 15, April 2003, Bank for International Settlement, Basle.

Keynes, J.M. (1937), 'The "Ex-Ante" Theory of the Rate of Interest', *Economic Journal*, 47, pp. 663–69.

Keynes, J.M. (1942), 'Proposals for an International Clearing Union', in: *The Collected Writings of John Maynard Keynes,* Vol. 25, Activities 1940–1944, E. Donald (ed.), London: Macmillan [1980], pp. 168–95.

IMF (2005), *Annual Reports on Exchange Arrangements and Exchange Restrictions.* International Monetary Fund. Washington D.C.

IMF (2006), *Annual Report.* Washington D.C.

IMF (2006a), *Economic Outlook,* September, Washington D.C.

List, F. (1841), *The National System of Political Economy*, English translation, London: Longmans, Green [1909].

Lu, K. (2003), 'An overview of the Taiwanese Qualified Foreign Institutional Investor System'. *BIS Papers* No 15, Bank for International Settlement, Basle.

Ma, G. and McCauley, R. (2003), 'Opening China's Capital Account Amid Ample Dollar Liquidity', *BIS Papers* No 15, Bank for International Settlement, Basle.

Mikuni, A. and Murphy, T. (2002), *Japan's Policy Trap: Dollars, Deflation and the Crisis of Japanese Finance.* Brookings Institution Press, Washington, D.C.

Naughton, B. (1994), 'Reforming a Planned Economy: Is China Unique?', in: C.H. Lee and H. Reisen (eds), *From Reform to Growth, China and other Countries in Transition in Asia and Central and Eastern Europe*, Paris: OECD, pp. 49–73.

Palley, T.I. (2006), 'The Fallacy of the Revived Bretton Woods Hypothesis: Why Today's System is Unsustainable and Suggestions for a Replacement', Paper prepared for an International Workshop on 'Currency Conflicts and Currency Cooperation in the Global Economy' held at the Institute for European Studies, University of British Columbia, Vancouver, 9–10 February.

People's Bank Of China (2006), *Quarterly Statistical Bulletin*, different years.

Prasad, E. and Wei, S.J. (2005), 'The Chinese Approach to Capital Inflows', IMF, Research Department, Washington, D.C., February.

Priewe, J. and Herr, H. (2005), *The Macroeconomics of Development and Poverty Reduction. Strategies Beyond the Washington Consensus*, Baden-Baden, also published in Chinese at the Southwestern University of Finance and Economics in 2006 in Chengdu, China.

Rodrik, D. (2005), 'Growth Strategies', in: P. Aghion and S. Durlauf (eds), *Handbook of Economic Growth*, edition 1, vol. 1, chapter 14, pp. 967–1014, Elsevier.

Rumbaugh, T. and Blancher, N. (2004), 'China: International Trade and WTO Accession', IMF Working Paper WP 04/36, Washington D.C.

Schumpeter, J. (1934), *The Theory of Economic Development. An Inquiry into Profits, Capital, Credit, Interest and Business* Cycle. Cambridge, MA: Harvard University Press.

Song, W. (1999), 'A Study on China's Capital Flight: 1987–1997'. Economic Research, May, Jingji Yanjiu (in Chinese).

Stiglitz, J.E. and Uy, M. (1996), 'Financial Markets, Public Policy, and the East Asian Miracle', *World Bank Observer*, 11(2), pp. 249–76.

Stiglitz, J.E. (2006) *Making Globalization Work*, Penguin Books.

Tian, B. (2004), *An Analysis of International Capital Flow and its Implications for Regulatory Policies*, China Finance Press.

Wade, R. (2005), 'Bringing the State Back', in: Lessons from East Asia's Development Experience. *International Politics and Society*, 2/2005, pp. 98–115.

Williamson, J. (1990), 'What Washington Means by Policy Reform', in: J. Williamson, (ed.) *Latin American Adjustment: How Much Has Happened?* Washington D.C.: Institute for International Economics, pp. 7–20.

Williamson, J. (2005), *Curbing the Boom–Bust Cycle: Stabilizing Capital Flows to Emerging Markets*, Washington D.C.: Institute for International Economics.

World Bank (1993), *The East Asian Miracle: Economic Growth and Public Policy*. New York: Oxford University Press.

World Bank (2001), *Finance for Growth. Policy Choices in a Volatile World*. Washington, D.C.

World Bank (2005), *Global Development Finance 2005*. Washington D.C.

Wu, F. and Tang, L. (2000), 'China's Capital Flight, 1990–1999: Estimates and Implications', *Review of Pacific Basin Financial Markets and Policies*, 3, pp. 59–75.

Zhu, A., Li, C. and Epstein, G. (2005), 'Capital Flight from China, 1982–2001', in: G. Epstein (ed.) *Capital Flight and Capital Controls in Developing Countries*. Cheltenham: Edward Elgar.

8
De-regulated Finance and Impact on Corporate Investments: The Case of Industry and Labour in India[1]

Sunanda Sen

8.1 Introduction

Financial liberalization has been subjected to divergent viewpoints, ranging from blanket approvals to critical evaluations, of measures, which follow with their impact on the economy concerned. Prescriptions of these reforms, as in mainstream doctrines, usually hover around an 'efficiency' argument for maximizing growth. Financial liberalization as held in these theories makes for higher growth by allocating the investible savings in the best possible manner.

Policy recommendations as above have, however, been contested, on grounds of conceptual logic as well as empirical validity (Davidson, 1978; Sen, 2003). As has been observed on the basis of country experiences, financial de-regulation is neither necessary nor sufficient to generate and sustain growth in real terms. It can be pointed out that while propelling upswings in financial markets, de-regulation does not necessarily generate real activities. This is because these financial booms are often driven by speculations on financial assets, a large part of which are not backed by real assets. New investments in the secondary market for stocks or in the real estate market do not mean new real activity, as construction of plants or new constructions of industrial plants. Moreover, the arguments have hardly paid the same level of attention to the structural effects of financial de-regulation on different segments of the economy, and in particular, on those for employment as well as investments in industrial activities.

We propose to draw attention in this chapter to the links between de-regulated finance and industrial growth and its impact in de-regulated labour markets. The arguments dwell on the frequently observed phenomenon of booming finance in the presence of a stagnating real economy, and the related portfolio adjustments which siphon off funds from real activities to speculation, with reactions on the part of industry to practise cost cutting by using labour in its most adaptable and flexible form while minimizing additional job creation.

In sections 8.2 and 8.3 we offer a conceptual background to this dual process, which connects the financial market to the status of corporate investments in industry and the related impact on labour. The arguments are corroborated in section 8.4 with a set of observations relating to the Indian economy. The three sub-sections that follow include the financial sector under deregulation, the portfolio adjustments in corporate industry that result under financial deregulation, and finally the status of labour, both with financial de-regulation and the flexibilization of labour in terms of economic reforms. We offer our conclusions in section 8.5.

8.2   De-regulated finance and the real economy

Advocacy of economic reforms including those relating to the financial sector rests on its possible impact in terms of growth via efficiency gains. Relying on the manuals of Pareto optimality or even the second best Pareto maxima, champions of free markets have been pushing reforms in different sectors of economies, while targeting developing areas in particular.

In the mainstream literature on financial markets, the role of uncertainty is by assumption ruled out, and despite the fact that it remains an integral aspect in actual functioning of these markets. This is justified by the further assumption that all operators in these financial markets behave rationally and have access to full information. These are the maximizing rational agents in neo-liberal theory who arrive at equilibrium in all markets with full utilization of all resources. Assumptions as above relating to the financial markets lead to the portfolio (asset market) equilibrium approach, postulating the much celebrated 'efficient market' principle for allocating capital on an optimal basis. It is important to point out that with uncertainty having no role whatsoever to play in the market for capital, speculation in these models is reduced to arbitrage, even in intertemporal space, which helps in recommending financial liberalization as a policy tool (Davidson 1978).

In an alternative approach to macroeconomic theory, which is identified as New Keynesian Economics (NKE), short-period disequilibrium in labour and capital markets are explained by incomplete (or asymmetric) information. With information constraining the capacity of the lenders to separate out the credit-worthy ('good') ones among the borrowers from those which are the defaulting (or the 'bad') types, lenders in terms of these models resort to credit rationing, which keeps out a section of borrowers from the market.[2]

Looking beyond the realm of received theory and its prescriptions we encounter the reality of de-regulated financial markets which are much different from what is postulated. First, we mention the heterogeneity of financial assets, subject to a range that spaces itself between assets according to whether these are liquid or fluid (Hicks, 1967) (held over a short period) and others which are not so.[3] The second aspect relates to the portfolio selection of investors in de-regulated financial markets under uncertainty. With prices subject to market forces, the portfolio choice of investors is influenced not only by current prices and returns on individual assets but, more significantly, by the *expected changes* in these. With uncertainty having a significant impact on expected earnings, the investor may in reality choose to move away, from long-term productive assets (which are relatively illiquid) to the short-run liquid types which are primarily speculatory. (As with Keynes's liquidity trap, the above characterizes, in a money/credit economy, tendencies to prefer liquidity to long-term financial or real assets.) Portfolio choices of investors in these situations are thus influenced not by material conditions of production alone but by the changing perceptions of future which are necessarily subjective (and subject to herd instincts, as held by Keynes) (Hicks, 1989).

Financial deregulation in the above situations initiates and sustains new demands in the market, for instruments to hedge and speculate, and for the requisite credit as are needed to finance these demands for credits. Instruments described as derivatives (forwards, futures, options, swaps and the likes), are often innovated and designed to provide covers against risks in uncertain financial markets. As pointed out in an analysis of derivatives, 'the explosive use of financial derivative products in recent years was brought about by three primary forces: more volatile markets, deregulation and new technologies' (Hicks 1989). It has been argued in the literature that derivatives provide an opportunity for the transfer of risks in the market, from risk-averse to risk-neutral agents. The consequence, as has been argued, may be a rise in efficient allocation of resources. Thus from a market-oriented perspective, 'the derivatives offer the free-trading of financial risks' (Siems, 1987).[4]

Theoretical explanations (as above) of the use of derivatives by financial agents thus originate from the claim that these instruments provide a better allocation of market risks over time, and thus welfare-enhancing instruments, as pointed out in the literature (Siems, 1987). However, as conveyed by the Black–Scholes–Merton formula for option pricing, the pay-off for an option can only be realized with a levered position in the underlying risky asset (for calls) or in cash (for puts). On the whole diversification and leverage are thus treated as the two key functions provided by derivatives like options and futures.

Incidentally, the demand for liquidity in the market to finance the purchase of equities, and specially the derivatives, follow a pattern that is different from what is needed to purchase the fixed rate–fixed price long-term bonds (Siems, 1987). The latter can be identified as the 'finance' motive of liquidity demand which is long-term, as distinct from other demand which is related to speculation or transaction demand in the short term, a position taken by Keynes in 1937. Separation of the long-term finance motive from the rest of liquidity demand has led post-Keynesians to point at the role of financial innovations in accommodating (endogenizing) the short-term demand for liquidity.[5]

With an uncertain future the market thus tends to have a tendency to offer short-term assets, which simultaneously generates the corresponding demand for liquidity, which in turn is accommodated and provided for under financial de-regulation. With uncertainty even the long term equities can generate a flow of short-term financial instruments by having a quick turnover in the secondary market. These transactions however, are incapable of generating demand for real investments. Contrary to what is viewed in mainstream economics as the facilitating role of financial innovations by providing intermediation it is possible for these to have a contractionary effect on the real economy. This can happen with (a) rising uncertainty in the financial market which draws away finance from the real sectors, and (b) financial exclusion of countries as well as households in general on grounds of low income, which reduces consumption, investment and as a consequence, dampens the multiplier effect for the real economy.

At this point we need to mention two additional aspects of these derivative instruments which remain critically important in their functioning. The first relates to the pre-condition that these markets are subject to risks and uncertainty. As it is claimed, 'in a perfect market with no transaction costs, no frictions and no informational asymmetries, there would be no benefits stemming from the use of derivative instruments'.[6] The second is related to the 'informational aspects' of derivatives, which in essence are linked to the prevailing uncertainty and risks in these markets Thus '... The true stochastic process followed by the underlying asset, and especially its volatility, must be known ex ante'. Arguments such as above become apparent in the option pricing formula of the Black–Scholes model where the rise in the call premiums as is caused by a rise in stock prices (known as the delta) is higher when the variance of stock price movement (whose probability distribution is known ex ante) is also higher (Siems, 1987).

However, the assumptions, as above, which include the full knowledge of the probability of stock price movements, subject to a normal distribution, turn out as untenable when the market moves fast and especially in an unpredictable manner (Siems, 1987). The process often involves a 'reflexive' pattern, where the realization of expected events (profits, asset prices, call premiums on options, and so on) in the market is also influenced by the subjective biases of the actors, which include the seller/buyer, lender, investor, and so on, in the market.

Critiques of the mainstream position have pointed out that derivatives, by concentrating capital in short-term speculative transactions, divert money from long-term investment. It is pointed out that derivative trading destabilizes the capital market by increasing the volatility of fundamentals such as interest rates, exchange rate of currencies, and so on. The rampant and wide-scale use of these instruments with a failure to prevent a stock market crash in different parts of the world also leads to the view that these risky instruments generate systemic disruptions in the market.

Volatility in the international capital market today includes, in addition to those relating to the volume of these flows of stocks, similar fluctuations in stock prices, exchange rates as well as interest rates. With a major part of financial flows geared to hedge funds, returns on finance today are very much sustained by the *volatility* itself of these flows of finance. Thus the calculations of the stock market call/put premiums in the much celebrated formulation of Merton (Merton 1990) and earlier of Black and Scholes (Black and Scholes 1973), in the standard models indicate that these premiums can move up only when stock prices are subject to a wider range of variance. The rising volume, the frequent instabilities, the changing pattern and their dissociation from real activities increase the importance of analysing their impact in recent times.

It is possible to visualize a situation where the end of a boom in the real sector (say due to external shocks or the saturation of technological innovations) increases the risks on extending credit. As a consequence financial institutions are encouraged to innovate financial products to cover risks (Soros, 1987). Thus each unit of new or old investments can now be backed, under the impact of greater uncertainty, by multiple instruments of hedging. The process may trigger off a rise in interest rate in the market which further dampens asset prices. As for banks, the shortfall in advances to the real sector is compounded by possible debt defaults with rising interest rates and falling prices of stocks. The banks/other financial institutions may react by extending credit to finance the hedge instruments, while lending cautiously to the 'best' customers in the market. This leads to a restructuring of bank credit, which not only moves away from the equitable as well as socially desirable channels of productive investments, but also generates a reduced level of effective demand in the economy.

A scenario such as above creates an atmosphere which Minsky has described as an 'euphoric economy' (Keen, 1996) one where capital appreciation rather than returns on such assets provide the firms the means to meet the rising liabilities due to the rising debt charges. The scene also characterizes a state of 'ponzi finance', namely, a situation where the returns from investments do not cover the costs of borrowings. The process of credit creation which starts off with hedging is transformed over time into speculation and then to ponzi finance (Minsky, 1982).

8.3 De-regulated finance and corporate portfolio

We draw attention, at this point, to the investment climate generated in the economy which affects the portfolio decision of investors including those in the corporate industrial sector. As with the banks corporate industry may also prefer to hold, in their portfolio, financial assets which are relatively more lucrative. The result often is a restructuring of portfolios, not only for the financial institutions but also for the industrial corporations, with greater incentives to invest in the financial sector products which include equities and the hedge instruments.

We try to capture the above aspect of corporate investment behaviour in the following formulation:

$$R = rV \tag{8.1}$$

Thus $r = 1/ V[r^f V^f + r^r V^r]$
From which

$$dr = 1/V[r^f \, dV^f + V^f dr^f + r^r dV^r + V^r dr^r] + dV/V^2[r^f V^f + r^r V^r] \tag{8.2}$$

where V^f, V^r, r^f, r^r are all positve and dV^f by assumption, is also positive
And the symbols stand for,

R: aggregate return on investment;

r: aggregate rate of return;

V: value added re-invested;

r^f and r^r: rates of return on investments in the financial and real
sectors;

and V^r and V^f: Value added which are re-invested in the financial and
real sectors.

In an extreme case of a low growth economy where the growth rate
approaches zero with $r \to 0$ we get, as a necessary condition, after
manipulations,

$$[dV^r/dr^r \cdot r^r/V^r + 1]V^r dr^r < 0 \tag{8.3}$$

where the first term can be written as ηV^r, the elasticity of value added
re-invested in the real sector in response to the rate of return therein. For
the expression in (8.3) above with a negative value we need, for $dr^r > 0$, a
negative dV^r which implies $\eta V^r < 0$ and also the absolute value $|\eta V^r| > 1$.

We witness, in the above formulation, the possibility that for a stag-
nant economy (where the overall rate of return in the economy tends
to approach zero), disparities between the booming financial sector and
the stagnating real sector works on the investor-response in terms of the
allocation of the reinvestible surplus (value added) between the respective sectors. An outcome as above, in the context of a financial boom in
the presence of real stagnation or low growth, thus comes out as a logical
possibility.

Delving further on the implications of the investment strategy of corporates as outlined above, we notice the incidence in terms of the status
of labour in these economies. With cost cutting practices under competitive capitalism in open economies, specially in stagnationist situations,
employers tend to pass on the brunt of adjustment to labour by having
recourse to what can be identified as flexible labour policies. Measures such as above are often considered by the capitalists as necessary
to keep their respective enterprises floating, especially in an environment of uncertainty in product markets and the intensified competition
from other enterprises in open economies. Flexible labour policies provide a convenient route for the employers to treat the wage bill (and
labour employed) as a truly variable cost of production (Keen, 1996).
The changes which come about entail both quantitative and qualita-
tive strategies to extract additional surplus value from labour employed.

To be more specific, the employers turn the workforce to a casualized, temporary status where workers are left with little bargaining power vis à vis the employers. Technology is also used in a manner that is labour-saving, thus using a large proportion of the value added to buy superior technology or else the high return financial assets. Labour flexibility also changes the fabric of labour participation in the production process. These include the stretching of working hours, payment of piece rates at less than the prevailing minimum wage rates, etc., which are quite common in the current regime. With these changes there emerges a new equation of power balance between the employer and the labourer, tilting in favour of the employers. Overpowering the same there emerges the absolute authority of finance which directs the investment decisions in the economy as a whole.

8.4   The Indian economy

8.4.1   De-regulated finance

As with the rest of the economy the financial sector in India has also been subject to sweeping reforms since 1991. The changes include, among others, the introduction of current account convertibility in 1993, de-regulation and unification of the interest rate structure, removal of priority credit, marketized borrowing by the fiscal authorities with an end to official borrowings from the RBI (known as deficit finance), introduction of credit-risk adjusted lending by commercial banks (in conformity with the Basel norms relating to capital adequacy), easier access to foreign capital including the FIIs and moves towards a gradual switch-over to the full convertibility of the rupee.

Measures such as above have led to a noticeable restructuring of the financial sector in the country. We consider the following six changes of special significance:

- Growth in capital inflows from abroad and the rising share of portfolio capital with the dominance of FII flows.
- The spectacular growth in market capitalization in the stock market, and especially in the secondary market turnovers.
- Greater volatility in stock prices as well as in trading volume.
- De-regulation in the capital market which includes the access of FIIs to the Indian stock market since 1992 and the introduction of derivative trading in stock markets, foreign exchange markets and lately in commodity markets.

- High returns on financial sector investments as compared to average returns in industry.
- Changes in corporate portfolios including those of banks with higher share of assets held as stocks.

Changes as mentioned above contrast the picture for the Indian financial system which prevailed before 1991. The system functioned in a regulated and controlled environment, with an administered interest rate structure in the credit market, quantitative restrictions on credit flows, high reserve requirements and the allocation of a significant proportion of lendable resources towards 'priority' sectors. An official committee under the chairmanship of N. Narasimham was appointed in 1991 to reform the financial sector. It recommended wide-ranging measures to de-regulate the financial market. These included, among others, introduction of stricter income recognition and asset classification norms; introduction of higher capital adequacy requirements; introduction of phased de-regulation of interest rates and the lowering of statutory liquidity ratio (SLR) and cash-reserve ratio (CRR) requirements, in a bid to ensure additional liquidity in the system. Reforms in the banking sector were promoted further in terms of the recommendations of the Second Narasimham Committee (1998). Among its suggestions which were implemented include the three-tiered risk-weight on assets and the need to maintain a minimum of 8 per cent of assets in the form of equities, which changed the structure of bank advances. In particular the zero-risk weight on investments in government securities made it attractive for banks to invest in the gilt market. It was also mutually convenient for the fiscal authorities to market the government bonds more easily, especially with the constraints they faced on the other route of borrowings through deficit finance.

Banks in India have been able to improve their performance, both with marked reductions in the percentage of non-profit assts (NPAs) as a proportion of total assets and with improvements in their capital adequacy ratios (CAR). The latter speaks of their ability to float equities in the market which conforms to the norms set by the Basel based Bank of International Settlement. Bank portfolios today can be held as securities issued by the government and others in the market. This has resulted in a fast growth in these categories of financial assets, and especially in government bonds, which far exceeds other channels of creating assets by banks including the traditional route of bank advances. (It is estimated that the banks currently hold 42 per cent of their net demand and time liabilities in government securities, as against the statutory

25 per cent requirement.) In addition, banks in India today can venture out to non-bank operations such as insurance and the security-related transactions, providing them sources of non-banking income. Intensified competition in the banking sector has been driving banks to obtain these alternate sources of income. The options to invest in risk-free government securities on the one hand and to pitch interest rates to higher market rates on the other (on most advances including those offered to the small and medium enterprises) are the new outcome. These are the alternative options or banks which may have affected the volume as well as the terms of bank credit flows to those who are only marginally bankable like the poor and the SMEs.[7] In the process credit is often denied to large segments of small and medium-sized enterprises which do not meet the eligibility criterion for credit ratings in terms of the Basel capital adequacy criterion. But these units are not necessarily less productive nor are they prone to default when compared with other borrowers who are considered to be eligible by banks. To give an example, the yield on loans to the SMEs at around 9.5 per cent has been comparable to those on car loans and even higher than the yield from mortgages. Despite the eligibility of the SMEs in terms of the returns on such loans, their percentage share in aggregate bank advances has dropped from 36 per cent to 23 per cent between 2000 and 2004. Advances to the priority sector as a whole also has so far been de-regulated, both in terms of the interest rates and also in terms of the additional types of priority credit as have been made eligible.[8]

Incidentally, one can draw attention here to the important role the SME sector plays in the Indian economy. The sector currently contributes 40 per cent of the total industrial production in the country and over 34 per cent of national exports. The socio-economic importance of these units is apparent from the fact that the total number of SMEs at 11.39 million units is nearly 95 per cent of all industrial units of the country, while providing employment to nearly 27.13 million people, which is nearly 86 per cent of the total employment in the country (Sen and Ghosh, 2005). Bank credit has thus been less accessible to a significant segment of the economy which is no less productive than that which prevails in the rest of the economy.

As for the role of de-regulated finance in the stock markets of the country, one needs to look at the transactions in the National Stock Exchange (NSE) which remains the main stock trading centre in the country today (followed by the second largest exchange in Bombay, the BSE). Between them the two have a turnover of almost 90 per cent of total stock transactions in India. De-regulation in India's financial sector has led to a structural shift in the pattern of financial flows for the economy. These include the spectacular growth in the turnover of the stock market, with the rank of the NSE at third highest after NYSE and the NASDAQ over the last three years. Thus the turnover in the NSE spot market went up by as much as 122.33 per cent between 2002 and 2005. However, even as the official survey puts it, 'This growth is partly merely arithmetic for rupee turnover goes up commensurate with stock prices'.[9]

As for the main players and instruments in the transformed capital markets, one has to recognize the crucial significance of the FIIs as agents and of derivatives as instruments in the liberalized regime of finance. The share of FIIs in total stock exchange transactions was around 81 per cent in 2005, as compared to 0.02 per cent in 2002. As for derivative trading since 2003, derivative turnover has *exceeded* spot market turnover. Share of derivative trading in the aggregate turnover of the two major stock markets during 2005 was about 65 per cent at Rs 12 000 cores of trading, which was *twice* the size of the equities market in India. Gross buying and selling by the FIIs in the equity market (at Rs 52 4860 crores) amounted to nearly the same as in derivative markets in 2005.[10]

As for the newly opened facilities to trade in the financial market which came with de-regulation, FIIs were allowed access to the Indian capital market in 2002 while derivative trading (which was in practice well-established), was formally treated at par with trading in securities in 1999.[11] Development of the exchange-traded derivatives market was made easier between 1993 and 1996 with a series of reforms in the stock market (Varma Committee)[12]. In 1999 the 30-year ban on forward trading was also lifted. Controversies, around the advance or carry forward system, in the stock market (known as 'badla') was formally allowed in 2001, on the plea that this will create liquidity in the system. While Over the Counter (OTC) forwards trading in stocks is still not legal, in practice it is widely used, in the form of interest rate swaps as well as currency forwards, instruments much preferred by the FIIs.[13]

An indirect impact of these changes (involving an increased involvement of both FIIs and derivatives) in the market has been the *growing volatility* in India's stock market. Thus volatility (as measured by the variance) of the weekly returns of the equity market has been consistently rising over the last three years. The variance in these weekly returns of stocks in the NSE, at 2.85 (for top 50 stocks) and 3.47(for the next 50), has been higher than those prevailing in major stock markets like the US (S&P 500) at 1.41 during January 2004 and for Korea at 2.81 for December 2005.[14] The trend in stock prices has also been in the upward direction, with the Sensex reaching newer peaks far exceeding its earlier records. It may be mentioned here that volatility itself of stock prices (and returns) provide the base for reaping higher profits from capital gains. As mentioned in a study from the Securities and Exchange Board of India (SEBI), 'Firms make a good deal of their money from exploiting the bumps and wrinkles in markets, which drive profits in derivatives, arbitrage and all kinds of market making'.[15]

8.4.2 Rates of returns in industry and finance

We now provide some evidence to indicate that growth as well as the rate of returns in the two sectors of finance and industry in India have actually been moving in opposite directions. The above confirms an on-going process of financial boom in the country in the presence of a moderate to slow output growth which includes the industrial segment. It also generates an atmosphere of deprivation and expropriation in the labour market by making use of flexible labour to the advantage of capital (Salama, 2006). We will return to aspects concerning labour in the following section.

Average returns on equities in the country's stock markets, according to official sources, ranged between 72.9 per cent (2003) 13.1 per cent (2004) and 42.3 per cent (2005) in the BSE over the last three years. Similar ranges of returns prevailed for equities traded at NSE as Nifty (Raju and Ghosh, 2004). Comparing these returns in the financial sector with those in industry (the data on which are available from Prowess on-line data sources), we find a confirmation of our hypothesis that by and large it has been far more profitable to invest in the financial sector compared with what it has been for investments in industry or even in other services. The above confirms the statement we made before that in India finance has been providing far more profitable channels of investment than those in industrial activities.

One can also observe tendencies on part of industrial corporates, to actually shift the investible surpluses in the direction of the financial sector. The evidence is provided by the statistics periodically released by the Reserve Bank of India, on non-financial Public Limited Companies in India[16] (Table 8.2). Profitability, as percentage of sales value, has been much higher in the services sector as compared to those in industry, which can be seen from the statistics on a representative sample of units in the two sectors. (Table 8.1)

Tables 8.2 and 8.3 both confirm the current tendencies in the public limited non-financial companies in India to switch their portfolio in favour of financial assets. Thus investment of these firms in industrial securities has actually fallen from 43 per cent to 34 per cent of their total

Table 8.1 Profit ranges: Number of industrial units as at end of March 2005

Profit range (percentages)	Industry	Services
Above 1000	1	4
Between 100–990	6	38
Between 50–99	7	257
Between 10–49	12	311
Between 0–9	1625	549
Between (−)0.01 to (−)20	499	176
Less than (−)20	363	324
Total no of firms	2513	1659

Source: Prowess Online data.

Table 8.2 Corporate investments (Rs crores)

	2002–3	2003–4	2004–5
Total investments	50200	73510	83841
Securities of financial institutions	12463 (24.82)	22053 (30.0)	25836 (30.81)
Shares and debentures* of subsidiaries	12928 (25.75)	15344 (20.87)	19560 (23.32)
Industrial securities	21942 (43.02)	30490 (41.47)	29053 (34.65)

Note: (a) *Debentures include privately placed debentures with financial institutions.
(b) Figures in brackets indicate percentages.
Source: Reserve Bank of India Bulletin September 2006.

investments between 2002–03 and 2004–05.The pattern tallies with the asset-liability structure of these units, with 'quick assets' (as defined in Table 8.3), covering more than half of total liabilities for the large firms having a sales value over Rs 1000 crores during 2004–05. The pattern was roughly of the same order for firms with lower sales values. It was but natural that the share of net fixed assets to aggregate net assets was at around 40 per cent for all these corporates. Financial liberalization has thus opened up profit opportunities in the financial sector, which in effect is mopping up a considerable part of the reinvestible surpluses in the industrial sector.

It is not difficult to observe, from the same data source on profits on sales, that the services sector proved a far more profitable outlet for

Table 8.3   Selected financial ratios of public limited companies (percentages) 2004–05

Sales range	Quick assets* to current liabilities	Gross fixed asset formation to total use of funds	Net fixed assets to total net assets
Rs 50–100 crores	51.9	43.2	40.0
Rs 100–500 crores	53.4	44.1	42.2
Rs 500–1000 crores	58.5	41.3	42.2
>Rs 1000 crores	50.4	38.0	40.8

Note: *Quick assets comprise of (a) sundry debtors (b) book value of quoted investments and (c) cash and bank balances.
Source: Reserve Bank of India Bulletin September 2006.

investment compared with the industrial sector. Table 8.2 provides an aggregative picture, with about 37 per cent in a sample of 1659 firms in the service sector that have been earning profits on sales as high as 50 per cent to 1000 per cent. This is a contrast to the industrial units with only 26 firms out of a total of a much larger sample of 2513 units that are listed within the same range of profits. The data relates to a recent period ending March 2005.

Disparities between the industrial and the service sectors are also apparent in the average profitability statistics for the two major stock exchanges of the country. The respective returns on equities transacted in the National Stock Exchange and the Bombay Stock Exchange were 39.82 per cent and 46.1 per cent during 2006[17] both of which are considerably high when one considers the much lower profitability in other sectors including industry.

Financial de-regulation has also considerably changed the mode of payments, especially for the senior executives in corporates who are these days often paid in part with stock options. This motivates corporate managers to monitor and keep up the stock prices of the company they work for, which is in addition to their traditional role. The drive to maintain and to push up the stock prices may at times run contrary to what is beneficial for the corporate unit in terms of real activities.[18]

In a recent paper it has been further observed that the industrial corporates today rely more on the internal savings compared with external bank borrowings or the floating of equities in stock markets. However, a major chunk of these savings are used to acquire assets in the financial rather than the industrial sector.[19]

Moreover, of the two external sources of finance for industrial corporations, viz. borrowings and equities, the former has been growing less compared with the latter, a fact reflected in the falling debt–equity ratio of these corporates (Bose, 2006). The limited role of banks as financiers of industrial investment raises an issue relating to the portfolio choice of banks with the current wave of financialization. We have observed elsewhere the limitations of the guiding principles of the financial reforms (which include the Basel norms) in a country like India where credit steadily moves away from borrowing units which are deserving, not only in terms of productive contribution but also in terms of social priorities.[20]

On the whole the changing pattern of corporate finance and governance that has emerged with the liberalization of the financial sector seems to have contributed to a much greater involvement of industrial corporates with the secondary market for stocks. Those who recommend the proximity to stock markets on the ground that the latter provides a better option to industry for access to resources and their efficient allocation do not realize the potential instability generated in the process. In addition to generating vulnerability at firm level, stock markets also create added incentives for firm managers to speculate, which, as pointed out earlier, is contrary to what makes for real investment in the economy.

8.4.3 De-regulated finance and industrial workers

We now focus our attention to the status of labour in the major Indian industries under de-regulated finance. This relates to India's labour market which is laden with flexibility under economic reforms. The first thing that is striking in this context relates to the phenomenon of 'jobless growth' in the economy which has been continuing over the last two decades. Annual growth rates of employment in India's organized sector over 1994–2004 has recorded a negative rate of (−)0.38 per cent, declining further from the low average rate at 1.20 per cent over the decade 1983–94. If one considers the industry groups at a disaggregate level (3-digit classification of Annual Survey of Industries) one witnesses a paradox of lagging employment growth, even in high growth industries. These are the industries that have been experiencing annual average growth rates at 20 per cent or above over the post-reform years since 1991. These include office equipment, aircraft and spacecraft, ships and boats, jewellery, electronics, furniture and motor vehicles, etc., which are the 'sun-rise' industries of the current decade. Jobs in manufacturing, which was around 57 lakh persons at end of fiscal years 1987 as well as 1988, has actually been *falling* since 1999, with the number at 47.44 lakhs at end 2002–03.[21]

The pattern, as described above, is all the more explicit in the *cumulative share* of industries, grouped according to their share of total output. Thus the relatively high growth industries in the organized sector with individual shares between 9.9 per cent and 5.8 per cent of output which collectively contributed 47.66 per cent of aggregate output have generated only 30.73 per cent of aggregate employment during the post-reform years. The pattern indicates, once again, the rather poor contribution of the high output growth industries in terms of employment. The pattern was similar in the low growth industries as well with growth rate on an average less than 5 per cent. These include the typical labour intensive items like man-made fibre, tobacco, publishing, etc.

We have sought elsewhere to explain employment growth by regressing it on technology, invested capital and labour productivity in these industries (Sen and Dasgupta, 2006b). Our results indicate a strong negative impact of technology (capital–labour ratio) on employment, especially in the high growth industries. Thus there has been a systematic tendency of labour displacement on the part of employers, by using the cost-cutting strategy under the new regime of competitive capitalism in the market economy. It is also interesting to observe in these results that labour productivity as such had a negative impact on employment. Labour thus generates more output per head, while failing to generate employment, given the labour saving biases in new technology. It probably implies that the use of labour saving devices have helped in cost cutting by increasing output per labourer while the scale expansions which could generate employment have been absent. Much of the latter can probably be interpreted by the tendencies, as mentioned earlier in this chapter, for corporate industry to shift investible surpluses in the direction of finance.

Fluctuations in output have been common with most industries, especially with liberalized entry of imports and uncertain export markets. Often these are matched by similar fluctuations in employment, which have been prominent even in industries with negative output growth rates, an aspect which indicates the extreme precariousness for labour in terms of the job situation. As has been mentioned in the literature, labour has become a 'risk-bearing factor of production' under liberalization (Jonsson, 1978). The synchronized pattern of variations in output and employment, observed for both high and low growth industries, indicate the impact of uncertain output markets on job opportunities. Labour thus seems to be having a raw deal, with fluctuating job prospects even in industries where output growth tends to be zero or negligible.

Looking a bit more closely at the pattern of employment in the Indian economy, one comes across *two* developments in recent years. The first relates to the casualization of labour and the second to the rising number of man-days per worker, both of which are substantiated by official statistics. As for the hours of work, both for permanent and casual, statistics on growth rates of working (man) days do not tally with the growth rate of workers, thus indicating more work per worker on an average basis. This partly explains the reductions in the reported employment figures due to the *stretching of labour hours through overtime* (and probably also non-payment of overtime labour) in industries. Both casualization and the incidence of unpaid/poorly paid labour with rising man days per worker reflect the incidence of labour flexibility. These provide a convenient route for employers to cut costs and maintain profitability on the already squeezed margin of re-invested surplus in industry which, as noted above, happens under financialization.

Of late, labour market flexibility has brought to the fore issues concerning the security aspect of labour. The notion dwells on aspects affecting livelihood which include, most importantly, employment status, both current and as expected during the future. Moreover, the terms of labour contract[22] to the extent people are with firm jobs, are also important. These include wages as well other benefits/costs related to the contract and include bonuses, housing, medical facilities, transport facilities, leave rules, tenure of job, etc. The economic and social status of labour is also influenced by different forms of support, to the extent available, from the state and/or the social network. For those without a firm job the latter remain the sole means of survival.

Both the unemployed and those with jobs of poor socio-economic status have generated wide-ranging debates on the success of economic reforms in India. In this chapter we have drawn attention to the new norms of corporate finance in the de-regulated regime, with short-term financial assets ('quick assets' as mentioned in Table 8.1 above) providing attractive options for industrial corporates, new investments in industry, and the need to earn competitive rates of returns as available elsewhere. Instead of following a path of scale expansion, industries adopt a strategy of extracting the maximum possible surpluses from labour already employed. This is achieved by augmenting labour productivity (with labour displacing technology) at a rate which far surpasses the rise in wages or other payments to labour. Data on related aspects for Indian industry confirms these developments (Sen and Dasgupta, 2006a).

Unemployment in the country as a whole (which includes the self-employed (Sen, 2007), unorganized industry and agriculture) has also been high, as indicated in the official National Sample Survey Statistics of India. The growth of employment (work force) at 2.48 per cent on an average during 1999–2000 has been less than the growth in labour force at 2.54 per cent over the same period. And latest available data for July 2004 to June 2005 shows a rise in unemployment as compared to 1999–2000, both for males and especially for females in rural areas when estimated on a 'daily status' of employment. The pattern has been no less dismal in urban areas and especially for females.[23]

Estimates such as above of employment of course overlooks the vast majority who are classified in official statistics as 'self-employed', having access to resources which are too meagre to provide them the bare means of even subsistence. On the whole labour in India's manufacturing sector thus seems to be in a state of crisis, which sharply contrasts with the booming business in the financial sector of the country.

8.5   Conclusion

It is now time to go back to the central argument of this chapter concerning financial de-regulation and the incidence on industrial activity as well as the state of employment. Our findings on the 'immiserization' of labour in India's manufacturing industries can be linked to both the flexibilization of labour and the financialization process, with disparate profit opportunities between the real and the financial investments. The latter leads to the drive on the part of employers to invest heavily in financial assets while making good in the real sector by using labour in the most profitable way. The quest for the latter is facilitated, this time by the state, with the induction of labour flexibility norms and the scrapping of protective labour legislations. The outcome thus is a unified process, with finance capital dominating over industry and industry extracting the maximum possible surpluses by exploiting labour.

Notes

1. Earlier drafts of this chapter was presented in a seminar in PERI, University of Massachusetts in September 2006 and also in a conference on 'Financialization of the Indian Economy' at the MSH Paris in October 2006. I thank Gerald Epstein of PERI and Pierre Salama, Ajit Sinha in the Paris conference, along with other participants in both meetings for comments on the earlier draft which have considerably helped reformulating it. A revised version of

it was presented in a conference at the Brazilian Centre at Oxford University in November 2006. I thank the organizers as well as the participants for providing the incentives to bring it to a final form. Errors as have remained, however, are entirely my responsibility.

2. Variants of the optimal portfolio models recognize the role of trading and information costs at equilibrium. However, it is also held that prices have a tendency to quickly adjust to information which is never in private domain. On the whole the system tends to set 'conventions' consistent with 'fundamentals', in terms of a process which is similar to what has been described as a 'random walk along Wall Street'! See in particular Fama (1969) and also Fama (1991).

3. The borrowers are assumed to have better information (compared with lenders) relating to their own inclinations for default. They are also assumed to have the capacity to choose among investment projects (thus often preferring the high-risk high-return ones) and, most importantly, have an ability to voluntarily exit by default. See Sachs (1982) and Cooper and Sachs (1985).

4. Assets in terms of these characterizations are, however, not subject to a binary classification as with money versus bonds in Keynes. Instead, assets here have a range with degrees of liquidity which vary along a whole spectrum. Accordingly the choice of the portfolio is susceptible to uncertainty by an even greater degree. See for the argument Hicks (1967).

5. See for the argument Harris (1996, pp. 60–73) and also Sen (1996, pp. 35–60).

6. See also Minsky (1982), Davidson (1978, Chapter 7) and also Sen (1996, pp. 35–60).

7. Details of these are easily available from official sources of statistics such as *The Economic Survey*, Government of India.

8. This has been a direct consequence of application of Basel standards and codes in India which is guided by the Standing Committee (on International Financial Standards and Codes), of the Reserve Bank of India (RBI) since December 1999. These norms require a minimum capital adequacy on the part of banks, which is determined by the risk component of its assets. Of late the Basel II norms are about to be implemented, which will impose even stricter capital adequacy norms in terms of the credit-risk-adjusted returns (CRAR). Impact of these regulatory norms on credit supply has been both contractionary and discriminating. See for details Sen and Ghosh (2006). See also Sen and Ghosh (2005).

9. *Economic Survey*, Government of India.

10. Ibid., p. 71.

11. *Economic Survey*, 2005–06, pp. 71–3.

12. See Varma (1998).

13. These included the screen-based trading system of the NSE in 1993, the lifting of bans on options trading in 1995 and a phased introduction of derivative products.

14. According to an unofficial source the volume of OTC transactions in 2004 was of the order of Rs 300 crores, a sum comparing (or even exceeding) the exchange traded derivatives.

15. Government of India, *Economic Survey*, 2005–06, p. 70.

16. Government of India, *Economic Survey*, 2005–06.

17. Reserve Bank of India, *Reserve Bank of India Bulletin*, September 2006.

18. Government of India, *Economic Survey*, 2006–07, p. 73.
19. These possibilities of using stocks as part payments have been used in advanced countries to finance mergers and acquisitions. The practice, as it has been pointed out, raises the level of vulnerability of corporates. See Singh and Zammit (2005).
20. Government of India, *Economic Survey*, 2006–07, p. S50.
21. See for a study on the impact of financial reforms under Basel norms on bank lendings, Sen and Ghosh (2005).
22. See, for an elaboration and application of this concept, Standing (1999; 2002).
23. Government of India, *Economic Survey*, 2005–06, p. 207.

References

Black, F. and Scholes, M. (1973), 'The Pricing of Options and Corporate Liabilities', *Journal of Political Economy*, 81 (3): 637–54.
Bose, P. (2006), 'Corporate Behaviour under Liberalised Finance: The Indian Experience', mimeo.
Cooper, R. and Sachs, J. (1985), 'Borrowing Abroad: The Debtors' Perspective', in G.W. Smith and J.T. Cuddinton (eds) *International Debt and the Developing Countries*, A World Bank Symposium, Washington, pp. 21–60.
Davidson, P. (1978), *Money and the Real World*, 2nd edn, London: Macmillan.
Fama, E.F. (1969), 'Efficient Capital Markets: A Review of Theory and Empirical Work', *Journal of Finance*, 25(2): 383–417.
Fama, E.F. (1991), 'Efficient Capital Markets II', *Journal of Finance*, 46(5), pp. 1575–617.
Government of India, *Economic Survey*, various numbers.
Harris, L. (1996), 'Financial Markets and the Real Economy' in S. Sen (ed.) *Financial Fragility, Debt and Economic Reforms*. Houndmills: Macmillan Press Ltd, pp.60–72.
Hicks, J.R. (1967), *Critical Essays in Monetary Theory*. Oxford: Oxford University Press.
Hicks, J.R. (1989), *A Market Theory of Money*. Oxford: Oxford University Press.
Keen, S. (1996), 'The Chaos of Finance: The Chaotic and Marxian Foundations of "Mynski's Financial Instability" Hypothesis', *Economies et Sociétés*, 30, special issue Monnaie et Production (10): 55–82.
Jonsson, E. (1978), 'Labour as Risk-bearer', *Cambridge Journal of Economics*, 2(4): 373–80.
Merton, R. (1990), *Continuous Time Finance*. Oxford: Basil Blackwell, 1990.
Minsky, H. (1982), *Can 'It' Happen Again? Essays on Instability and Finance*, Armonk: M.E. Sharp.
Raju, M.T. and Ghosh, A. (2004), 'Stock Market Volatility – An International Comparison', *SEBI Working Paper* No 8, April.
Reserve Bank of India (2006), *Bulletin*, September.
Rousseas, S. (1986), *Post-Keynesian Monetary Economics*. Basingstoke: Macmillan.
Sachs, J. (1982), 'LDC Debt in the 1980s: Risks and Reforms' in P. Watchel, *Crisis in the Ecconomic and Financial Strucure*. Lexington: Lexington Books.
Salama, P. (2006), 'From Flexibility to Social Cohesion through Finance', mimeo.

Sen, S. (1996), 'On Financial Fragility and Its Global Implications' in S. Sen (ed.) *Financial Fragility, Debt and Economic Reforms*. Houndmills, Macmillan Press Ltd, pp. 35–59.

Sen, S. (2003), *Global Finance at Risk: On Real Stagnation and Instability*, Houndmills, Palgrave Macmillan.

Sen, S. (2007), *Globalization and Development*, Delhi: National Book Trust.

Sen, S. and Dasgupta, B. (2006a), 'Labour in India's Manufacturing Sector', *Indian Journal of Labour Economics*, March.

Sen S. and Dasgupta B. (2006b), *Political Economy of Labour under Globalisation: A Case Study of Labour in Indian Manufacturing Industries*, mimeo.

Sen, S. and Ghosh S.K. (2005), 'Impact of Basel II on Credit in India', *Economic and Political Weekly*, Special number on Money and Finance, April.

Sen, S. and Ghosh, S.K. (2006), 'Basel norms, Indian Banking Sector and Impact on credit to SMEs and the Poor', *IDS Working Paper* (forthcoming).

Siems, T.F. (1987), '10 Myths about Financial Derivatives', *Cato Policy Analysis*, no. 283, 11 September.

Singh, A. and Zammit, A. (2005), 'Corporate Governance, Crony Capitalism and Economic Crises: Should the US Business Model replace the Asian Way of Doing Business?' Centre for Business Research, University of Cambridge, Working Paper No. 329.

Soros, G. (1987), *The Alchemy of Finance*. New York: Simon and Schuster Inc.

Standing, G. (1999), *Global Labour Flexibility – Seeking Distributive Justice*. London: Macmillan Press Ltd.

Standing, G. (2002), *Beyond New Paternalism – Basic Security as Equality*. London: Verso 2002.

Varma, J.R. (1998), Government of India, Committee on Derivative Trading.

9
Does Ownership Explain Bank M&A? The Case of Domestic Banks and Foreign Banks in Brazil

Fatima Cardias Williams and Jonathan Williams

9.1 Introduction

Higher levels of banking sector consolidation are one outcome of financial liberalization and technological developments over the past quarter century. Spawning a global wave of consolidation, beginning in the US and Europe in the mid-1980s before reaching emerging markets in the 1990s, liberalization and technology continue to raise competition while the market for corporate control reflects newer influences, such as cross-sector and cross-border financial linkages.[1] Gelos and Roldós (2004) note three differences between the consolidation processes in mature and emerging markets. (1) cross-border mergers and acquisitions (M&A) is a more important source of consolidation in emerging markets; (2) consolidation is used to restructure emerging market banking sectors following episodes of financial crisis rather than to eliminate excess capacity; (3) emerging market governments are active participants in the consolidation process.

Two events have neatly dovetailed to equate market forces. As competition in mature banking markets intensified, banks looked further afield for opportunities to diversify risks and generate profits. Concomitantly, emerging market governments deregulated banking sectors, repealing restrictions on foreign investment and foreign bank activities, and privatizing state-owned financial institutions. The rising incidence of financial crises in emerging markets in the mid-1990s highlighted a shortfall in domestic capital, and the need to encourage foreign participation to recapitalize and consolidate domestic banking sectors. Hence, international banks had *demand* for access into new markets which emerging markets could *supply*, and emerging market banking systems had *demand* for additional capital which international banks could *supply*.

Slager (2004) contextualizes motives for international bank M&A. Several motives are cited: banks follow customers to new markets; to increase earnings and diversify risk; to exploit growth potential in host countries; to circumvent limited growth opportunities in highly concentrated home markets; to realize efficiency gains and improve profitability. Expected scale and scope economies are considered to yield improvements in bank productive efficiency (Berger, 2000). One strand of the bank M&A literature uses discrete outcome models to explain M&A. Generally, banks with stronger financial profile are more likely to buy banks, whereas weaker banks are more likely to be targets. Some indicators affect the probability of an outcome more than others, and quantifying relative importance can be used to derive inferences about banks' strategic decisions.

Our objective is to determine if acquiring and target banks are distinguishable from non-merging banks in terms of financial profile, and, if found, whether differences exist across bank ownership – between domestic-owned and foreign-owned buyers and targets. Financial profile is defined by a vector of covariates based on the CAMELS taxonomy. A multinomial logit model (MNLM) is applied to the sample of 1242 observations on 192 commercial banks operating in Brazil from 1992 to 2005. This approach is consistent with Vennet (1996, 2003), Focarelli et al. (2002) and Koetter et al. (2005), among others. Our contribution rests as follows: since many emerging market authorities have actively courted foreign banks as a means of furthering the development of domestic banking sectors, we consider if the strategic preferences of foreign and domestic buyers are homogeneous. Understanding the behaviour of new entrants as well as expansionary domestic banks is a relevant exercise for banking sector policy makers and regulators, alike. So far as we are aware, this is one of the earliest studies to be applied to an emerging market. Since Brazilian banking is characterized by a restructuring of domestic banks and foreign bank penetration, we classify sample banks according to five discrete outcomes: (1) domestic buyer; (2) foreign buyer; (3) target of domestic buyer; (4) target of foreign buyer; (5) control group of non-merging banks.

The remainder of the chapter is organized as follows. Section 9.2 reviews the literature. Section 9.3 outlines the consolidation of the Brazilian banking sector. Section 9.4 introduces the statistical model and data. Section 9.5 presents the results and section 9.6 concludes.

9.2 Literature review

The research on bank M&A has two main strands. First, event studies investigate if M&A deals create value for bank shareholders around announcement date; studies consider intra financial industry deals, cross-border deals, and pre-and-post risk valuation (see Cybo-Ottone and Murgia, 2000; DeLong, 2001; Amihud et al., 2002). Empirical evidence from the US suggests value gains are distributed in favour of target bank shareholders at the expense of acquiring bank shareholders (Berger et al., 1999), but value destruction for the latter offsets the value creation implying insignificant joint returns (Houston and Ryngaert, 1994). European deals create value: gains accrue to target bank shareholders with no significant value destruction for acquiring bank shareholders (Cybo-Ottone, 2000; Beitel and Schiereck, 2001). Secondly, bank operating performance (measured by ratios or estimated efficiency) is compared pre-and-post merger (Altunbaş and Marqués Ibáñez, 2004; Humphrey and Vale, 2004). Berger and Humphrey (1997) review several studies and report that on average there are no cost efficiency gains accruing from M&A, although cost efficient banks with superior management are expected to raise efficiency in acquired banks. However, sizable profit efficiency gains accrue when large banks merge (Akhavein et al., 1997). Piloff and Santomero (1998) compare these two approaches. However, neither approach explains the motives underlying bank M&A. This issue is addressed in a literature which uses discrete outcome methods to model the probability of an outcome occurring given a set of covariates. Discrete outcome models are applied to explain bank failure (Wheelock and Wilson, 2000; DeYoung, 2003; Lanine and Vennet, 2006), and bank location (Focarelli and Pozzolo, 2001; Berger et al., 2003).[2]

Koetter et al. (2005) discuss studies that model the probability of bank M&A: financial profile explains M&A outcomes with acquirers and targets having profiles different to non-merging banks. With regard to domestic M&A, banks most likely to be acquired are characterized by low capitalization (Hannan and Rhodes, 1987; DeYoung, 2003; Koetter et al., 2005); poor profitability and earnings (O'Keefe, 1996; Focarelli et al., 2002; Lanine and Vennet, 2006); low liquidity (O'Keefe, 1996; Worthington, 2004); and poorer management quality, measured as cost efficiency (O'Keefe, 1996; Koetter et al., 2005) though exceptions due to bank ownership exist (Lang and Welzel, 1999; Worthington, 2004). In brief, underperforming banks are more likely to become targets, with targets tending to be smaller than acquirers (Wheelock and Wilson, 2000; O'Keefe, 1996; Worthington, 2004; Koetter et al., 2005) though size, like profitability, is not always a significant covariate (Hannan and Rhodes, 1987). Re-expressed, acquiring banks tend to be larger, more efficient, and have a stronger financial profile than target banks.[3]

Studies of cross-border bank M&A consider country-level and firm-level characteristics. Large, relatively poor countries tend to be targets for international banks that use cross-border M&A to reach widely-spaced populations. Cross-border M&A positively relates to shared language and geographical proximity (Buch and DeLong, 2001). Relatively more open countries can be expected to receive a higher share of cross-border M&A activity (Buch and DeLong, 2001; Focarelli and Pozzolo, 2001). The importance of productive efficiency (cost efficiency and scale economies) in determining M&A is emphasized by several authors. Focarelli and Pozzolo (2001) write that large banks originating from competitive and well regulated domestic markets are more likely to expand overseas; this is consistent with the limited form of the global advantage hypothesis (Berger et al., 2000). Finally, cost efficiency is considered more important than the overall degree of economic integration in explaining internationalization in banking.

Few cross-border studies use bank-level characteristics to explain M&A. Vennet (1996) distinguishes between (1) cross-border takeovers and (2) domestic acquisitions where over 50 per cent of the target is acquired yet both banks continue to operate. Generally, in the case of cross-border M&A, targets are less profitable and less cost efficient than acquiring banks. Similar results hold for domestic acquisitions, except target banks do not differ from the non-merging control group. The exercise is carried out on a larger dataset of cross-border deals with consistent findings (Vennet, 2003): acquiring banks have lower cost and higher profitability than targets; target bank cost efficiency and especially profit efficiency is less than acquiring banks' (supporting Akhavein et al., 1997).

9.3   Bank consolidation in Brazil

The consolidation of Brazilian banking is explained by: (1) changes due to government-led restructuring; and (2) changes due to increases in cross-border M&A activity.

9.3.1   Domestic restructuring

During the inflationary period of the 1980s and early 1990s, Brazilian banks earned large profits from inflationary transfers (Fritz, 1996; Barros and Almeida, 1997); banks' inflationary revenue had grown to 4 per cent of GDP over 1990 to 1993, accounting for 38.5 per cent of bank revenue. The implementation of a stabilization plan (the Real Plan) in July 1994 brought easy profits to an abrupt halt, and banks tried to compensate by increasing credit. In the eight months following implementation, credit growth was 43.7 per cent (Nakane and Weintraub, 2005). Yet, banks did not properly assess credit risks and non-performing loans grew from around 7 per cent in December 1994 to peak at 16 per cent in August 1995 (Barros and Almeida, 1997). Government intervention prevented bank insolvencies.

In November 1995, the Programme to Promote the Restructuring and Strengthening of the Financial System (PROER) kick-started bank consolidation. It gave the Central Bank rights to require banks to (1) increase capital; (2) transfer shareholder control; and (3) be merged or acquired by another bank. The authorities later launched PROES (for state-owned banks with the proviso that the banks could be privatized) and PROEF (for banks owned by the Federal government) in August 1996 and June 2001, respectively. The outcome of restructuring is summarized as follows: the number of banks fell from 246 to 155 between 1994 and 2002; the number of majority-owned foreign banks increased from 37 in 1994 to 70 in 2001 with asset share increasing from 7.17 per cent to over 30 per cent; bank privatization reduced the number of state-owned banks from 32 to 14 between 1994 and 2002 (Nakane and Weintraub, 2005).

Gelos and Roldós (2004) claim market forces are the dominant driver of consolidation in mature banking markets. In Brazil, market forces became a driver of M&A in the late 1990s (Paula and Alves, 2007). Since 1999, the large, private-owned Brazilian banks have been more active than foreign banks in M&A transactions, with the former acquiring domestic and foreign-owned banks (Paula, 2002).

9.3.2 Foreign bank entry and cross-border M&A

The market share of foreign banks in Brazil has increased since the mid-1990s: in 1996, foreign banks (majority controlled) held 10.83 per cent of banking sector assets before a peak was reached at 30.13 per cent in 2001. More recent Central Bank data (June 2006) shows foreign banks hold 23.42 per cent of assets. The data highlight two structural changes: foreign bank penetration as a solution to the problems of the mid-1990s (Carvalho, 2002);[4] and, the positive reaction particularly by large, private-owned domestic banks, which improved efficiency, realized revenue economies through cross-selling activities whilst expanding their activities either organically, or via M&A (Paula and Alves, 2007). Typically, foreign banks have acquired medium-sized domestic banks though there are exceptions (Paula and Alves, 2007). Western European banks have aggressively expanded in Brazil and Latin America. Paula (2002) rationalizes this activity. Expansion is the strategic response to increasingly competitive home markets. European financial deregulation has pressurized interest margins and bank profits. Thus, geographic expansion is not only a source of earnings diversification but a means to strengthen European banks in their home markets via high profits generated elsewhere. Latin banking markets, especially Brazil, are characterized by high interest margins that offer foreign banks considerable opportunities to increase returns (Afanasieff et al., 2002; Beck, 2000; Claessens et al., 2001). Although the higher spreads found in Brazil take account of risk – particularly risk due to a weak institutional and legal environment – the higher margins translate into high profit margins compared with other emerging markets and mature banking sectors (Claessens et al., 2001; Paula and Alves, 2007).

Latin America is a target for European banks because of its growth potential, together with the fact that regulatory restrictions have limited opportunities in Asia until recently. Spanish banks entered Latin America because of perceived competitive advantages (over other foreign banks) in terms of language and culture (Sebastián and Hernansanz, 2000). Other causal factors include asset seeking (in markets allowing faster growth and higher margins); asset exploiting (a belief that Spanish management would be more efficient than domestic); and oligopolistic reaction (Spanish banks follow each other into the same markets) (Guillén and Tschoegl, 1999). On the contrary, US-owned banks have focused on organic growth (Paula, 2002).

Finally, Brazil offers potential efficiency gains to foreign banks (Paula and Alves, 2007), especially in light of the relatively high operating costs of Brazilian banks (Beck, 2000; Claessens et al., 2001). The issues of whether foreign banks are more efficient than domestic banks, and whether competition has led to higher efficiency at Brazilian banks, lie outside the scope of this chapter. For information, the empirical evidence is mixed: whereas Vasconcelos and Fucidji (2002) find foreign banks more efficient than domestic banks, Carvalho (2002) finds no significant difference in efficiencies, prices charged and loan portfolios. While foreign banks appear more risk averse and exhibit a clear preference for safer loans, this is true of large, domestic banks.

9.4   Methodology and data

In this section we introduce the multinomial logit model, describe the number of discrete outcomes in the model, and discuss the covariates which are to be specified.

9.4.1   Multinomial logit model (MNLM)

In our model, a bank can experience four M&A outcomes or remain in the non-merging control group, with the probability of being in an outcome explained by a vector of bank-specific covariates. Formally, the MNLM is written in equation (9.1).

$$\ln \Omega_{m|b}(x) = \ln \frac{\Pr(y = m|x)}{\Pr(y = b|x)} = x\beta_{m|b} \quad \text{for } m = 1 \text{ to } J \qquad (9.1)$$

where b is the base category or control group and m is the number of alternative outcomes. Since $\ln \Omega_{m|b}(x) = \ln 1 = 0$, it must hold that $\beta_{m/b} = 0$. Thus, the log odds of an outcome compared with itself are always zero, and the effects of any independent variables must also be zero. The J equations may be solved to find the predicted probabilities of an outcome – see equation (9.2).

$$\Pr(Y_i = j) = \frac{\exp(x_i\beta_j)}{\sum_{k=1}^{J} \exp(x_i\beta_k)} \qquad (9.2)$$

where Y_i is the categorical dependent variable that takes one of the values 1 to J and J is the number of outcomes. The estimated parameters per group, β_j, yield the effect of the covariates, x, on the logged ratio of probabilities relative to the control group, that is, $\ln(\Pr_{ij}/\Pr_{i0}) = \beta_j x$.

In equation (9.3) the MNLM is written to illustrate the measurement of the influence of an identical set of covariates, x, for J outcomes with respect the common control group.

$$\ln\left(\frac{\Pr_{ij}}{\Pr_{i0}}\right) = \beta_{0j} + \beta_{1j}x_{i1} + \beta_{2j}x_{i2} + \beta_{3j}x_{i3} + \ldots + \beta_{ni}x_{in} \qquad (9.3)$$

Following Koetter et al. (2005), we report relative risk ratios (RRR), which measure the change of the probability of being in outcome j relative to the probability of being in the control group, for a unit change in the variable x. Equation (9.4) shows how the RRR is calculated for a one unit change in covariate x from the value of x to x$'$.

$$RRR_j(x, x') = \frac{Pr\,(y = j|x)/\,Pr\,(y = b|x)}{Pr\,(y = j|x')/\,Pr\,(y = b|x')} = e^{\beta j} \qquad (9.4)$$

The RRR is interpreted as follows: a RRR of one is analogous to a zero coefficient implying a change in the variable does not affect the probability of being in outcome j relative to the probability of being in the control group. A RRR greater than one indicates an increase of the probability ratio as x increases, while an RRR less than one signifies a decrease in the relative risk to be in outcome j as x increases.

9.4.2 M&A outcomes

Our conjecture is that bank financial profile explains participation in M&A: the financial profile of buyers and targets exhibit differences from the control group of non-merging banks. Following Vennet (1996, 2003), we identify five discrete outcomes arising from the Brazilian consolidation process: banks are classified as (1) domestic buyer; (2) target of domestic buyer; (3) foreign buyer; and (4) target of foreign buyer; plus the control group of non-merging banks. Banks may experience more than one outcome, which reflects observed behaviour and captures the dynamics of M&A activity. The analysis covers 1992 to 2005, with 1242 observations on 192 commercial banks. Several sources were used to identify M&A and classify banks: BankScope, Paula (2002), Nakane and Weintraub (2005).

Table 9.1 shows M&A outcomes over time. The larger number of observations on domestic buyers compared to their targets implies that some buyers are multiple acquirers – notably the large private-owned banks. Domestic bank acquisitions begin in 1996 and accelerate over 1997 and 1998. After a brief lull, activity resumes over 2002 to 2005. The number of observations involving foreign buyers is understated because in some cases the shares of resident banks were acquired by banks based outside Brazil; the data in outcome (3) relate to acquisitions where the 'foreign buyer' is the Brazilian subsidiary of a foreign bank. This explains why the number of foreign bank targets exceeds the number of foreign banks. Foreign acquisitions of Brazilian banks occur in jumps; in 1997–98, 2000 and 2003. Despite the consolidation process, outcomes (1) to (4) account for less than 6 per cent of observations in the sample.

9.4.3 Covariates

To ensure compatibility with the literature, we select a vector of covariates consistent with the CAMELS approach to quantifying bank financial

Table 9.1   Numbers of M&A outcomes, 1992–2005

Year	Domestic buyer (1)	Target of domestic bank (2)	Foreign buyer (3)	Target of foreign bank (4)	Control group	Total by year
1992	0	0	0	0	7	7
1993	0	0	0	0	11	11
1994	0	0	0	0	41	41
1995	0	0	0	0	93	93
1996	2	0	1	0	104	107
1997	4	2	0	4	100	110
1998	4	2	0	5	100	111
1999	1	1	1	0	109	112
2000	1	2	1	6	113	123
2001	1	1	2	0	131	135
2002	4	2	1	1	123	131
2003	3	1	2	4	95	105
2004	5	1	1	1	80	88
2005	2	0	0	0	66	68
By outcome	27	12	9	21	1173	1242

Source: BankScope.

profile.[5] Bank financial statement data are sourced from BankScope and converted into millions of US dollars at 1995 prices. Initially, we constructed 18 indicators but reduced this number to 12 following correlation and step-wise regression analysis. Table 9.2a describes the 12 covariates whilst Table 9.2b presents descriptive statistics for each covariate by outcome.

Equation (9.3) may be rewritten as equation (9.5) to show the MNLM to be estimated:

$$\ln(Pr_{ij}/Pr_{i0}) = \beta_{0j} + \beta_{1j}EQTA_{i1} + \beta_{2j}Sec_{i2} + \beta_{3j}LLP_{i3} + \beta_{4j}Growth_{i4}$$

$$+\beta_{5j}Ceff_{i5} + \beta_{6j}Peff_{i6} + \beta_{7j}RoA_{i7} + \beta_{8j}Liq_{i8} + \beta_{9j}TC_{i9}$$

$$+\beta_{j10}LTA_{10i} + \beta_{11j}Spread_{11i} + \beta_{j12}TA_{i12} \qquad (9.5)$$

Where J = number of outcomes (1 to 4); EQTA = equity/assets; Sec = securities/assets; LLP = loan loss provisions/gross loans; Growth = annual rate of asset growth; Ceff = cost efficiency; Peff = profit efficiency; RoA = return on assets; Liq = liquidity; TC = rate of technical change; LTA = loans/assets; Spread = interest spread; TA = total assets. All data are in percentages and the covariates are specified with a lag of one year.

Table 9.2a Covariates used in MNLM

Covariate	Proxy	Expected relationships
Equity-assets	Capitalization	Poor capitalization raises probability of bank failure, increases probability of a bank being a target (Wheelock & Wilson, 2000; Lanine & Vennet, 2006; Hannan & Rhodes, 1987).
Securities-assets	Asset quality	Higher ratio implies bank is more diversified with lower overall level of asset risk (Koetter et al., 2005).
Loan loss provisions – Loans	Asset quality	Banks with poor credit risk profile are more likely to be targets (Koetter et al., 2005).
Annual growth in assets	Asset quality	Captures risk of expanding too quickly or too slowly. Slower growth expected to raise probability of being a target.
Cost efficiency, profit efficiency[a]	Management quality	Less efficient banks expected to be targets (O'Keefe, 1996; Vennet, 1996, 2003; Koetter et al., 2005). On average, there are no cost efficiency gains from M&A activity (Berger and Humphrey, 1997) but large profit efficiency gains are found (Akhavein et al., 1997).
Return on assets	Earnings performance	Mixed results in literature.
Cash + interbank assets-assets	Liquidity	More liquid banks expected to be involved in M&A either as buyer or target.
Technical change[a]	Systems	More technically advanced banks expected to be buyers & to use technological advantages to lower costs at merged entity.
Loans-assets	Loan intensiveness of balance sheet	Increase in loan intensity lowers probability of foreign involvement in M&A.
Interest spread[b]	Bank risk profile	Increase in spread raises probability of bank being a domestic buyer and/or target.
Total assets	Size	Small size banks expected to be targets (Wheelock & Wilson, 2000; O'Keefe, 1997; Worthington, 2004; Koetter et al., 2005).

Notes:
[a]We use stochastic frontier and Fourier flexible functional form methodologies to estimate cost efficiency and alternative profit efficiency (see Berger and Mester, 1997). Technical change is derived by differentiating the cost function with respect to time (see Altunbaş et al., 1999).
[b]Interest spread is calculated as interest received on earning assets less interest paid on purchased funds and it quantifies bank risk profile. Rojas Suarez (2001) highlights problems associated with applying performance indicators commonly used in mature banking sectors to banks in emerging markets. Citing the behaviour of poorly managed banks operating in emerging markets, she claims these institutions grow market share by advancing loans to risky borrowers. Funding for these loans is obtained by offering higher deposit rates which increases funding costs, but the higher cost is not proportionately translated into increases in loan rates. Thus, interest rate spreads remain low and can actually decline in periods of excessive risk taking (which in an analysis of mature banking sectors would be interpreted as greater efficiency of financial intermediation).

Table 9.2b Descriptive statistics; by outcome, %

	Equity/assets	Securities/assets	LLP/Loans	Asset growth	Cost efficiency	Profit efficiency	RoA	Liquidity	Technical change	Loans/assets	Interest spread	Assets, $m
Control group												
Mean	21.75	38.75	10.41	25.09	78.75	71.55	2.76	23.47	-35.88	34.95	6.68	3669
Median	14.78	35.03	3.08	6.36	82.27	77.04	2.48	19.08	-32.83	34.94	5.91	655
Std dev	20.90	25.77	38.09	165.62	13.15	15.92	8.05	18.55	24.44	23.89	19.10	11233
Min	-45.56	0.00	0.01	-93.40	2.20	1.14	-96.67	0.00	-181.31	-0.97	-166.49	4.89
Max	99.52	99.86	750.00	3315.02	100.00	100.00	63.92	98.77	72.46	98.04	164.05	110760
Domestic buyer (Outcome 1)												
Mean	15.99	34.22	5.15	8.32	79.44	74.41	1.21	28.16	-33.27	37.89	8.14	26811
Median	10.20	37.80	3.89	7.75	82.09	78.11	2.20	23.68	-32.28	36.58	7.81	16141
Std dev	18.00	15.06	7.20	27.36	12.02	11.90	6.67	19.44	19.45	15.88	8.63	26548
Min	3.65	0.00	0.25	-82.91	21.33	32.27	-32.14	7.69	-83.67	0.00	-4.67	23.70
Max	95.05	65.58	38.75	68.57	88.29	86.65	6.65	99.20	-9.50	91.05	48.20	82911
Domestic target (Outcome 2)												
Mean	15.03	34.60	37.29	14.26	73.37	73.85	0.47	27.81	-34.52	35.45	7.51	2364
Median	14.31	33.78	10.14	-5.47	80.96	72.69	2.46	22.30	-40.03	35.90	6.63	1243
Std dev	24.60	23.65	104.80	80.12	20.25	10.95	9.06	22.36	24.04	22.20	17.36	3001
Min	-79.57	3.36	0.16	-55.17	8.47	51.13	-32.17	0.73	-75.42	0.00	-59.38	64.67
Max	71.55	99.27	528.85	347.91	94.36	100.00	13.44	96.49	36.03	75.10	54.02	10995
Foreign buyer (Outcome 3)												
Mean	14.58	40.88	3.77	92.16	84.09	76.21	1.61	29.16	-31.41	27.50	5.09	9737
Median	12.80	37.87	1.49	44.61	84.66	77.03	2.39	27.17	-26.82	38.35	5.04	6682
Std dev	7.52	17.70	5.25	104.37	3.55	6.68	1.65	10.34	12.28	16.21	6.20	6902
Min	7.23	19.60	0.02	-7.72	76.73	62.08	-1.49	12.97	-54.31	1.94	-5.32	937
Max	33.35	74.47	17.90	262.79	88.77	83.70	3.51	47.43	-12.54	45.61	12.17	20005
Foreign target (Outcome 4)												
Mean	13.29	40.83	8.79	13.29	77.20	68.75	2.62	31.59	-30.38	25.15	5.43	4016
Median	5.24	38.19	6.01	5.24	80.59	73.81	1.93	25.91	-23.81	29.98	6.21	2512
Std dev	41.16	22.00	8.35	41.16	13.63	15.32	4.45	20.22	18.15	16.70	9.17	4757
Min	-43.48	0.00	0.15	-43.48	16.61	24.96	-6.77	2.72	-72.19	0.00	-16.76	9.46
Max	147.64	95.52	30.19	147.64	88.19	87.89	13.57	98.37	-0.62	50.82	36.75	19829

9.5 Results

The results section is divided into three sub-sections. First, we report specification analysis of the MNLM. Second, the relative risk ratios are presented and discussed. Finally, we consider differences in financial profile across discrete outcomes.

9.5.1 Specification analysis

For the MNLM model, we specify four discrete outcomes of the consolidation of the Brazilian banking sector. The outcomes are logical and take account of domestic restructuring and increasing internationalization in the banking sector, important structural changes shaping the financial industry in Brazil. A Wald test is employed to verify if the data support the choice of outcomes. The null hypothesis is $H_0 = \beta_{1,m|n} = \cdots = \beta_{K,m|n} = 0$ with the test statistic being drawn from the χ^2 distribution. If none of the independent variables significantly affect the odds of alternative m versus alternative n, it implies that m and n are indistinguishable with respect to the variables in the model (Long and Freese, 2006). The test statistics and their p-values are shown in Table 9.3. Domestic buyers are distinguishable from the control group, domestic and foreign targets, but not foreign buyers. At the 15 per cent significance level, foreign buyers and the targets of domestic buyers are distinguishable from the control group, and foreign buyers are distinguishable from targets of domestic buyers. Statistically, we cannot distinguish between domestic and foreign buyers, and domestic and foreign targets.

A second Wald procedure tests the effect of multiple independent variables; that is, $H_0 = \beta_{k,1|b} = \cdots \beta_{k,J|b} = \beta_{I,1|b} = \cdots = \beta_{I,J|b} = 0$. The test statistics

Table 9.3 Wald tests for combining alternatives outcomes

Alternatives	χ^2	d.f.	$P > \chi^2$
Domestic buyer – Domestic target	29.904***	12	0.003
Domestic buyer – Foreign buyer	12.157	12	0.433
Domestic buyer – Foreign target	22.706**	12	0.030
Domestic buyer – Control	47.442***	12	0.000
Domestic target – Foreign buyer	17.028	12	0.149
Domestic target – Foreign target	8.086	12	0.778
Domestic target – Control	17.740	12	0.124
Foreign buyer – Foreign target	9.344	12	0.673
Foreign buyer – Control	17.565	12	0.130
Foreign target – Control	10.839	12	0.543

Note: ***, **, * significant at 1, 5 and 10 per cent.

and their p-values are shown in Table 9.4. The test is flexible in that it allows the null to be tested for each covariate. The null is not accepted for any covariate at the 20 per cent level of significance.

Finally, a likelihood ratio test compares the estimated model (5) with a restricted model specifying only the intercept as a covariate; that is, $H_0 = \beta_{k,1|b} = \cdots = \beta_{k,J|b} = 0$. The test statistic at 142.04 with 48 degrees of freedom shows the null is overwhelmingly rejected by the data. Generally, the MNLM is well specified.

9.5.2 Relative Risk Ratios (RRR)

The relative risk ratio (see equation (9.4)) measures the change of the probability of a bank being in outcome j relative to the probability of being in the control group, for a unit change in a covariate. The RRRs are shown by outcome in Table 9.5. Clearly, the probability of a bank being a domestic buyer, and to a lesser extent a foreign buyer, is explained by the covariates. In accordance with expectations, a relationship exists between bank capitalization (equity/assets) and the probability of participating in M&A activity; a one percentage point increase in capitalization increases the probability of a bank being a buyer (either domestic or foreign) by nearly 8 per cent.

Three asset quality covariates are specified. An increase in the share of securities relative to bank size positively raises the probability of being a domestic buyer, suggesting better diversified banks – with lower overall asset risk – are more likely to acquire other banks. A positive, albeit insignificant, relationship is observed for foreign buyers. Similarly, the

Table 9.4 Wald tests for independent variables

Variable	χ^2	d.f.	$P > \chi^2$
Equity/assets	13.658**	4	0.008
Securities/assets	6.762	4	0.149
LLP/Loans	11.711**	4	0.020
Asset growth	7.708	4	0.103
Cost efficiency	10.851**	4	0.028
Profit efficiency	7.092	4	0.131
RoA	8.094*	4	0.088
Liquidity	6.281	4	0.179
Technical change	16.605***	4	0.002
Loans/assets	7.402	4	0.116
Interest spread	8.695*	4	0.069
Total assets	53.378***	4	0.000

Note: ***, **, * significant at 1, 5 and 10 per cent.

Table 9.5 Relative risk ratios by outcome

Variables	Domestic buyer	Target of domestic buyer	Foreign buyer	Target of foreign buyer
Equity/assets	1.079***	0.978	1.077**	1.017
Securities/assets	1.466**	1.076	1.155	1.034
LLP/Loans	0.937	1.008***	0.865	0.998
Asset growth	1.366	0.649	5.642**	1.040
Cost efficiency	1.101*	0.967**	1.189*	1.008
Profit efficiency	1.065**	1.013	1.065	1.003
RoA	0.927***	0.998	0.966	1.006
Liquidity	1.415**	1.095	1.154	1.038
Technical change	1.073***	1.003	1.057*	1.016
Loans/assets	1.537**	1.081	1.142	1.023
Interest spread	1.113***	0.995	1.025	1.002
Total assets	4.183***	1.113	2.625***	1.407**

Notes: Number of observations = 1 123; Pseudo R2 = 0.1818; Log likelihood = −319.68499.
***, **, * significant at 1, 5 and 10 per cent.

probability of being a target of either domestic or foreign banks grows if the target is better diversified, but the statistical relationship is weak. The coefficients on LLP/loans (credit risk) show that banks with relatively poor asset quality have a greater probability of being a target of domestic buyers. On the contrary, foreign buyers appear to opt for targets whose asset quality is superior to the control group (although the relationship is insignificant). Finally, foreign buyers have significantly faster asset growth relative to the control group; similar yet insignificant relationships are observed for domestic buyers and the targets of foreign buyers but not the targets of domestic buyers.

Improving cost efficiency raises the probability of being a domestic buyer and foreign buyer by 10.1% and 18.9%, respectively. The results show that targets of domestic buyers are relatively cost inefficient banks. This is consistent with expectations that better cost managers (buyers) are likely to believe they can realize efficiency gains in target banks. While our results appear at odds with the previous literature, which claims profit efficiency is relatively more important than cost efficiency in explaining M&A, we do not disagree: an increase in profit efficiency raises the probability of a bank being a domestic buyer by 6.5 per cent, but the RRRs are insignificant elsewhere.

We find more profitable banks less likely to participate in M&A. This is not too surprising since M&A could erode profits thereby lowering shareholder value, which should be an important strategic objective. An increase in RoA actually lowers the probability of a bank being a domestic buyer; the same relationship is observed for foreign buyers and targets of domestic buyers but the coefficients are insignificant. The descriptive statistics showed that, on average, banks involved in M&A are more liquid than the control group and this is confirmed by the RRRs. Yet, only the probability of a bank being a domestic buyer is significantly increased (by 41.5 per cent) by a single unit rise in liquidity. A logical hypothesis suggests that banks benefiting more from technological developments are more likely to acquire banks and apply their competitive advantage to lower overall costs and improve efficiency. Our results offer support: a unit improvement in technical change raises the probability of a bank being a domestic buyer and foreign buyer by 7.3 per cent and 5.7 per cent, respectively.

The final three covariates extend the analysis beyond CAMELS. The results show that a rise in loan-intensity increases the probability of a bank being a domestic buyer (by 53.7 per cent). Greater loan-intensity raises the probability of being a foreign buyer (by 14.2 per cent) and a foreign target (by 2.3 per cent) though the relationships are insignificant. This suggests acquiring banks seek to strengthen their loan portfolios. Wider interest spreads raise the probability of a bank being a domestic buyer (by 11.3 per cent) but reduce the probability of being a domestic target albeit insignificantly. In keeping with Rojas Suarez (2001), the result implies risk aversion raises the chance of being a domestic buyer. Finally and consistent with expectations, an increase in bank size raises the probabilities of a bank being a buyer (domestic or foreign). The assets of the average domestic buyer are $26 811 million, more than seven times larger than the average bank in the control group, whereas the size of the average foreign buyer is roughly 2.7 times that of the average control bank. The data on targets suggest foreign buyers acquire relatively larger targets (1.7 times the size of targets acquired by domestic buyers). Tentatively, this implies foreign banks grow market share via M&A, and that the probability of being a target of foreign banks increases with target bank size. The magnitude of the RRR suggests bank size is the most important covariate in explaining M&A in Brazil.

9.5.3   Intra-outcome differences

The previous section identified those aspects of bank financial profile which explain the probability of a bank being in one of J outcomes rather than the control group. Here, the discussion centres on differences in profile across J outcomes: to limit the discussion we do not discuss the odds involving the control group (see above). In Table 9.6, we show only

Table 9.6   Comparison between outcomes, percentage change in odds ratio

Outcomes per explanatory variable	b	z	P > z	%	%StdX
Equity/assets					
Domestic buyer – Control	0.076***	2.678	0.007	7.9	260.4
Domestic target – Domestic buyer	−0.098***	−3.040	0.002	−9.3	−80.9
Foreign buyer – Domestic target	0.096**	2.375	0.018	10.1	411.7
Foreign buyer – Control	0.074**	1.978	0.048	7.7	251.4
Securities/assets					
Domestic buyer – Control	0.383**	2.242	0.025	46.6	6 42 779.1
LLP/loans					
Domestic target – Control	0.008***	2.758	0.006	0.8	36
Asset Growth					
Foreign buyer – Domestic target	2.162***	2.727	0.006	769.2	193.7
Foreign buyer – Control	1.730**	2.530	0.011	464.2	136.8
Foreign target – Foreign buyer	−1.691**	−2.030	0.042	−81.6	−56.9
Cost efficiency					
Domestic target – Domestic buyer	−0.131**	−2.286	0.022	−12.2	−74.7
Domestic target – Control	−0.034**	−2.117	0.034	−3.3	−30.1
Foreign buyer – Domestic target	0.208**	2.143	0.032	23.1	789.4
Profit efficiency					
Domestic buyer – Control	0.063**	2.279	0.023	6.5	173.2
RoA					
Domestic buyer – Control	−0.076***	−2.792	0.005	−7.3	−44.5
Domestic target – Domestic buyer	0.074***	2.021	0.043	7.7	77.7
Liquidity					
Domestic buyer – Control	0.347**	2.018	0.044	41.5	36 646.6
Technical change					
Domestic buyer – Control	0.070***	3.572	0.000	7.3	458.3
Domestic target – Domestic buyer	−0.067***	−2.985	0.003	−6.5	−80.9
Foreign target – Domestic buyer	−0.054**	−2.296	0.022	−5.3	−73.4
Loans/assets					
Domestic buyer – Control	0.430**	2.433	0.015	53.7	13 77 762
Foreign target – Domestic buyer	−0.407**	−2.175	0.030	−33.5	−100
Interest spread					
Domestic buyer – Control	0.107***	2.898	0.004	11.3	540.7
Domestic target – Domestic buyer	−0.112***	−2.847	0.004	−10.6	−85.8
Foreign target – Domestic buyer	−0.105**	−2.573	0.010	−9.9	−83.7
Total assets					
Domestic buyer – Control	1.431***	6.266	0.000	318.3	1468.9
Domestic target – Domestic buyer	−1.324***	−4.935	0.000	−73.4	−92.2
Foreign buyer – Domestic target	0.858***	2.703	0.007	135.9	421
Foreign buyer – Control	0.965***	3.396	0.001	162.5	540.1
Foreign target – Domestic buyer	−1.090***	−4.142	0.000	−66.4	−87.7
Foreign target – Foreign buyer	−0.623**	−1.990	0.047	−46.4	−69.9
Foreign target – Control	0.342**	2.462	0.014	40.7	92.9

Notes: b = raw coefficient; z = z-score for test of b = 0; P > |z| = p-value for z-test;
% = percentage change in odds for unit increase in X; %StdX = percent change in odds for a standard deviation increase in X.
***, **, * significant at the 1, 5 and 10 per cent.

significant differences in the odds of a bank being in one outcome relative to the odds of being in another outcome. The beta coefficients (b) show how much the odds of being in a J outcome increase (decrease) in response to a unit increase in each covariate relative to another J outcome. Standard errors (z) and p-values (P > z) are given in columns three and four. Column five (%) shows the percentage change in the odds ratio whereas column six (%StdX) gives the percentage change in the odds ratio for a standard deviation increase in the covariate. When interpreting a statistical relationship it is assumed all other variables are held constant.

The results are calculated on the assumption that the first outcome's covariate is greater than the second. Our focus lies in establishing changes in odds between domestic buyers and their targets; foreign buyers and their targets; domestic buyers and foreign buyers; and targets of domestic and foreign buyers. First, we discuss domestic buyers and their targets. The results suggest the following: a unit increase in total assets (bank size) lowers the odds that a bank is a target of a domestic buyer by 73.4 per cent; the odds of being a target are lessened (in decreasing order) by unit increases in cost efficiency (12.2 per cent), interest spread (10.6 per cent), capitalization (9.3 per cent) and technical change (6.5 per cent), but the odds are increased by a unit increase in earnings (RoA, 6.5 per cent). Fewer relationships exist between foreign buyers and their targets. While only two covariates are important in explaining changes in odds, the odds are extremely large: a unit increase in asset growth reduces the odds of a bank being a target for foreign buyers by 81.6 per cent whereas an increase in assets reduces the odds by 46.4 per cent.

We do not observe any meaningful changes in odds between domestic buyers and foreign buyers, or between their targets. However, the odds of being a target for foreign buyers – rather than a domestic buyer – are lessened (in descending order) by unit increases in total assets (66.4 per cent), loan intensity (33.5 per cent), interest spread (9.9 per cent) and technical change (5.3 per cent). On the contrary, the odds of being a foreign buyer – over a target of domestic buyers – are increased by unit changes in asset growth (769.2 per cent), total assets (135.9 per cent), cost efficiency (23.1 per cent) and capitalization (10.1 per cent).

9.6   Conclusions and implications

Our principal objective has been to validate empirically whether financial profile explains why some banks engage in M&A while others do not. A multinomial logit model is employed that specifies the four discrete outcomes that we select to characterize the dynamics of bank consolidation in Brazil. A vector of covariates based on the CAMELS method plus three additional covariates are our proxy for bank financial profile. The model specification is supported by statistical tests. Our findings concur with the established literature; financial profile can explain M&A participation better performing and larger banks more likely to be buyers while poorer performers and smaller banks have a higher probability of being targets.

A second objective has been to determine if the financial profiles of buyers and targets are sensitive to bank ownership. Generally, several common factors explain the probability of a bank being a buyer irrespective of ownership: buyers tend to be better capitalized (implying safer or more prudent institutions), relatively more cost efficient and loan-intensive, benefit more from technological developments, and are larger firms. The implication is that buyers believe they can utilize superior management skills and technologies to generate efficiency gains (including scale economies) in target banks. Yet, we find non-shared factors that differentiate domestic buyers and foreign buyers from non-merging banks: domestic buyers are more diversified (in terms of securities), profit efficient, liquid, but with lower earnings capacity whereas foreign banks are faster growers.

Domestic buyers and foreign buyers, despite their similarities with respect to non-merging banks, acquire different types of target. The targets of domestic buyers, for instance, have poorer credit risk levels and are cost inefficient compared to the control group. Targets of foreign buyers, on the contrary, tend to be larger than non-merging banks. This tentatively suggests foreign buyers use M&A to grow their assets and market shares whereas domestic buyers acquire banks with difficulties. We find foreign bank targets have better credit risk levels than non-merging banks, which suggests foreign buyers buy asset quality although the relationship is insignificant.

Having established differences between merging and non-merging banks, we considered differences between M&A participants. Targets of domestic buyers – in relation to their buyers – tend to be smaller, cost inefficient, have narrower spreads indicative of higher risk, are poorly capitalized, and benefit less from technological developments. Yet, targets have stronger earnings capacity which is a powerful motive for M&A. It appears domestic buyers acquire under-performing banks; this is consistent with the efficient operation of the market for corporate control. Foreign buyers in comparison with their targets are faster growing and larger. The M&A strategy of foreign buyers differs from domestic buyers: we suggest foreign buyers use M&A to increase asset size and market share, but targets must be adequate performers in terms of credit risk management because of foreign banks' search for asset quality.

Generally, the results for Brazil are consistent with evidence from other countries; financial profile does explain bank M&A. Arguably, the salient contribution of this study is the empirical verification that domestic buyers and foreign buyers acquire target banks which have contrasting financial profiles. This suggests a clear pattern exists in the M&A strategies of banks operating in Brazil. As such, one can make inferences concerning the continuing consolidation process in the Brazilian banking sector.

Notes

1. The uneven pattern of foreign bank entry in emerging markets reflects intertemporal differences in regulatory reforms. Clarke et al. (2003) and Barth et al. (2001) note the rapid and extensive increase in foreign bank ownership of banking system assets in Latin America and Central and Eastern Europe. Consolidation and cross-border bank M&A in Asian banking markets has increased after deregulatory reforms were implemented following the financial and economic crises of 1997–98.
2. Failed banks often exit the market via their acquisition by other banks.
3. Focarelli et al. (2002) distinguish between mergers and acquisitions. Mergers are driven by a strategic aim to expand revenues by selling more services (implying integration of acquiring and target banks' networks). Expectations are that higher non-interest income offsets initially higher costs, which together with lending growth yields greater profitability. Acquisitions are associated with desired improvements in the quality of the loan portfolio, and this is expected to realize additional profits without altering the bank's cost base.
4. Carvalho (2002) argues the decision to widen foreign bank penetration was not a conscious policy, rather a solution to the problem of an increasing number of banks requiring intervention after the mid-1990s banking crisis. Although the number of foreign banks in Brazil was frozen by the 1988 Constitution, a loophole allows the President right to authorize, on a case-by-case basis, foreign bank entry as national interests demand. Foreign bank entry, however, was conditional upon the acquisition of a troubled state-owned bank. Paula (2002) suggests the authorities have used foreign bank penetration to strengthen the Brazilian banking sector as well as to weaken local monopolies.
5. The acronym CAMELS stands for capital adequacy, asset quality, management ability, earnings performance, liquidity, and systems.

References

Afanasieff, T.S., Lhacer, P.M. and Nakane, M. (2002), 'The determinants of bank interest spread in Brazil', *Banco Central do Brasil Working Paper Series*, 46, August.

Akhavein, J.D., Berger, A.N. and Humphrey, D.B. (1997), 'The effects of megamergers on efficiency and prices: Evidence from a bank profit function', *Review of Industrial Organisation* 12, 95–130.

Altunbaş, Y., Goddard, J. and Molyneux, P. (1999), 'Technical change in banking', *Economics Letters* 64, 215–21.

Altunbaş, Y. and Marqués Ibáñez, D. (2004), 'Mergers and acquisitions and bank performance in Europe: The role of strategic similarities'. *European Central Bank Working Paper Series* No. 398.

Amihud, Y., DeLong, G.L. and Saunders, A. (2002), 'The effects of cross-border bank mergers on bank risk and value', *Journal of International Money and Finance* 21, 857–77.

Barros, J.R.M. and Almeida, M.F.D. (1997), 'Restructuring Brazil's Financial System', Secretariat of Economic Policy.

Barth, J.R., Caprio, J. and Levine, R. (2001), 'Bank regulation and supervision: what works best? A new database', *World Bank Policy Research Paper*, No. 2588.

Beck, T. (2000), 'Impediments to the Development and Efficiency of Financial Intermediation in Brazil', *World Bank Policy Research Paper* No. 2382.

Beitel, P. and Schiereck, D. (2001), 'Value creation at the ongoing consolidation of the European banking market', Institute for Mergers and Acquisitions (IMA), *Working Paper* No. 05/01.

Belaisch, A. (2003), 'Do Brazilian banks compete?', *IMF Working Paper* No. 113.

Berger, A.N. (2000), 'The integration of the financial services industry: Where are the efficiencies?', *North American Actuarial Journal* 4, July, 25–45.

Berger, A.N., Dai, Q., Ongena, S. and Smith, D.C. (2003), 'To what extent will the banking industry be globalized? A study of bank nationality and reach in 20 European nations'. *Journal of Banking and Finance* 27, 383–415.

Berger, A.N., Demsetz, R.S. and Strahan, P.E. (1999), 'The consolidation of the financial services industry: Causes, consequences, and implications for the future'. *Journal of Banking and Finance* 23, 153–94.

Berger, A.N., DeYoung, R., Genay, H. and Udell, G.F. (2000), 'Globalization of Financial Institutions: Evidence from Cross-Border Banking Performance', *Brookings–Wharton Papers on Financial Services* 3, 23–157.

Berger, A.N. and Humphrey, D.B. (1997), 'Efficiency of financial institutions: International survey and directions for future research', *European Journal of Operational Research* 98, 175–212.

Berger, A.N. and Mester, L.J. (1997), 'Inside the black box: What explains differences in the efficiencies of financial institutions?', *Journal of Banking and Finance* 21, 895–947.

BIS (2004), 'Foreign direct investment in the financial sector of emerging market economies', Committee on the Global Financial System, Bank for International Settlements, March.

Borooah, V.K. (2002), 'Logit and probit: Ordered and multinomial models', *Sage University Papers* 138.

Buch, C.M. and DeLong, G.L. (2001), 'Cross-border bank mergers: What lures the rare animal? Kiel Institute of World Economics', *Working Paper* No. 1070.

Carvalho, F.J. Cardim de (2000), 'New competitive strategies of foreign banks in large emerging economies: the case of Brazil', *Banca Nazionale del Lavoro Quarterly Review* LIII, 213, 135–70.

Carvalho, F.J. Cardim de (2002), 'The recent expansion of foreign banks in Brazil: first results', *Latin American Business Review* (ed. Paula, L.F.R.), 3(4), 93–119.

Clarke, G., Cull, R., Martinez Peria, M.S. and Sánchez, S.M. (2003), 'Foreign bank entry: Experience, implications for developing economies, and agenda for further research', *World Bank Research Observer* 18, 1, 25–59.

Claessens, S., Demirgüç-Kunt, A. and Huizinga, H. (2001), 'How does foreign entry affect domestic banking markets?', *Journal of Banking and Finance* 25(5), 891–911.

Cybo-Ottone, A. and Murgia, M. (2000), 'Mergers and shareholder wealth in European banking'. *Journal of Banking and Finance* 24, 831–59.

DeLong, G.L. (2001), 'Stockholder gains from focusing versus diversifying bank mergers', *Journal of Financial Economics* 59, 221–52.

DeYoung, R. (2003), 'De novo bank exit', *Journal of Money, Credit and Banking* 35(5), 711–28.

Focarelli, D. and Pozzolo, A.F. (2001), 'The patterns of cross-border bank mergers and shareholdings in OECD countries', *Journal of Banking and Finance* 25, 2305–37.

Focarelli, D., Panetta, F. and Salleo, C. (2002), 'Why do banks merge?', *Journal of Money, Credit and Banking* 34(4), 1047–66.

Fritz, B. (1996), 'The art of living with inflation: The Brazilian banking system', in Schuster, L. (ed.) *Banking Cultures of the World*, Frankfurt: Verlag Fritz Knapp.

Gelos, R.G. and Roldós, J. (2004), 'Consolidation and market structure in emerging market banking systems', *Emerging Markets Review* 5, 39–59.

Guillén, M. and Tschoegl, A.E. (1999), 'At last the internationalization of retail banking? The case of Spanish banks in Latin America', Wharton Financial Institutions Center, *Working Paper* 99–41.

Hadlock, C., Houston, J. and Ryngaert, M. (1999), 'The role of managerial incentives in bank acquisitions', *Journal of Banking and Finance* 23, 221–49.

Hannan, T.H. and Rhodes, S.A. (1987), 'Acquisition targets and motives: The case of the banking industry', *Review of Economics and Statistics* 69(1), 67–74.

Houston, J.F. and Ryngaert, M.D. (1994), 'The overall gains from large bank mergers'. *Journal of Banking and Finance* 18, 1155–76.

Humphrey, D.B. and Vale, B. (2004), 'Scale economies, bank mergers, and electronic payments: A spline function approach', *Journal of Banking and Finance* 28, 1671–96.

Koetter, M., Bos, J.W.B., Heid, F., Kool, C.J.M., Kolari, J.W. and Porath, D. (2005), 'Accounting for distress in bank mergers', Deutsche Bundesbank Discussion Paper, Series 2: *Banking and Financial Studies*, No. 09/2005.

Lang, G. and Welzel, P. (1999), 'Mergers among German cooperative banks: a panel-based stochastic frontier analysis', *Small Business Economics* 13, 273–86.

Lanine, G. and Vennet, R.V. (2006), 'Failure prediction in the Russian bank sector with logit and trait recognition models', *Expert Systems with Applications* 30, 463–78.

Long, J.S. and Freese, J. (2006), *Regression Models for Categorical Dependent Variables Using Stata* Texas: Stata Press.

Nakane, M.I. and Weintraub, D.B. (2005), 'Bank privatization and productivity: Evidence for Brazil', *Journal of Banking and Finance* 29, 2259–89.

O'Keefe, J.P. (1996), 'Banking industry consolidation: Financial attributes of merging banks', *FDIC Banking Review* 9, 18–38.

Paula, L.F. (2002), 'Expansion strategies of European banks to Brazil and their impacts on the Brazilian banking sector', *Latin American Business Review* 3(4), 59–91.

Paula, L.F. and Alves Jr, A.J. (2007), 'The determinants and effects of foreign bank entry in Argentina and Brazil: a comparative analysis', *Investigación Económica* LXVI (259), 65–104.

Pilloff, S.J. and Santomero, A.M. (1998), 'The value effects of bank mergers', in: Amihud, Y. and Miller, G. (eds), *Bank Mergers and Acquisitions*, Dordrecht: Kluwer Academic Publishers.

Rojas Suarez, L. (2001), 'Rating banks in emerging markets: What credit rating agencies should learn from financial indicators', *Institute for International Economics Working Paper* No. 01–06.

Sebastián, M. and Hernansanz, C. (2000), 'The Spanish banks' strategy in Latin America', *SUERF Working Paper* No. 9, Paris.

Slager, A.M.H. (2004), 'Banking across borders: Internationalisation of the world's largest banks between 1980 and 2000', Erasmus Research Institute of Management.

Vasconcelos, M.R. and Fucidji, J.R. (2002), 'Foreign entry and efficiency: Evidence from the Brazilian banking industry', State University of Maringá, Brazil.

Vennet, R.V. (1996), 'The effect of mergers and acquisitions on the efficiency and profitability of EC credit institutions', *Journal of Banking and Finance* 20, 1531–58.

Vennet, R.V. (2003), 'Cross-border mergers in European banking and bank efficiency. In Herrmann, H. and Lipsey, R. (eds), *Foreign direct investment in the real and financial sector of industrial countries*, Springer Verlag, 295–315.

Wheelock, D.C. and Wilson, P.W. (2000), 'Why do banks disappear? The determinants of US bank failures and acquisitions', *Review of Economics and Statistics* 82(1), 127–38.

Wheelock, D.C. and Wilson, P.W. (2004), 'Consolidation in US banking: Which banks engage in mergers?', *Review of Financial Economics* 13, 7–39.

Worthington, A.C. (2004), Determinants of merger and acquisition activity in Australian cooperative deposit-taking institutions', *Journal of Business Research* 57, 47–57.

Index